No New Messages

By Pat Tiffin

To Kit, Sharon (Annie), and Judy

Three amazing women who have believed in me when I struggled
to believe in myself.

She stepped off the curb into the path of a cab. The driver swerved, horn blaring, shouting as he flew by, flipping her off. She jumped back, startled, heart racing, head already pounding. But now was nothing compared to what was coming. Every time she thought about it her throat shut down until she could hardly breathe. The light changed and the crowd carried her across Sixth Avenue.

She fumbled in her purse for a small bottle of Advil that she knew was in there somewhere. She couldn't fathom how she would work today. But she couldn't stay home. She finally found the pills, next to her cell phone, vibrating against her hand. Voice mail. She hadn't even heard it ring.

She stopped halfway up the block, dumped out couple of tablets and swallowed them dry. She flipped open the phone to check the missed call. She didn't need to, she already knew who it was, but she checked anyway. It was him. She rubbed her eyes. God, how was she gonna get through this day.

The vibration persisted, irritating, like a circling mosquito that she couldn't swat. She hadn't even had her coffee. She couldn't deal, okay, not right now. Starbucks was up ahead, slammed by the morning crowd. She pushed in the door, fighting to find the end of the line. The phone rang again. She ignored it. Another message. She hit dismiss to stop the buzzing, a battle of wills now. She wouldn't pick up, he couldn't make her.

She watched the girl with the hot pink hair and the nose ring, marking cups, singing out the orders. Like she did every day. Like everything was fine. The phone rang again. Screw you, she thought. You can wait.

***

It was America's tragedy, not hers. She hated the day. The month, the week and the day most of all. She could imagine herself, forty years from now, frail and wizened, standing on some stage somewhere to accept a flag or a plaque. Like the soldiers from Normandy or the people at Pearl Harbor, fewer and fewer of them every year. Each ceremony smaller, sadder because no one cared anymore.

But for now there was no hiding, just geographic cures, moving from one place to the next until she became known. Then it was sad, sidelong looks and strangers squeezing her arm. Dedications and podiums and polite requests for interviews. She turned them down. All turned down now.

They all remembered where they were, what they felt. They watched CNN for days, horrified and paralyzed, no way to help. Just watch the news and send the money. So much money. She lived on it now. She would have preferred to work, but it was impossible. It always got out, she was never sure how. Then she'd hear the whispers as she passed, feel the eyes on her back. It was only a matter of time until someone had to ask. They meant well. They wanted to connect. Not to her, to it. Cocktail party chatter, coffee klatch tidbits. *Did you hear? Susan Kearney. They were married six years. North tower. One hundred and first floor.*

It was closer to seven actually. And they'd lived together a year before that. Sean Patrick Kearney. Born June 21, 1965. Died September 11, 2001. Nothing left but the memorials. Endless.

Chapter 1: July 17, 2006

The boxes, all meticulously labeled, had been left in the appropriate rooms. She was experienced now with moving trucks and men, most of the cartons never opened just moved from place to place. Still, it was more like Sean than Susan. He liked order. She wasn't inclined toward organization. They used to argue about the clutter that drove him mad and she never saw. Susan was creative, or at least she used to be. Not an artist, just a thinker. Outside the box, her bosses always said. That Susan. She stayed in the box now. Colored between the lines, labeled the cartons and wrapped her breakables in newsprint and bubble wrap. There was something to be said for structure. Playing by the rules. Stray outside them and a building can fall down. Twice.

She had visited North Carolina as a child. Her father's mother's sister lived here, dead now. No reason to have stopped here, to stay here. She remembered it as full of flowering trees and bushes, scent on the air, with pansies that bloomed in the winter. Beautiful. So different from New Jersey where she grew up, with its outlet malls and ozone alerts. So different from Manhattan, the magic city that she and her best friend Maggie had dreamed of as teenagers, with its lofts and galleries, everyone clubbing in fabulous clothes with rich men. They read the magazines. They knew the score. But Maggie never made it across the river. She lived in Pennsylvania, outside of Scranton, raising two boys and doing the books for her husband's plumbing business. It was the first place Susan went when she left New York. She stayed less than a year. The unrelenting compassion was more than she could bear.

She'd headed west and tried Idaho but couldn't handle the snow. The long cold dark nights at first were a comfort. The sunny days and endless blue sky less so. *Make your outsides match your insides, the shrinks said. However you feel, Susan, it's okay.* They were so full of shit. There was nothing okay about how she felt. Not then, not now.

She had tried in the beginning. Stood with the rest of the families, devastation on parade. She was one of them, or at least she wanted to be. She joined the victim groups, first for support, then advocacy, eventually adversarial, the driven demanding answers for the downtrodden. She'd hugged hundreds of women and men, mothers and wives and brothers and grandfathers. Strangers, so many strangers who wanted to touch her skin. She met the mayor and the governor, too many senators and most of their wives. Time Magazine printed a photo of her at Ground Zero with former President Clinton, pointing out Sean's picture on the endless walls of missing faces. It was picked up all over the world.

His father Patrick had put up the flyers, not her. Blurry with drink and tears, he had hoped. Susan had known better, even before she watched the buildings fall on TV. When everyone's hopes were crushed, like the bodies and desks and lunch bags left too long in the break room refrigerator.

After Idaho, there was no attempt at permanence. She got a storage locker, lots of boxes and a new SUV to hold them, paid for in cash. There was so much money. Sean's life insurance, double indemnity in effect. The company generously sent checks, gifts, promised partner profits and health care benefits. Then there were the donations. Divvied by some insane system, based on what they would have earned, as if a financial analyst was worth more than a bus boy. All men created equal. Not if they're dead.

The public outpouring was overwhelming. Millions and millions, in small change and large checks. Every dollar was sticky with horror and pity and pain. It was a gruesome lottery. She thought of the money every time she saw the footage from right after the planes hit, before the towers fell. Papers everywhere, oversized confetti floating lazily down, luggage and laptops falling from the sky. Like a game show. Her husband died on 9/11. Please phrase your answer in the form of question. She didn't know what to do with the money. Her husband's company did so she let them. Between his investments and all the rest, she was a millionaire. Sean would have been proud.

After Idaho, she had meandered her way cross-country, stopping different places at different times. Sometimes just a night or two, sometimes a week, one time a month before she moved on. In Arkansas she walked into a diner that had the Clinton picture framed on the wall under an American flag. She didn't notice, but the waitress recognized her right away. Breakfast was free, for the price of a dozen shaking hands and a few more stories about where they'd been when they heard. So many "I'm sorrys." The owner, John, spent a half an hour telling Susan about what should be done to the goddamn rag-head A-rabs. His son had enlisted. Just home from basic training, off to Afghanistan in less than a week, Robbie would blow those terrorist bastards to kingdom come. John called him over and pulled out his camera. Just one, he asked. She couldn't say no. So it was Susan and Robbie, with his olive flak jacket and pimpled cheeks, lined up against the paneled wall, his gangly arm around her shoulder offering a thumbs up salute. She didn't know if he had survived the shock and awe.

That's when she ended up in North Carolina. The desire to stay caught her by surprise. She hadn't been connected to any place since New York. It was home in her head, but she couldn't live there anymore, in their third-floor walk-up in Chelsea. Their apartment had an eat-in kitchen and a sometimes-working fireplace that she had loved. Sean liked the fires but not the soot. Their windows overlooked the plant district, hundreds of lush green trees and tropical plants edging out the sidewalk. She loved to walk through them, her own little paradise.

At first it was soothing, the sameness, the plants a gentle arc where nothing had changed. But after the first year, she started to feel a need to wipe the shiny leaves. Get the ash off. Would have to stop, using her sleeve or her shirt, trying to be sly, she wasn't crazy. It was everywhere, on the streets, in the house, those long green leaves. She didn't sleep, pacing with a wet washcloth, T-shirts pressed into the cracks around the windows, under the door. Had to keep it out, who knew what it was, who it was. She couldn't stop cleaning. Everything she saw was dusted in ash. She felt it on her skin, in her eyes, woke up with grit in her mouth. She threw up every night until she finally made herself leave. She hadn't been back.

No one lived there now. The accountants paid the rent.

She found this house by accident, driving aimlessly as always, through a small town called Wendell. Not Wend-ell, like Oliver Wendell Holmes, but "when-dell," accent on the dell. It was a pop quiz for strangers, Yankees notorious for failing. Susan didn't disappoint.

The realtor's sign was almost hidden by the golden rod and spider grass. The land was fronted by low stone walls, no mortar, probably standing for decades, only a few stones gone. There were four acres for sale, covered with pines and overgrown azaleas, gum trees with spiky seed balls that punctured bare feet. A long drive down a long dirt driveway to even know someone lived there.

The house was old, a decrepit bungalow with a wrap-around porch and a small deck added off the back. Ancient crepe myrtles huddled over the drive, and an overblown rose bush had taken over the side yard, vines spreading through the knee-high grass, blossoms peeping between blades. There was a carport instead of a garage, a small barn in back with a fenced in paddock, tumbling for the most part. The door to the house wasn't locked. No one had been home for a very long time.

Inside, the small kitchen was grimy, old grease and ugly wallpaper. It's only saving grace was a huge picture window that looked out where the horses used to graze. Water stains dotted the ceilings and spread down the walls in the square dining room. More ghastly wallpaper, a small bathroom off to one side with a stand up shower and a washer dryer hook up. The living room was L-shaped with a big blackened fireplace in the corner and another giant plate glass window looking out on the overgrown front lawn. There was a tiny sunroom off to the side, screens ripped and in some spots, carefully sewn with navy blue thread. Everywhere wood floors, old wide planks without any luster, bowed and cracked, with scratches and paint splatters throughout.

Susan made her way upstairs, a narrow steep corridor without a railing. There were three more rooms. A big bedroom, the ceilings so sloped half the space was lost. A tub and toilet were tucked to the side of a walk-in closet. Susan bumped her head, hard to remember to duck. The other two rooms were long and narrow, a window seat in one, tucked beneath the eaves. Its cushion had disintegrated, not more than a nest for mice or rats or whatever lived here now. More water stains, broken windowpanes.

The house was quite possibly beyond repair.

Yet she found herself wanting it with an urgency that was undeniable and unexplainable. The owner wanted more money than it was worth. She paid what was asked, the realtor her friend for life. And now she was here. Until she had to go.

***

Jack pulled into the dirt lot, rough and rutted from years of truck tires spinning in the mud, gravel sprinkled here and there. He'd stopped to see his mother. Gotten the news. He was reeling. At a loss, he'd struggled to meet her eyes, say the right things. She listened, loving that he loved her enough to lie. Knowing how much it was hurting him, she lied right back, nodding, promising. She'd beat this. A piece of cake. Stage Four cake, metastasized to her lymph nodes, so many already engaged. She smiled and patted his hand, her only child, fed from the very breasts in question. She'd always kept him safe, put him first and if he needed her not to be dying, then she wouldn't be.

His dad's truck was parked in its usual spot, to the right of the store. Jarvis Grocery and Gas Since 1941, according to the sign, though there hadn't been any gas since the Vietnam war. Skeeter Jarvis' daddy owned it, his daddy before that, though Skeeter ran it mostly now days. Would own it some day soon. The building was long and low, two large windows in the front, littered with flyers for pancake breakfasts, pit bull puppies, lawnmower repair, a handyman for honey-do lists or used truck tires for sale. Unwashed for decades. That's what the rain's for, Skeeter had been heard to say, having learned it from his daddy.

Jackson pulled hard on the door, hinges grimy, the frame warped, his eyes adjusting to the dim light. It wasn't a real store, a few shelves of dusty canned okra and creamed corn, overpriced bread and packages of cookies that never went stale. There was cold beer and Coca-Cola, ice cream coolers with cups of Hershey's chocolate or vanilla. A round rack hung with little bottles of lighter fluid, batteries, breath spray and car deodorizers. Way over-priced. Not much sold. They did sell plenty of cigarettes and chew, the occasional loaf of bread and bottle of milk that a man always seemed to need to pick up for his wife or his momma.

Jack heard a rumble of greeting from the back, a circle of mismatched chairs behind the coffee pots, next to the broken Slushy machine. They filled up every day, some folks coming and going in the mornings or the late afternoon, others staying to pass the time. All men, John Deere caps and hunters camo, cigarette smoke and bad jokes as thick as fog. It was a man's place, none of the trappings required in the company of women. His dad had been dropping in for years, more so now that he couldn't work. Jackson could remember the first time coming here as a boy, trying for nonchalance, thrilled to be included, that his daddy thought he could hold his own with the other men.

"Hey." Jackson sat on overturned blue plastic crate.

"Son." His father sipped from a coffee cup.

"I stopped by the house." He waited. "Talked to Mom." Again a pause. Silence filling it. "I wanted to make sure..." he fumbled. "If you were okay."

"Your momma's the one who's sick." Ben Wyle blew on his coffee, as if it were still hot. His elbows on his knees, the coffee cup at his lips, nestled in both hands. Blowing gently, his eyes followed the ripples out to nowhere. A Styrofoam infinity pool.

"She's gonna be okay," Jack said. No response. "What did the doctor say?"

"That she's sick."

"Dad!" Frustration showing.

His father finally turned to him. "Some things you can choose, like your car or where you wanna live. But some things..." He cleared his throat. "You got no control, you can't pick it or fix it."

"There must be something she can do," he protested. "There's chemo..."

10

"Like falling in love," his father continued, as if he hadn't spoken. "Can't explain it, can't change it. One day you're living your own life, and the next you can't get her outta your head."

"Hey Ben." A big man, beard and mustache, heavy around the middle, poured a cup of coffee. "That Jackson sitting there? Hey boy, ain't seen you for a while."

"Hey Dutch," Jack said, shaking his hand. "How's everything going?"

"Can't complain," he said. "Well, I could but the wife beat me to it." He nudged Jack in the ribs. "Married by a judge when I shoulda asked for a jury."

His father's coffee trembled in the cup. "Seems like there should be an easier way for a men to get his laundry done," Ben agreed.

"Cheaper too," Dutch added. "You hear about the Garrett place? Old lady finally sold it." He added sugar to his coffee, sipped, dumped in some more.

"Yankee girl," one of the others grunted.

"Heard they took her good, got asking price," Bubba Sykes said.

"Where'd you hear that?" Skeeter asked from the counter.

"Wanda told her cousin Ginny, she's my girl's husband's sister. Straight from the horse's mouth."

"Don't need no more Yankees coming down here," another observed. Everyone agreed.

"Must have some money."

"Don't they all."

"Little bit of a thing, a blondie." Everyone looked. "That's what Randy says," Bubba added, nodding toward one of the other men.

"Saw her signing the papers at the bank," Randy replied. "Looks like that girl with no underpants. In that movie. You know." There was a brief debate about the name of the movie. No one could remember. They all remembered the lack of underpants.

"Dad," Jack said, "you wanna go to the Waffle House?"

"Hey, what do you call a smart blonde?" Bubba didn't wait for an answer. "A golden retriever." Laughs all around, a couple of groans.

"Dad? You wanna go eat?"

"This guy walks into a bar carrying an alligator," Skeeter said, leaning on the counter. "And he says, 'If I put my privates in that gator's mouth and come out without a scratch, I drink for free tonight.' Well, everybody wants to see it so the bartender gives the go-ahead. The man whips out his boys and puts 'em in the gator's mouth, and the jaws snap shut. The man waits for a second, hits the gator on the head with a beer bottle. Them jaws pop open and there ain't so much as a scratch on him. 'Anybody else wanna give it a try,' he asks." Skeeter paused, savoring the set up. "Course, nobody says nothing. Then a blonde in the back puts her hand up and says, 'I will, if you promise not to hit me with that bottle.'"

Everyone howled.

"Thanks, son, but you go on," Ben said. "I think I'll just sit here for a spell."

Chapter 2: July 21, 2006

The first three nights it rained. Poured. Every pot and bucket paying tribute to the rotting roof. The thunder was so close it shook the windows, lightening snapping and popping. Strikes lit up the sky, deer caught racing through a backyard strobe, jerky like the stick figures she and Maggie would draw down the side of their Spanish books, flipping the pages to make them run. As mesmerizing at thirty-two as it had been at fourteen, Susan waited and watched, hoping more would come. A drop of water plunked on her forehead. She was running out of pans.

The phone company came in the morning. There was an old thermometer outside the kitchen door. Eighty-two degrees at 10:00 a.m., as humid as if the rain had been a dream. The house was a sweatshop. The two men went about their business cheerfully, bickering back and forth as men do when they know each other well. They put jacks in the bedroom and living room and kitchen. She only had one phone to plug in.

She still kept his name. S. Kearney, that's how it had been listed in the telephone book, lots of goofing about whether the S stood for Sean or Susan, jokes about male chauvinism and female supremacy. They were so happy in that first little apartment on Avenue A, before Sean finished school and went to work for Cantor Fitzgerald. Long talks into the night, vibrant music, silly nicknames and sex all the time.

She loved him so much then, more than she could imagine loving anyone. Done now. Most times she hated him. It was wrong, she knew, in spite of the five stages of grief that had been shoved down her throat at every turn. Because she hated him not for dying, but for dying how he did. Nine eleven, tattooing her life, like faint blue numbers on old Jewish skin.

She'd taken off the wedding ring, hung it on a long cheap chain around her neck. She could have changed her name back to Dennison, her original name. The lawyer had the papers ready. She'd been ready. But in the end, she never did sign. So it was S. Kearney still, just a different number in a different town.

"Y'all from New York?"

"He wants to know if you're from New York City," said the younger man.

"Yes, I am."

"Told ya," the older one crowed, slapping his friend's shoulder. "I can always tell." He held out a hand, pulled it back, wiped it on his jeans and stuck it out again. "Wilton Earl Mayes, ma'am."

"Susan. Kearney."

"That's Bobby there." The younger man grunted, bent over a wire in the baseboard. "I can always tell, New York," Wilton continued. "Been there myself once."

Thousands of people had come, lining the streets of lower Manhattan, candles in Dixie cups, clutching little flags, some holding up pictures of lost friends. A respectful mob. No cheers for the limousines and motorcades. The quiet was a fortress, built too late for too many. They stood for the families, for the city, for the world, heads bent in prayer, cheeks wet with tears. She had watched their faces fly by, her forehead against the cool glass of the town car that carried her, Sean's father Patrick holding her hand.

Inside, it was all priests and politicians, rabbis, firemen, bagpipe bands. A parade of celebrities, fame buying them a seat on the stage and a moment at the mike. The families sat on rented chairs, threw roses in a ring. Ground level at ground zero, down a long walk down a long ramp into a mass grave. Susan threw her shoes away after, couldn't stop wondering who had been underfoot.

"…proud to be American," Wilton continued. She tried to smile and nod. A small tic pulsed on edge of her lower lip. "We weren't more than ten yards away."

"Whoopee shit," Bobby muttered.

"Don't see you goin' no where."

"It was 1972!" Bobby spun a finger next to his ear.

"I'm sorry, I…?" Confused on cue.

"Willie Mays. We got the same name," he added, as if she might not get it. She didn't. "I was right there, first game he played for the

14

Mets! Colored or no, he's still the greatest baseball player of our time, right? I was this far from him, this far!" He spread his arms for Susan's benefit. She blinked.

"The Mets!" Bobby scoffed. "Wanna talk about a player, Derek Jeter, that's a player."

"I don't really follow baseball."

Willie deflated. "And you're from New York?"

"Could I get either of you something cold to drink? Orange juice?"

"I best go test the line," Willie muttered.

Bobby looked up from the floor. "Fifty years old and another man's name his only claim to fame."

"Butt hole." The screen door swung shut.

"I'm sorry, really. I never...."

"Don't go minding him for a minute, ma'am. Ain't too many folks round here he can tell that tired ole story to." He grinned. "I'll have some of that juice, with ice if you would." Bobby wiped sweat from his forehead and turned back to the wire. "Just about got you hooked up."

She walked him out when he was finished.

"You're gonna need some help with that roof," Willie told her while Bobby loaded equipment into the van. "My brother, he does roofing, all kinds of work, painting, electrical. You want, I can have him drop by."

"Thank you. Does he have a card or..."

"That'd mean he knew how to spell," Bobby sniped.

"Shut your trap. I'll have him drop by, ma'am. Works reasonable."

"Works for beer," Bobby added. "Have a good day and you call us if there are any problems." Willie hit the horn, two short beeps, and they headed off in a cloud of dust.

The phone worked. She checked her cell phone while she was at it. No new messages.

Chapter 3: July 25, 2006

"You Miss Cartney?"

"Kearney."

"Shoot, and here I was thinking you might be related to Paul." The woman on the porch was petite, flat-chested, with saddlebag thighs and thin blonde hair trailing down her back.

"Paul who?"

"The Beatles. You know. Hey Jude, don't be afraid," she sang, trying to help her along. "Don't mind me, easily amused. Jolene Mayes." Susan stayed behind the door. "Wilton Mayes, he's my husband's brother? Said you needed some work on your roof."

"Oh right, hello. Sorry. I was expecting your husband."

"No point in waiting on a man when there's a woman to do the job. We get things done, don't we?" She stepped through the screen door and looked around. "Hell's bells, honey, you got yourself a problem here. Shoot." She shook her head. "Whaddya say your name was, sugar?"

Jolene worked her way through the house, Susan trailing behind. The roof was just beginning of the problems. She ticked them off as they walked along, cracking drywall, rotting boards, suspicious electric. "You gotta spray for termites, see here, that dust? And that pipe over there, going to the upstairs bathroom, I'm betting that's bust. See how the stain's a different color and shape?"

"No."

"Take my word for it and try not to flush. Boy, this place is worse off than I thought," she said, shaking her head. "How much they take you for?"

"I beg your pardon?"

"This house been up to sale forever, Miz Garrett's a shrewd old bird, figured sooner or later some high-flying developer'd be needing to buy up her land. Holding out for top dollar, like prices folks got in Cary," she explained. "What am I saying, you never heard of Cary." She laughed. "Anyway, I bet they soaked ya good, no offense. Selling

16

to a Yankee, well, the only way that would happen is if they could take you for a ride. No offense," she added again.

"None taken."

Jolene was up and around the roof in less than a half hour, nimbly skipping over holes and gleefully pulling up shingles to expose the rot beneath. "Ain't no insulation, either," she yelled down. "You gonna spend the money for a roof, you might wanna think about adding that to your bank note. Save ya in the long run."

"I don't need a loan."

"Fine by me, cash is good too," Jolene replied, sliding down the ladder. "You married, sugar?"

"No."

"Good for you. One less headache and a lot less laundry. Unless of course you're lookin', in which case I gotta a cousin over in Louisburg? Get past the hair on the back and he is the nicest man alive."

Susan laughed, surprised at herself. "I think I'll pass."

"Am I driving you crazy? My husband says I could out talk a lawyer at a ten-car pile up. Let me write this up for you, Miss Susan, and I'll give you a number for those termites too."

It took more time to write up the estimate than examine the roof. Susan found herself offering lunch. She brought tuna fish sandwiches and Diet Pepsi's to the front steps. "I don't have a table yet," she apologized. "Haven't even started to unpack."

"It's overwhelming, that's what moving is," Jolene replied. "I won't do it, couldn't imagine trying to move all the shit we've piled up, excuse my French. Been in the same house for twenty-three years. Hell, if I had half a brain, I'd bulldoze the place and start over. We're just down the road a piece, cross the crick. You come visit sometime, let me return the favor." She took a bite of tuna.

"You've always lived here then?"

"Grew up on a tobacca farm just this side of Smithfield."

"Kids?"

"Two. One's in college, over in Winston-Salem, that's Mickey, my oldest. Lost my little one, years back. Got run over by her grampa's tractor." Susan's knees jerked. "Here, careful." Jolene steadied the paper plate on her lap. "Darlene, my baby girl. She was the sweetest little thing. You wanna see her picture?"

She didn't. "I'd love to."

"I keep her right here," Jolene said, pulling a locket from her shirt, splitting it open. The little girl was freckled and gap-toothed. "Close to my heart." She kissed the picture and snapped the locket shut. "She'd be seventeen now."

"I'm sorry."

"It was a long time ago." The Nextel on her hip crackled and spit.

"Jolene, where are you? Over."

"None of your business, Billy, but if you have to know, I'm at Miss Susan's."

"Who?"

"The roof Willie Earl told you about."

"The Yankee?"

"And where are you? Over." She waited. Nothing but static from the Nextel.

"I'm telling ya," she griped, rolling her eyes at Susan. "Billy, I know you can hear me, so listen up. You best be over at the Caine's place fixing that crack in their foundation. Jerry Caine's gonna beat your butt if it ain't done this week. Over and out." She hung up. "And to think I married him of my own free will."

Susan walked her to a beat up Dodge pickup.

"I can start on Saturday, get the materials and all." She seemed to be waiting.

"That's fine." Not sure for what.

"I was thinking, we normally get a deposit for a job this big."

"Oh, I'm sorry, of course." Susan dashed back in the house, came back with a check. "I did it for half, is that okay?"

"That's great," she beamed. "I'm gonna leave the ladder if you don't mind." She climbed in the truck, carefully tucking the check in her pocket. "All righty, I will see you then." She started the truck. The muffler, if there was one, was clearly on its last legs. She gave a cheery wave.

"Hey Jolene?" Susan yelled over the engine. "It's McCartney."

"What?" Leaning out the window.

"Paul McCartney."

She slapped her forehead. "Damned if it ain't. Don't forget about them bugs."

Chapter 4: July 27, 2006

Susan didn't sleep much. Not without the pills that the doctor seemed to think she shouldn't need anymore. It's been almost five years, Susan. There were different doctors. She would find one here. She put up the calendar on the wall in the kitchen. September on top, all later months ripped away and tucked behind, the blocks from the twelfth through the thirtieth blacked out like teeth on a pumpkin. Carefully she counted backwards, through September and August into July. She drew an X across the 26th. Forty-seven days until the new year.

The first anniversary she was still in the city. Their apartment had been deluged with flowers, more than countertops and coffee tables could hold. One night after a jug of wine, she lined them up on the stairs, two flights full. People in the building added to the piles, teddy bears, mylar balloons, cellophane bouquets from the Korean grocer. A shrine to Sean. As the days passed, the flowers died. Eventually someone took them away.

People in the neighborhood tacked up flyers, with pictures of Sean, a woman and two other men who had lived on the block. REMEMBER 9/11. All in caps. They needed to remember, she needed to forget. Everyone knew her. They touched her arm, reached out to catch her eye or her sleeve. *How ya doing, huh? You doing okay?*

Sometimes they would tell her about a friend, a fireman, a secretary, a sous chef. Lots of could-have-been claims too, about people who called in sick that day, got stuck in traffic or missed their train. She never paid for her coffee anymore. The dry cleaner wouldn't take her money either. No chance to get back to normal. All the tiny kindnesses defining her forever.

On September 10, she'd paced the apartment, anxious, as if 2001 had been just a dress rehearsal. Now they would fix it, stop it, change it. We know now. She almost expected him to come home, bitching about annoying clients and crowded trains. *What's for dinner, Suz?* He never called her Susan. Always, Suz, sometimes Suzie, Suz the Cuse, Suz the

Insatiable. She would do it different now. Planned it over and over in her head, what she'd say and do, how to keep him home, make him late, so she could tell her own stories of what might have been.

But he never came home.

The next day, she'd gone to the ceremony, draped in black, sitting beside her mother, his father and sisters, listening to the silence in the city. From 8:46 to 9:03. Commemorating the people on the planes, those in the towers. The second hit fell first. Twenty-nine minutes later, they were both gone. By 10:28, it was over. She'd gone home alone afterwards, refusing all offers from family and friends.

Susan stacked some boxes in the living room to make a chunky chair, adding another carton for a footstool, one for an end table. She had no furniture, except a mattress. She hauled that upstairs, never slept there. An hour or two, it wasn't worth the effort.

There was a TV and a DVD player somewhere, but she hadn't looked for them. Silence was the best way to meet new surroundings. She spent the better part of each night tucked between the cardboard arms, looking out the window. The night noises were deafening. No trucks or sirens, cicadas, crickets, bull frogs baying at the moon. It reminded her of the jungle and the old black and white Tarzan movies she'd watched as a kid on Sunday morning TV.

She plugged her cell phone into the charger. Checked the messages, nothing new. She fussed with phone, lining it up straight to the edge of the box table. Tweaking the position until it was just right. Little things mattered.

Susan roamed around the house, peering into cupboards and closets. Upstairs, under the eaves, she found thirty-year-old newspapers, a hammer with a broken handle and a dead mouse, mummified in the heat. She picked it up with a towel and threw the whole bundle in the trash. There was a tiny pantry to the right of the garbage can, with long levered doors hinged in the middle. More junk and a small grimy dishwasher on wheels that hooked up to the sink with a hose. She rolled it out, but the hose didn't fit. The hoses from the fire trucks from New Jersey didn't fit the hydrants in New York either.

There was no standard size. Hundreds of miles of heavy canvas hose, splayed limp and useless in the streets. Not that it would have mattered, but somehow it did.

When they moved to the apartment in Chelsea, Sean was happy to have a dishwasher. They didn't have much else. He was still starting out, the rent was astronomical. Whatever was left, they spent on suits and shoes, dressing him for the future. Susan wasn't sure what she wanted to be, happy with a part time job at Macy's dressing windows.

"You be the grown up now, I'll take over at the mid life crisis," she told him as they snuggled together on a mattress on the floor.

"I'm having a mid life crisis?"

"It's a given. I figure it will go one of two ways, red corvette or organic goat cheese."

"No goats," he said firmly.

"Penis car," she groaned. He tickled her half to death.

They hardly had any furniture worth mentioning, a good TV and stereo, a leather armchair from his dad, a lumpy pull out loveseat from her old apartment. Susan would go out on pre-dawn garbage raids along Sutton Place and Park Avenue South. The things rich people would throw away. She crowed over each find, sanding scratches and slipcovering pillows, proudly displaying each finished piece. Sean hated that his living room was filled with other people's trash. One time, they'd fought passionately over a coffee table, surprising themselves. After an hour of stiff silence, they made it to the mattress, urgent to repair the damage. Pulling at each other's clothes, making promises about forgiveness and forever, finally laughing, eating cold sesame noodles and lemon chicken from containers stuck in the tangled sheets.

She hadn't unpacked the sheets. She didn't need them. She only unpacked what she needed as she needed it. Sometimes it was easier just to buy new than try and find something. It was exhausting, the management of stuff. The trivia of possessions, crock pots and cookie sheets, a bowl for earring posts, pictures in frames, pictures in books, CDs, silverware. No more meaning than thirty year old newspapers.

The kitchen wallpaper had rows of teapots and cups, red and gray and green, probably better faded than new. The dining room was eagles and flags, likely gold once, brown now, buckling down to dirty baseboards. The ghosts of possessions past left smoky outlines on the walls. A sideboard perhaps or a buffet, a family heirloom loaded up with gilded china used twice a year for holiday dinners. Never used again as the children got older and moved away. Neat squares of missing frames moving up the staircase. Faces long gone.

It was a homeless house. Teetering on the edge of terminal neglect, no care, no proud displays of carefully placed pieces. So far away from what it used to be. The floors must have been beautiful once. Like Susan. She wasn't even pretty now, hadn't been for a long time. Neither were they. Just a nip away from being ugly, worn too hard, dirt and time ground into the creases. She owned no mirrors. No need to view a face that was never painted or hair that was just as likely to be dirty as clean. It was best left alone. But floors, floors could be saved.

***

Becky, or Rebecca as she had decided to be called in later years, grew up in the country just outside Rolesville. A family farm, with three brothers and a baby sister who died sleeping in her crib when she just ten weeks old. They'd met at a church picnic when Jack was no more than fourteen. Becky was fifteen, an older woman, a girl who seemed to know more than most. Always quick on her feet, she could catch you off guard with a smart remark, teasing, tossing that long hair over her shoulder with a wink and shrug, a flash of a smile, lips always shiny as if they were wet. No chapstick for Miss Becky Lee Howe – lip gloss all the way. The other girls hated her or worshiped her. Becky never seemed to care which.

Jack stood in the doorway, surveying the mess in the shed. Half the crap was hers. Stuff from the old Becky. Rebecca had left it behind when she went, like a snake shedding its skin. It stung still, though he knew it shouldn't. He was better off without her, everyone knew that. All through the separation, a year's wait to get divorced in North

Carolina, folks were on his side. Couldn't stop them from telling him so. They cornered him in the Food Lion, corralled him at the coffee shop, relating stories, rumors, things that he didn't want to know. Things he already did. Why was it that kind, nice people need to twist the knife? How could anyone think he'd want to know that his wife was lying tramp who'd made a fool of him all over town.

The shed was so full of junk he couldn't get more than a foot in the door. It must have been hundred degrees inside, air thick with moisture and dust. He tossed some old mini-blinds out into the yard, a big coffee can with an inch of orange water and rusting nails. Behind a cardboard box of old books was a broken rocking chair, a snarl of Christmas lights on its seat. It was theirs, hers, bought at a garage sale with big plans to strip the old varnish, re-cane the rotting back. Abandoned, along with all the other vows.

He never should have married her. But he did. And though he pretended otherwise, he'd probably still be if he had his way. Thank god no one knew that, he'd be the butt of every joke from here to Raleigh. A man walks into his own house and finds his wife tangled up on the couch, another man's hand up under her sweater, the two of them flushed with more than guilt. He should have kicked her to the curb. Should have wanted to.

She had gall, that Becky Howe, always did. He'd liked that, how she would always say what she thought, whether folks wanted to hear it or not. For a Carolina girl, she was less than gentile, bold, ambitious and sometimes brutal, though not above the wiles and ways that had served southern women for decades. Jackson was fascinated, a moth to the proverbial flame. No clue how hungry fire can be.

When she laughed it was loud and genuine, straight from the belly. She did as she pleased, a free spirit with a narcissistic bent. When friends would cringe at restaurants or malls or churches, she'd roll her eyes. "I'm gonna live my life, do whatever you want with yours," she'd say. The implication being if you didn't like it, you could get lost. She never seemed the least bit bothered if they did.

He'd seen it happen with her friends and family, here today, gone tomorrow. Amazed how comfortable she was with herself, he admired her. Mistaking selfishness for self-esteem. It never occurred to him that she wasn't capable of connection, discarding people as easily as a Big Mac wrapper. Not until it was his turn.

In less than two years of marriage, she grew bored, restless, discontent. Always on the look for a better offer while Jack scrambled to make her happy. She didn't need him for that and had no qualms telling him so. When he pleaded for their marriage, her disdain was absolute. She knew what she wanted and he wasn't part of it. She just walked out, as if he was the one at fault. He'd literally chased her to the car, ashamed of how much he loved her.

He tried to keep track of her, careful, subtle surveillance. She moved to an apartment in North Raleigh, began going to clubs and nice restaurants with music in the bar. He followed her, sitting outside for hours, parking where he could watch the door. Only one time did he go in, the compulsion to see her so overpowering. He only wanted to talk to her, tell her how much he missed her. He fantasized an apology, a reunion, happy ever after.

Irritation flashed across her face the second she saw him. Then her chin came up, she titled her glass a hairbreadth in his direction, deliberately leaning in, open mouth and lazy tongue to circle the ear of the man of the minute. The cruelty stunned him. He stopped chasing her that night, stopped calling, couldn't stop thinking. But his apparent lack of interest peaked hers. She started to call, drop by. At her convenience, never his request.

She got a job at a local TV station, qualifications not in question after a chance encounter with the station manager. His mom called him the first time she saw Becky on the news, standing in front of the courthouse, giving background on the most recent politician to be under investigation by the FBI. She didn't want him to turn on the TV and be caught off guard. He suspected his mother knew how he really felt. No one knew he taped the news every night, skimming through it in his bed in the dark, hoping and hating to catch a glimpse of her.

Jack yanked the snarl of Christmas lights free from the chair and fought with the kinks, sweat sticking his shirt to his skin. A mess, everything was a mess. He threw the stupid lights against the stupid wall. They caught on two nails where the hose was supposed to hang and dangled there. A grown man mocked by twinkle lights.

"Shit, shit, shit," he muttered, wiping his forehead. He was only doing this so he wouldn't think about the cancer. Stay busy. Keep his mind off his mother.

"Accomplished that, " he said out loud. He hadn't given his momma a thought. Becky, Becky, Becky. He was pathetic. He had to keep his mind on the job. Clean the shed. He opened a box marked Miscellaneous. Inside was like a junk drawer had been turned upside down and dumped. Scotch tape dispenser, a bunch of pens, an old remote for a long gone TV, a bag of nuts and screws and bolts. To the dump pile. He bent and hefted the box, had it to his chest when the bottom gave out. Everything went everywhere. Shit, shit, shit.

Chapter 5: July 28, 2006

Lyman's Hardware was just off Main Street in Wendell. Right in between Dorothy's Coffee Cart and the Mortell Factory outlet, seconds mostly, made in a local mill off Route 231. The hardware store was family-owned, three generations still at work. It was the grandfather who helped her. She told him her plan. He told her about a Lowe's in Knightdale where they rented commercial sanders. She could get one if she wanted. She could buy everything there, probably cheaper, and still he offered.

"But I could do it by hand, right?"

"The way it used to be done," he agreed.

She bought gallons of stripper and rubber gloves, sand paper by the yard. They talked about wood putty and replacing planks, considered stains, the pro's and cons of cherry, walnut, oak. His name was Charles Lyman. He was a tall man, broad shoulders and trim hips, straight back. "My friends call me Charlie," he said, slow as syrup. His hands were big and veined, knobby, joints just starting to twist. Young Charlie, his forty something son, carried the five-gallon buckets to her car. Little Charlie only worked the weekends, being seventeen and all.

"So you bought the Garrett place," Charlie said, as he was ringing up the tab.

"How did you know where I lived?"

He laughed. "Ain't too many who haven't lived here their whole life. Though more than there used to be, that's for sure. You all alone out there?" She nodded. "Hmm. You need help with those floors, I can come by. If you can tolerate an old man fumbling around, that is."

"Thank you, I will." The bell over the door jangled on her way out.

The Coffee Cart proved a pleasant surprise, with a long list of flavored coffees, lattes and frozen confections written on a blackboard above the counter. There was coconut cake and red velvet cake with cream cheese icing. Cinnamon biscuits, not really buns, hand-rolled and sugar-glazed. The brownies were bigger than a man's wallet, thick moist slabs in Saran Wrap twists. During lunch hour, the Coffee Cart sold cold sandwiches and hot dogs from a little rotisserie that sat on the counter. They were served with coleslaw and chopped onions, chili on demand.

"Cappuccino, please."

"What size?'

"Venti?"

"Don't see no foreigners working here, missy," snapped the woman behind the counter. "We got two kinds of big, middle-sized big or big-big?"

"Big-big."

Miss Dottie was a large woman, lots of weight sitting around her waist and hips like an oversized inner tube. Her skin was dark, black with a bluish tint, hair dyed red a few months back. Now the color hemmed the tips, like bric-a-brac sewn on the legs of short jeans, poking up around her head, sticky with the steam.

"Cake?"

"No thanks."

"You don't like the cake?"

"I've never had the cake."

"Well, lookie here, Betty Jane, she's never had my cake." An ancient woman at the corner table looked up and shook her head. "And she says she don't want to try none." The head kept swaying. Tsk, tsk. Dottie's hands landed on her wide hips. "You sure you don't want any cake?"

"Thank you, but…"

"Ahh leave her alone, Miss Dottie. Not everybody can build a booty like yours," a man's voice drawled. Susan hadn't heard him come in. He had a pleasant smile and neat, even teeth. Braces as a kid, she thought.

"Hush your mouth, young man, making eyes at an old woman's behind," Dottie scolded, already filling a cup. "I saw your momma the other day. Looked a little peaked."

"Excuse me," Jack said, stepping past Susan to get his coffee. He smelled like cinnamon. "Her bark is worse than her bite," he murmured.

28

"But her ears work just fine," Dottie retorted, dishing froth into a cup.

"Cut me a piece of coconut too, for the road."

"At least some folks got sense," Dottie muttered, handing over Susan's cappuccino. She slammed the cash register drawer and counted out change from a twenty. Susan stuffed it in her purse and stepped out into the heat. Over ninety today the radio promised, already close to that now. No air conditioning at the old Garrett place. She had to find a Wal-Mart.

"She's right, you know, you have to try the cake."

Susan turned quickly. He was taller than she was, tanned, blue eyes, big nose, plain brown hair, a little too long. He wore jeans and a button down shirt with the sleeves rolled up. Lived-in boots. He pushed a small white box toward her.

"No, really, I couldn't..."

"You don't try the cake, you might as well never go there again. And it's the only place in town to get a decent cup of coffee." Still she hesitated. "Come on, it's just cake. Dottie doesn't take kindly to strangers as it is, but without this, well…"

She took the box. It weighed a ton. "If I had only known."

"You're new in town," he said kindly.

"Well, thank you, umm…?

"Jackson Wyle. Welcome to Wendell. Susan Kearney," he added, grinning as he walked away.

"How the hell does everybody know," Susan called after him.

He kept walking. "Welcome to Wendell."

Chapter 6: July 29, 2006

A hijacking was the worst they could conceive back then. They had no protocol for this. A hijacked plane would have to land. Negotiate. There would be time. There was no time. New York air traffic controllers were still trying to locate American Flight 11 minutes after it exploded into the North Tower.

It was the first plane, the one that trapped Sean. It had taken off at 7:59, two flight attendants stabbed by 8:15, an emergency call by 8:20. Rapid descent, we're in rapid descent. Heading for Kennedy, or so they thought. We're flying low. Oh God we are way too low.

Susan fell asleep in her chair and woke up a little after three am. She checked the cell phone before making coffee. No new messages. The water from the sink ran orange, then beige. At least it didn't smell. The coffee would have to take care of the rest.

She had yesterday's cake for breakfast. It was a fork scraper, lick-your-fingers-like-when-you-were-a-kid slice. Butter rich, coconut sweet, not overly concerned with portion control. Each mouthful so incredibly rich, pleasure so extreme even Susan felt it. She found herself wondering about the red velvet. Seriously considering the brownies.

She swept the floors, piles of dirt and dust, working in the dark in the dining room. The overhead light was nothing more than capped wires in a ring of painted tin. Her footsteps resonated through the empty house. Twice she stopped, sure it was someone. Just herself. She took off her sneakers and worked in stocking feet, pushing the boxes to the walls.

"Hello," she called. Hello, the house echoed back. "Hello, hello." Hello, hello. She leaned against the wall, arms outstretched. "Ground control to Major Tom."

"This is ground control to Major Tom," she sang, her voice thin, out of pitch. "You've really made the grade." She paused, listening to the play back. "Your circuit's dead, there's something wrong." She stuck out her arms and spun. "Can you hear me, Major Tom?"

Can you hear me, Major Tom? She stopped, the room spinning for just a second longer. Slowly she brought her arms down. All still. Nothing to be heard.

"Get to work," she said out loud. To work, the house whispered.

She went to the car, stubbing her toe in the dark on a cinder block. She pulled out the bottles of Murphy's Oil soap. When she turned, a cat had materialized on the porch railing. It was thin as two sticks, with a belly close to bursting. The tip of one ear was shredded and gook ran from its eye. Wary golden eyes, white mittens long gone gray.

It jumped and ran, disappearing in the long grass next to the deck. Susan set the Murphy's on the kitchen counter and went back for the five-gallon bucket of stripper. By the time she got to the porch, she was sweating. "God, this is heavy."

A raucous meow came in response. The cat was back, sitting two feet from the steps. "I don't have anything to give you," she said. "Go home." It didn't move. Susan went in the house, filled a bucket with water. The cat jumped back to railing. "This is not home," she told it, watching through the window. The cat pulled at a mat on its hind leg, hindered by its belly. She opened the refrigerator and scraped yesterday's tuna onto a paper plate.

"Don't get any ideas," she said, opening the door. The cat ran. She set the plate on the porch. "And I don't have any milk." She waited but the cat stayed away. Susan sighed and turned back to the task at hand.

The floors were filthy. She started in the kitchen, on her hands and knees. She worked sections, the water in the bucket black in minutes, greasy to the touch. She loved the smell of Murphy's Oil Soap, the rhythm of the scrub brush. The layers of grime peeled off reluctantly, almost part of the floor. Underneath the boards were tired, no gleaming hidden treasures. Just wood, bared to the world, plain grain, no shine or wax or lipstick to hide behind.

***

Jolene leaned into the mirror, picked a little sleep from the corner of her eye before loading her toothbrush. "Hey, I need you to go to the

BB&T today and talk to Dick Liddle," she called, over the running shower. "We can get caught up on the house this week, least part ways, got Miss Susan to thank for that. That place is a mess, I'm telling ya. Be more to come, that's what I'm thinking." She waited. Nothing but water running.

"I'm conversating here, Billy! Least you could do is pay attention. Dick Liddle, you hear me?" A grunt. "All right then, don't be pretending later that you didn't." She pulled on a baseball cap, took a last look in the mirror. "I'm gonna go, I'll call you later. Don't be running the hot water all day, can't keep up with the electric as it is. And don't use every towel in the house neither." She started to go, turned. "And you best not be hanging around that Skeeter Jarvis all day, we got work to do." No response from the shower. She sighed. "Okay, I'm going. Love you," she said.

She made a run to Dottie's, took a minute to catch up on the news. Jimmy Hastings was there, Young Charlie, Jackson, of course Betty Jane. Someone had been breaking into cars over in Stallings Crossings, everybody figured it was kids, lots of speculation about whose. They were adding a Dick's Sporting Goods to the shopping plaza in Knightdale, the boys were happy about that. There were rumors that the library was going be cutting its hours again, Dottie grumbling about the government.

"Hey Jack," Jolene said, "I gave your number to Susan, out at the Garrett place? She needs you bad." The men hooted. Jolene glared. "I meant she's got bugs."

"Careful boy, don't wanna be catching nothing," Jimmy chuckled.

Jolene rolled her eyes. "Lord spare me from a man with a one-track mind."

"He done that, wouldn't be any left on earth," Dottie replied. "Girl was in here yesterday, skinny little thing, snooty. Yankee," she added.

"Didn't want no cake," Betty Jane said. Dottie nodded, point made.

"Give her a break," Jack said. "How's she supposed to know you got the best cake in the county? Thanks, Jolene," he added. "You got her number?"

"No, but I'll find out. Let me have two bigs, Dottie, to go," she said. "How'd things go with your momma, Jack?"

"I better take off," Jack said, tossing a dollar on the counter.

Jolene turned to watch him go. "Not so good, huh?"

"Not good at all," Dottie replied.

Jolene pulled into the driveway a little before eight. Susan came out on the porch. She didn't wave or smile, just watched. There was something about her, it wasn't hard to see. It reminded Jolene of using her great-grandma's china, each piece so fragile that she worried herself sick all through dinner, watching each cup and plate in fear that it would break.

"Morning," Jolene called. "You're up early, I figured you might be. Got that look about you. Brought you a coffee. Shoot," she said, seeing the mug in Susan's hands. "You already got some."

"Thanks," Susan said, coming down the steps. "Hey, what's red velvet cake?"

"Angel on the tongue and devil on the thighs," Jolene replied, slapping hers. "They don't have red velvet cake up north?" She didn't wait for answer. "Can't believe that, hell of a shame. It's the devil's food, chocolate cake with a buncha dye in it to make it red. Don't know who thought that up, but they got it at the Coffee Cart," she added.

"I was there yesterday."

"I know. You shoulda got some cake."

"So I heard."

"And trust me, the brownies can do more for ya than a romance novel, if you know what I mean," Jolene said, winking as she tugged a toolbox off the back of the truck.

"Can I help you?"

"Nah. I'm waiting on my boys, bunch of good for nothing Mexicans that should be grateful for a job. Billy lets 'em get away with hell. They're always late." She pulled out a beat up air compressor and an armload of orange extension cords. "Got someplace I can plug this in?"

They had to snake it from the dining room. "You've been busy," Jolene said, surveying the floors. "You know my grandma used to say how she'd scrub her floors with sand. Can you imagine! I got mostly linoleum, except in the bedroom and that don't matter none cuz you can't see the floor for the socks. That man, he can dirty up a sock. And the smell, whew, worse than the dump on an August day." She shook her head. "I'm saying, the things no one tells ya. Wouldn't have to worry about sex education if they'd tell those girls a thing or two about foot odor," she said. "You eating tuna fish for breakfast?"

Susan had trouble switching gears. "What?" Saw the can on the counter. "Oh no. There's a cat." Jolene raised her eyebrows. "I don't know who owns it but it looks like it could be pregnant. I was thinking I'd catch it and maybe…"

Jolene burst out laughing. "You ain't gonna catch any cat. Shoot, girl, you crack me up. It's a barn cat. Lives in the barn."

"It was on the porch."

"And you fed it?"

"Just the tuna fish," Susan said. Feeling foolish.

"You feed it, you own it," Jolene told her, checking her watch. "Where are they? Oughta call immigration, that's what I oughta do."

"I don't want a cat. Especially a pregnant cat."

"Maybe you oughta tell that to the cat. Hey, you found a church yet?"

"A church?"

"Billy and me, we go to First Baptist, church with the red roof off Highway 64, you get to Wal-Mart, you've gone too far. We'd be pleased to take you along on Sunday, introduce you around. There they are," Jolene exclaimed, attention shifting to a dirty white van chugging down the drive. She pushed out the front door, stood on the porch with her hands on her hips. "You're late. Late, comprendo?"

She tapped her watch. They grinned at her, clearly unfazed, then shyly shook Susan's hand, their eyes on their feet. Jolene bossed them about, mixing languages, getting ladders set up and hauling tools to the roof. "And don't any of you be thinking about falling through none of

34

them holes, I'll be darned if I'm paying workman's comp." She scrambled up the ladder after them. "You can let me know," she called down. "About church."

***

They had been married in a church. Catholic, Sean's family was. She'd gone through weeks of pre-Canaan classes with the priest, learning her responsibilities as a Catholic wife and mother, everyone pointedly ignoring the fact that she had shared his bed for over a year.

It was no big deal to her, but so important to Sean, or at least to his father. Susan hadn't been brought up as anything, her parents didn't go to church at all. Catholicism seemed mystical, heavy on ritual, robes and history. At the rehearsal dinner, Patrick had made a fine speech, kissed the top of her head and gave her his dead wife's rosary, blessed by the bishop. Delicate blue beads on a fine silver chain, she draped it among the flowers in her bouquet and carried it down the aisle.

He was a sweet man, Sean's father. They were both widowed now. Susan could hardly stand to hear his voice, only called when the guilt became unbearable. Each call made her guiltier still. The rosary was packed in one of the boxes. She'd left the wedding album behind. Sometimes she wished she had left the ring, hanging a long cheap chain, cold and constant against the skin between her breasts.

About 4:00 am, she headed out to find the Wal-Mart.

She used to make fun of Wal-Mart shoppers, she and Sean and their pseudo sophisticate friends. Manhattanites all, young, bright, the world just waiting for them to arrive. They were mostly co-workers of Sean's. They met on Fridays for happy hour, chic in shades of black, drinking apple martinis and Sam Addams, making fun of lives they'd never lived. All but two of them were gone now and Wal-Mart had become her salvation. Open twenty-four hours a day.

She only went at night with the other vampires. Perusing the empty aisles, always something to buy, fill another box that she would never have to open. Because she could always go to Wal-Mart and buy whatever had been inside. A plate, a pepper mill, a T-shirt, duct tape. She needed duct tape.

She bought that, a flashlight and batteries, paper towels and plates, a few tank tops and elastic waist shorts. She browsed the air conditioners, not sure what to buy and not many Wal-Mart employees on hand to help. She picked two, one for each floor, guessing at the ratio of square feet to BTUs. On the grocery side, she got more coffee, English muffins, toothpaste and a bag of dry cat food.

"You feed it, you own it," she muttered.

"Ma'am?"

"Just talking to myself," Susan said to the checkout girl. Not a girl at all, a woman, probably in her late fifties. Rough around the edges, showing the lines and creases of a hard life. Susan set the Meow Mix on the conveyor belt. "Is dry food okay? If a cat is pregnant?"

"I don't know. Kim, hey Kim, you got cats, right?" She repeated Susan's question, yelling across two aisles. Opinions bounced back and forth, a stocker and a customer adding their two cents. Consensus was such that Susan went back for a twelve pack of Nine Lives, tuna in sauce, seafood sampler and ocean whitefish. Easy open cans.

Sucker. Jolene might as well have been in her head. She struggled to lift the air conditioners in the car. The dawn was splendid, pale pink and gold with wispy gray clouds. People were getting up, getting out. One more stop to make.

The Coffee Cart opened at six. Dottie was reading the paper, looked up with a scowl. The only advantage of being a Yankee in Wendell was that the locals expected her to be stupid. The same old lady sat at the same table, quite possibly wearing the same clothes.

"So now you want cake."

"Yes, ma'am." A truant child.

"Thought you didn't like the cake."

"It wasn't that I didn't like it, I just hadn't had it."

"All the more reason to want it."

"I know, I know," Susan replied. "It's the best cake I ever had."

36

It took two brownies, a slice of red velvet and a half a coconut cake to make it right. Big-big coffee. Susan pushed out the door, balancing the cup and a box tied with string.

"No cinnamon buns," Dottie remarked as the door closed behind her. "Betty Jane, you see that? Doesn't want no cinnamon buns." Betty Jane shook like a bobble head.

***

"I'm telling ya, it's solid," Skeeter insisted, taking a swallow off a long neck beer. "All the way." The faces looking back were doubtful, sipping their coffee. Big Jim Harrigan snorted outright. "Been testing it down at the barn, gotta work out a few kinks and I'll be good to go."

No one said anything. Bubba Sykes changed the subject. "Heard things ain't looking so good for Cordelia Wyle."

"The wife went over there the other day, brought some peach cobbler," Dutch said. "Came back all teared up. Darn shame."

"I'm telling you," Skeeter interrupted, "this is a chance to get in on the ground floor."

"Yeah, right fore the ceiling caves in," Big Jim replied. "Did I tell you my old lady got herself a job at the Wal-Mart? Working nights." He winked. "Gives a man room to breathe."

"Breathing into your hand." From Billy.

"Shut up." From Big Jim.

The door jangled and a girl from the trailer park down the way came in. Skeeter set the Budweiser below the counter, settled himself on the stool behind the old cash register. He was in his early forties, coulda been fifties or sixties, one of those sinewy men, skinny, with a long face. Broken veins on his cheeks and nose, drinking so steady for so long he'd have seized up without it. Didn't so much get drunk as stayed drunk, maintenance required, the first beer cracked when he opened the doors at five am.

He rang up the girl's pack of Basic cigarettes and a Diet Mountain Dew, handing over the change. He wasn't much for women. Trouble that's all they were. And this one in particular, coming in whining, trying to use foodstamps for tobacco and beer. Willing to go two for one. Not that he was above it, but he didn't need to be doing nothing that somebody could look at funny. He ran a cash business, kept a tab when folks ran tight, they paid on it as they could. He didn't hold with them ATM cards or the like, no checks. Cash kept it simple, even the tax man had to take his word on how much come in.

Skeeter was an idea man. A big thinker, lots of schemes and plans, always coming up with something that was gonna make him rich. Back in the day, he'd gotten in trouble a time or two, when his ideas leaned more toward vices than devices. Corn liquor so ripe it blew the tops off the bottles, near took out Tommy Lee Chappell's left eye. Little bags of marijuana stretched thin with dried herbs until they were nothing but, plenty of folks pissed at him that time. But nothing so bad that he had more than a black eye or a weekend in jail, with a bawling out from his momma after his daddy posted bail. He didn't like jail, couldn't even smoke a cigarette like any decent man might wanna do, so he started putting his mind to a different bent.

"See, it's a ball, got weights in it, you know, to make it roll along? And there's these blades on the outsides that chew up the leaves and stuff, pieces go right down the spout." Skeeter drank some more beer. "I'm telling ya, this is the one that's gonna do it," he added hoping for interest. "Gutter Balls, that's what I'm gonna call it." The men laughed themselves stupid.

"How does the thing turn on anyway," Bubba gasped, wiping his eyes.

"Whaddya mean?" Skeeter's face bright red.

"It's gotta spin. You stick some razor blades on a tennis ball and roll it down hill, it ain't gonna cut your lawn."

"I know that, course I knew that, that's what I'm working on now," Skeeter blustered. Grins turned to hoots. "I said I was working out the kinks."

"Old Gutter Balls working out the kinks," Dutch howled.

"And how the weights gonna make it roll? Not like most gutters go down hill."

38

"Less Billy put 'em up," Big Jim snickered.

"I'll be sitting pretty, you wait and see. Ignorant bastards," Skeeter muttered. "See who's laughing then." He stalked into the back room, slamming the door. Everybody grinned.

"Dumb ass," Big Jim said.

Chapter 7: July 31, 2006

"Found a bunch more holes in the side roof there," Jolene said, "but we're making progress. Ain't supposed to rain for a day or two, but I'll tarp it just the same. Help keep the bugs out. Speakin' of bugs, did you call Jackson?"

"The guy with the cake?"

"The one and only Bug Doctor."

"That's scary. You want some more?" She'd split the piece of red velvet.

Jolene wiped her mouth, dropped her napkin in the trash. "Better get back to work. Don't want folks thinking I'm a slacker. Lord knows, Billy's already got that covered." Jolene had insisted that the boys put in the air conditioners, they'd argued a bit before she agreed to let Susan pay them. "What's taking them so long, see you're spoiling 'em, no better than Billy. Juan, Jose, Manuel," she bawled up the staircase, "plug that damn thing in and get your butts back up on the roof." She paused at the screen door. "See you got yourself some cat food."

"Don't say it."

"Okay." Two seconds later her head popped back into view. "Sucker."

"Slacker."

The light on the answering machine was still blinking. Florida area code on the caller ID. Last night, she'd listened as her mother left a bright message, wondering if Susan had any interest in taking a cruise over the holidays. "It will be fun, honey. I promise." There was a long pause, as if her mother knew that she was standing right there, not picking up the phone. "Okay, well, call me. I miss you. And Stephen says hi."

Stephen was her mother's new husband. Her father had died of cancer in 1999. Her mother lived in Florida now. Susan hadn't gone there, not once in all the years that she moved around the country. All the cosseting and worry, it was too intrusive to consider. Her mother was hurt which had upset Stephen. *Your mother loves you, Susan. Don't shut yourself off from your family.* She wasn't. She was shut off period, the breaker thrown, the bulb blown. *This isn't what Sean would have wanted. You're a young woman. You deserve to have a life.* Her mother's constant refrain, Susan's knuckles white against the phone. She wasn't young and she knew what she deserved. She stopped answering the phone. It was better for everyone. She erased the latest message and the light went dark.

Very few families can withstand madness. It was hard to explain, how it manifested itself. Contrary to popular belief, a crazy person can know she's crazy. It's other people who don't want to believe it. In the beginning, right afterward, she would see them. The towers. Never Sean, not like his father or friends, chasing after a face in the crowd only to catch themselves. She'd be out somewhere and out of the corner of her eye, there they'd be, hoarding the skyline. Twin sentinels, the gatekeepers. She'd look again and they were gone. She knew she was losing it. *It's okay, Susan, the doctors said. It's normal.* Like hell it was normal. She wasted years listening to them. The only thing she missed was the pills.

She slept for a while. Jolene and the boys had packed up and gone when she awoke. The air conditioners hummed, a new noise to incorporate, the house slowly cooling. She dug through the Wal-Mart bags and found the duct tape. It was time to get it done.

In the downstairs bathroom, the old medicine cabinet had a mirrored door, going moldy around the edges, silver flaking away. It was the only mirror in the house. She'd been trapped in it, her second night, unaware, coming in and flicking on the light. Her face, that face, in the glass. She'd fled the room, her heart pounding so fast, trying not to gag. Anxiety is to be expected, Susan. She bent her forehead to her knees, waiting for the panic to subside.

Life was not about living. Endurance, that was it. There was a price to pay for drawing a breath. She knew hers. And she hadn't unpacked it. Thought maybe it would go away, leave her alone. She had the phone. But nothing had changed, the rules still the same here as in any other place. It was supposed to be out, where she could see it. And they could see her.

She'd begun pawing through the boxes in the living room, looking for it, stumbling on towels in the third box she checked. She paused in her search, grabbed one and taking a deep breath, gone back to the bathroom. Eyes averted, she inched inside, feeling her way, fingers trembling as they found the cabinet, blindly pushing the door open. Mirror, mirror to the wall. She forced herself to look.

It was just a metal cabinet. The shelves were nasty with contact paper, rusty corners, dead spiders. A big fat bug the size of her thumb, upside down dead, the stuff of bad Japanese movies. The old Susan would have been creeped out. The new Susan knew more about monsters.

Then she'd gone to the living room and searched until she found it. A picture frame, brassy gold, cheap, the kind that hinged in the middle and held two pictures. On one side was a blonde man, a good picture of a good-looking guy. He smiled at her. The other man was dark, the picture a bit grainy. He was looking up, young, a bit chubby, caught by surprise. Susan had positioned the frame on the mantle, gently running her fingers over his face.

Now she took the duct tape and went to bathroom. The mirror stood as it had been, to the wall, the towel protecting her from any sudden sightings. Carefully she pulled it off, feeling her heart rate pick up. She ripped a strip of tape with her teeth and looped it over the door, working from behind. Another, then another, then another, using touch to guide the edges, carefully overlapping them. After half a roll, she was safe enough to face it, extra strips lined up on the edge of the sink, ready to fill any holes. A few slivers and it was over. A new silver, over glass not under, solid and dull, nothing staring back.

The cat was on the porch railing again, same story, running when she put out the food. She understood being afraid of people. Susan had never been one of a pack, not a girl with girlfriends, never one of a gang that emptied the table for trips to the ladies room. It had always been her and Maggie, the two of them against the world. Maggie was nice, sweet. Susan was outspoken. Too assertive for a girl, one of her eighth grade teachers had noted on her report card. She did tend more toward temper than calm. She was smart, everyone thought so, funny though sometimes caustic. One time, she overheard one of Sean's friends telling his date that Susan could be quite the bitch. She probably could, but hadn't realized that people thought so.

She watched from the kitchen as the cat peered warily from the long grass. Finally slinking up on the deck, she wolfed down the food. When she finished, she jumped to the railing and began to groom. A graceful basketball on toothpick legs, such a big belly, nipples already gone to teats.

She and Sean hadn't wanted children. We're young, he used to say. Let's enjoy it, she'd agree, wrinkling their noses at friends whose lives had been overrun by diaper bags and baby wipes. She was so grateful not to be one of the 9/11 mothers. All the pregnant women. All the fatherless children, gifts from God, people said. If that was the best God could do, Susan wanted no part of him. She remembered watching them on Oprah, holding up the last remnants of their husbands and lovers for all the world to see. Smiling. Brave women, better than her. She had to turn off the TV.

Sean's office was above where the fuselage hit. Where the jumpers jumped. She sometimes wondered if he had. They would have found the body, Patrick always said, not wanting to believe his son could have thrown himself out into the sky. Tumbling down through the smoke and the flames to shatter on the street. They'd have found the body, he insisted. Susan wasn't sure. There were so many bodies that were never found.

She paid attention back then. Watched everything, read everything, wrote letters to the editor, gave speeches for groups and committees. A public face, hiding in plain sight. Then one day she woke up and realized there was nothing new to add. It was simple, really. Nineteen men had gotten on four airplanes and drove them toward buildings. One to a field. Ashes, ashes, we all fall down.

43

The deer were back in the back yard again, grazing in the moonlight as clear as day. It made her heart ache, the simplicity of it. The beauty. She sat on the steps of the deck, fingering her wedding ring. Circling the rim, never putting it on. When she lifted her head, two golden eyes were staring, close, closer than ever before. Wary but motionless. Susan sat there most of the night, till the deer moved on and little cat curled into a ball and slept on a moldy cushion forgotten in the weeds by the steps of the deck.

Chapter 8: August 1, 2006

"You've got to be kidding," Susan said.

People always reacted that way when they first saw the car. It came with the franchise. A lime green hatchback with a giant insect leering from the roof, six furry legs and ping-pong ball eyes. Bug Doctor, proclaimed big purple letters across the hood and doors, a phone number and website smaller in black.

"Think of it as a conversation starter," Jackson said, extending a hand. She shook it, small hands and an awkward grip.

"I guess Jolene told you I needed an exterminator?"

He nodded, pulling a clipboard from an crate of papers in the trunk. He closed the hatchback and the bug eyes bounced cockeyed down to the windshield. Attached with Slinkys. Susan turned away, trying not to laugh.

"It's okay, I'm used to it," he said. He watched her as she walked, instinctively comparing her to Becky, as he did with all the woman he met. They were similar height, Susan much thinner, dressed in baggy shorts and a T-shirt with the tag poking out the back. Pretty in a faded kind of way. None of Becky's color and flair. No light inside.

"…thank you for the cake," she was saying. "Or maybe I shouldn't. It's an addiction."

"That's how we hook ya, first slice is free," he joked.

"I'm turning into a beached whale."

"Not likely," he scoffed. He felt her bristle. Not sure why, but he turned his attention to the house. "I'm gonna take a quick look and let you know what's what."

When he came to the door, she was scrubbing the walls in the bathroom. Citrus scent. "Sorry to interrupt."

"No that's fine. So what's the verdict?"

"I got good news and bad news, which do you want first?"

"Bad."

"You got termites up the wazoo," he said.

"Technical term?"

"I am the Bug Doctor, you know."

"So what's the good news?"

"I'm gonna get them gone."

He walked her around the house, pointing out the telltale signs, poking boards with a pen, so she could watch them go to dust. At some point, the little black cat began to follow, picking a careful path through the grass. "Got yourself a friend?"

"Came with the house. Like the bugs," she added. "I think she's gonna have kittens."

"You think?" He squatted, wickering deep in his throat, hand outstretched. Carefully the cat ventured forward, touched her nose to his finger. "What's her name?" She ran at the sound of his voice.

"I can't believe she got that close to you." She seemed upset. There was something about this girl that wasn't right. None of your business, he thought. "Are you okay?"

"I'm not keeping it," she blurted. "It's not mine or anything."

"Okay."

"It's somebody else's cat," she said, hugging herself, fingers fidgeting.

"You've never lived in the country, have you?" She shook her head. "Folks can't be bothered with getting a cat spayed, or can't afford it, they end up with too many cats. So they take 'em out on some old country road and dump 'em."

"That's awful."

"I suppose it beats drowning, but not by much." She'd gone pale. "Are you sure you're okay, it's pretty hot..."

"Why do you keep asking me that," she snapped.

"I'm sorry, didn't mean anything." They reached the bug mobile. "I had a cat when I was a kid. Callie, that was her name." She didn't answer, didn't ask any questions. This girl was strange, too used to being alone. The words came out before he had time to think. "Would like to let me show you around sometime, maybe get something to eat?"

"Doesn't seem like there's that much to see."

"Classic Yankee mistake, we've got..."

"Thanks, but I don't think so," she interrupted, fingers plucking at her shorts. "Do I pay you now?"

"No, when I'm done." He felt stupid. Hadn't dated since the divorce and here he was hitting on some girl with cardboard furniture. Who just blew him off. Nice, he thought.

"It's an out of state check."

"I know where you live. You're not planning on packing up and leaving in the dead of night, are you?"

"What I do is none of your business!"

"Hey, I wasn't…"

"Let's get one thing straight. I need an exterminator, period. Nothing else. We clear on that? Doctor," she added sarcastically.

"I don't think that will be problem," he snapped back. "But you're right, with an out of state check, I should get it in advance."

He climbed into the car, shoving aside a bug leg as she stalked to the house. Temper rising, memories playing in his head.

"Oh stop whining. You are so freaking needy."

"What's that supposed to mean?"

"Please Jack, you follow me around like a puppy!"

"I'm sorry that I want to spend time with my wife!"

"Wah, wah, wah. If I wanted a baby, I'd have one."

"Jesus, Becky," he protested, *eyes dark with hurt.*

"Trust me, sugar, I treat you exactly the way you want me to."

"Here." Susan was suddenly at the car window, thrusting the check forward.

He blinked. *"Start as soon as it clears,"* he said, snapping it from her fingers.

***

Dinner was late. Again. The stupid bitch couldn't even get dinner on the table on time. He opened the refrigerator and pulled out a beer.

"I gotta warm it up, need to warm it up," he mocked, watching his wife put together a plate for the microwave. "Been ready in the first place wouldn't hafta warm it up."

She didn't bother explaining he was over an hour late. It was torture, watching the clock tick, no win no matter what. If she kept the food on the stove it would be overcooked, dried out. If she didn't, it would need to be warmed up. She tried to listen for his truck, get the plate in microwave before he got in the door. But the baby had been coloring in her room, called her to see a drawing. She'd gone. Stupid, just like he said.

"I set up a tray at the TV," she murmured. Trying to anticipate, to avoid, to manage. "Why don't you get yourself comfortable and I'll bring your dinner in."

He was on her at the sound of her voice, grabbing her face with one hand, cheeks contorted, lips squeezed tight. She went up on her tippy toes, his nose inches from her face. "Think you're smart, do ya?" He hissed, breath ripe with beer. "Do ya?" Mute, she shook her head. He let go of her face and shoved her against the counter. No avoiding it now.

He slapped her, almost casually, the back of his hand across her cheek. "You know what you are, I'll you what you are. You're lucky I stay with you, that's what. Who else would take ya?" He stepped closer, flipping her hair, poking her breasts, slapping at random. He grabbed her arm and flung her across the room. She stumbled, fell to the floor. "Dumb bitch," he snarled and kicked her. Once, twice, she curled, trying to cover herself. He stood over her, breathing hard. "Now get your ass up and get my dinner done." She didn't move fast enough. "You hear me," he yelled, jerking her up by the hair.

"Yes, yes," she cried. "I'll get it. I'm sorry. I'm sorry."

"You sure as shit are," he snapped, throwing her back down.

***

She'd met Sean at an art opening in Soho. A friend from work had a friend who was an artist, his first show. Susan came alone. The paintings were hideous, big canvases smeared with black and brown paint. Stick figures in red and orange.

"Ugly, aren't they?"

She glanced at him. He had dark hair, blue eyes. Black Irish, they called it.

"That does seem to be the point."

"You a friend of the artist?"

"A friend of a friend of the artist." She finished her paper cup of sweet wine. "How about you?"

"Just looking to meet a pretty girl," he grinned.

They had been together ever since.

***

No one had thought to notify the dispatchers at 9-1-1. So when everyone started calling them, they didn't have a clue. People on the street knew more. It was hard to conceive now what they didn't know then. Dedicated men and women, sitting at their consoles wearing headsets in a building without windows, they were trained for emergencies. Not this one. Their lines were jammed. Cell phones breaking up, everything overloaded, no way to access information.

They told people to wait for the firemen or to exit the building in an orderly fashion. Stay off the elevators. Wait for instruction. Go to the roof if you can't get down. They didn't know the helicopters wouldn't be able to land. They didn't know anything, but how could they? Susan wondered how many of them still lay awake at night, agonizing over the calls they took, the advice they had given.

She arranged the boxes in the dining room to fit a rectangle on the floor, a bit of shine protected by a long lost table. It took her a while to get the order right, the size of the boxes not quite in perspective with the space. She dragged two of the big Rubbermaid containers from the kitchen and positioned them on either side. Chairs. She rearranged the table boxes again to make room for legs. She drove into Wal-Mart and bought three bowls, a blue and white flowered tablecloth, a six pack of beer and bands to keep her hair off her face.

When she got home she put food out for the cat and waited for the deer, but they didn't come. The cat did, watching her, leaving herself enough room for a head start.

"You weren't afraid of him," Susan said. The cat didn't blink. "I won't hurt you." At least I won't mean to, she thought. The cat ventured closer, rubbing its chin on the concrete steps. Susan kept very still. "Is your name Callie? You like that," she asked, slowly extending her hand like he did. "Come on, here kitty." She felt the whiskers, the cat rubbing its jaw on her finger tip. "Callie," she crooned.

Sean was allergic to cats. Sneezed like a mad man whenever they were around. She'd never had one. They'd had a dog when she was growing up, Hokey was his name, like Hokey-Pokey, her mother said. Susan had tried to train him to do it, spent hours putting one foot in, the other foot out. Funny the things a person remembers.

***

"Hey, sugar," Jolene drawled, plopping down in the cardboard chair. "Love what you've done with the place." She gestured toward the dining room.

Susan glanced over her shoulder, on her hands and knees at the fireplace. "Hey. You done already?"

"Already? It's after four."

"Really?"

"Another stack of shingles and you'll be snug as a bug in a rug," she said. "Wonder where that came from, snug as a bug, gross when you think about it."

"You know anything about chimneys?"

"Some, I suppose. Don't think there's much to know." Jolene crouched down next to her, dropped to her knees and peered up the hole. "You gotta open the flue."

"I did, at least I think I did. I can't tell if it's open because I can't see anything."

"It's stuck." Jolene rattled the handle, stuck her head in farther. "You know we'll be eating soot if this sucker comes loose."

"Be careful."

"There's something stuck up there. Leaves or a dead squirrel. Could be a bat's nest."

50

"Bats?"

"Nothing to be scared of, they eat spiders you know." Susan wasn't convinced. "They only fly at ya cuz they're blind. If you navigate by noise and somebody starts screaming, well, duh, what do you expect them to do! You got a broom or something?"

It took three pokes before a lump of leaves, pine needles and a dead bird came tumbling down. The soot followed suit. They both jumped back, tipping over.

"Damn!" Jolene coughed. Her face was black, rings around the eyes. Susan giggled. "You don't look much better."

"But I can see the sky," she crowed, sticking her head in the hearth.

"Still need to have it cleaned, probably enough creosote up there to blow the place to kingdom come." Jolene wiped her face with her sleeve, looked at Susan and laughed. "You're the better half of a minstrel show."

"I'll get some towels. You want a coke?"

"Got any beer?"

"Bottom shelf."

They sat outside on the front porch. The heat was shocking after the air-conditioned house. Solid, a wall of thick moist steam. Jolene ran the cold bottle over the back of her neck before she took a long pull.

"Nothing like it. A hard day's work, a cold beer." She nudged Susan with her shoulder. "Even better with a friend." Susan didn't answer. "We're friends, right."

"I guess."

"Don't sound so excited," Jolene said. "Hard being alone, not all the time, god knows I'd cut off my arm to have a moment's peace, but...life's better with some back up." Susan nodded. "How long's it been?"

"What?"

"Since he's gone?" Susan stared. "A woman doesn't hang a wedding ring around her neck for no reason." Jolene reached over and touched the chain, the gold band dangling outside the shirt. Susan looked down, quickly stuffed it back inside, a perfect circle carved out of the soot on her shirt.

"I don't want to talk about it."

"Sure. Okay. Sorry." Jolene leaned back and took a long swallow. Susan stiff as a board beside her, she half expected to get tossed off the porch. Need to mind your own business, she said to herself. Weren't too many folks around with a messed up house and plenty of money to fix it. She was so far behind with everything and the car note was coming up next week. They needed this money. Susan cleared her throat.

"He died. I just don't like to talk about it."

Jolene lifted her beer in silent assent. Susan rolled her neck, tried to loosen her shoulders. The quiet stretched.

"I ever tell you about Billy's momma?" Jolene asked. "That old woman is crazier than a shithouse rat. I mean, out there. Got this patch of weeds in the front yard, sticks a tomato plant in it every spring and calls it a garden. Well, she's decided the reason she don't get nothing growing is because of the crows. What crows, there ain't no crows because there ain't nothing for them to eat! It's like talking to a wall," she said, shaking her head. "Next thing I hear she's down at the pawnshop and talks Duke Merry into selling her a damn shotgun." Jolene polished off her beer. "You think you got problems, well, let me tell you."

Chapter 9: August 3, 2006

The phone rang. She checked the caller ID and picked up the phone.

"Maggie!"

"I had to call your mother to get the number, what's up with that?"

"I'm sorry, I was going to call but..."

"Yea, yea, yada, yada. So you're in the Carolinas?"

"Wendell, to be exact."

"Yee ha."

"Hey, Scranton's not exactly the culture capital of the world."

"But we are known for our construction. So what are you doing in Wendell?"

"When-dell."

"Whatever."

"I don't know. I just found a house and...I don't know."

"You got a house? Wow, Susan!" You're finally getting better, Susan. Thank god you're not still crazy, Susan.

"I probably won't stay."

"Don't get huffy. What's the house like?"

"Oh shoot, Maggie, it's the termite guy," Susan exclaimed, looking down the empty driveway. "This place is a mess and here he is and I gotta go. Can I call you back?"

"Can you?"

When they were kids, they'd done everything together. Swimming lessons and bike rides, Barbies, science projects, proms and summer jobs at Mickey D's. Then high school was suddenly over and Maggie went to college. Susan went to New York. For the first time, they were living different lives. Maggie studied accounting, got a two year degree. Susan sneaked into classes at NYU, art history, philosophy, women's studies. She worked three jobs to pay the rent on a studio apartment she sublet from a friend of her mother's.

After she and Sean moved in together, she ditched two of them and worked at Macy's, helping to set mannequins and props in the store windows. Maggie got engaged and instead of coming to New York, followed her boyfriend Eric to Pennsylvania. Susan was her maid of honor. Two years later Maggie would repeat the favor. Eric and Sean never hit it off. Susan and Maggie pretended not to notice.

***

When Jack got to the house, his dad's car was gone. He checked the workshop in the garage anyway, but it was empty. Neat and organized, a place for everything, everything in its place. His dad had been a school bus mechanic, same job for over twenty-five years. One day he'd bent to pick up a tire and couldn't straighten up. A ruptured disk, degenerative. He went back to work, but it was only a matter of time. After three more incidents and two more surgeries, he went out on disability. A hard thing for a man who had worked hard all his life.

Jack went up the back deck and saw his mother sitting at the kitchen table. The sun streamed through the sliding glass doors, bathing her in light. She was looking at something, a photo album, a pile of them on the table top. He tapped on the glass and she looked up, smiled over her reading glasses.

"What a nice surprise," she exclaimed, hugging him. Cordelia Wyle was a pretty woman. In her sixties, hair carefully colored a pale blonde, wide set hazel eyes. Her skin was fine, wrinkled around the eyes, cheek bones carved by the disease.

"What are you doing here? Let me get you some tea."

"I'll get it, Mom, you sit down," he said. "What are you looking at?"

"Oh just some old pictures. You remember this, when we went to Asheville?"

"Oh wow," he said, looking over her shoulder. "That tent leaked so bad!"

She chuckled. "Your father tried so hard. Out there in the pouring down rain, draping that tarp over the top, remember?

"I remember the mud puddle."

54

"Bless his heart, he was covered. And so mad that he fell." She ran her fingers gently over the page. "You and I laughed like fools."

"Dad didn't think it was so funny."

"Not then, but I've heard him tell the story. That mud puddle gets bigger every time." She flipped a few pages, both of them smiling.

"Where is he?"

"Oh, I imagine he's down to the hardware store or over at Skeeter's. A bit upset with me today."

"He's not upset with you. Why would he be upset with you."

"It's no matter, Jackson." Eyes on the album.

"Why is he upset with you?"

"I wanted him to help me with something." She turned a page. "Oh look, there you are at boy scout camp. My goodness, is that Bobby Germaine? What a chubby child."

"Mom, what did you want him to do?"

"Don't bother yourself about it, Jackson. It will take care of itself."

"Just tell me," he persisted.

She got up and turned on the kettle on the stove, taking a teabag out of a old tin canister on the counter, chipped around the cover, a decal of roses circling the base. "Why don't you go to church anymore, Jack?" She got down a cup and saucer. "I used to see you there every week." Before Becky left, she wanted to say.

"I haven't had time."

"Don't lie to your mother." The kettle shrilled. She poured hot water into her cup, let the bag steep, carefully squeezed it between thumb and spoon. "Her leaving, it's not the end of the world, Jack. There's more to come."

"I don't want to talk about this now, okay."

"Two years and the hurt's as fresh as strawberries in the spring. It makes my heart ache to see it." She came back to the table, touched his shoulder. "Oh I know, you're fine, everything's fine. God will carry you through, Jack, if you just ask him."

"If God was going to help, he might have stepped in before I made a complete ass of myself." He felt her eyes on his face, kept his on the photo album, flipping page, page, page, page.

"I'm sure your father felt the same way about that mud puddle." His eyes came up and she smiled. He couldn't help but smile back. "I love you, Jackson."

"What did you need done, mom?" She hesitated, debate plain on her face. Her hands had always been so beautiful, long and slender, nails ending in an arc, always polished. She shifted one of the photo albums, a pair of shears underneath. Her eyes were too bright. "I can probably do this part," she said, so soft he leaned in to hear it. "But I need help with the razor. For the back." He didn't understand. "The lady at the...the hospital, she said she shaved hers off, it's better, you know. Then just letting it fall out." A tear slid down her cheek. "I hate that I'm so vain," she whispered.

He put his arms around her, his cheek to hers. Then he picked up the scissors and cut off his mother's hair.

***

She never heard the car. The knock at the door scared her silly.

"Miz Kearney?" Charles Lyman stood at the screen, a gangly younger version of himself waiting in the yard. "Hope I'm not intruding?"

"Mr. Lyman."

"Charlie. And this is my grandson." The teenager mumbled hello, shuffled his feet. "How them floors coming?"

"I'm not too far along, scrubbing mostly." She still stood behind the door. "Oh, I'm sorry. Would you like to come in and take a look?"

"Fetch that pot of stew on the front seat, boy, and then you can get started." The boy turned and Charlie stepped inside. "My son's wife, wanted me to bring you some of her stew. She said I'm to tell you that you should add the dumplings right before it starts to bubble."

"That's so nice. Thank you."

"I'll tell her you said so." She offered him some coffee and put the stew in the refrigerator. Little Charlie vanished out the front door. "Looking good. Lots of elbow grease there, I betcha."

"They were pretty dirty. Kind of lost momentum though."

"Something worth doing always takes time." His eyes drifted over the cardboard table. From the front yard, an engine roared then settled in a steady growl.

She went to the window. The boy was on a rider mower. "Oh no, I can't..."

"Little Charlie, he needs to keep busy. A boy his age, too much time on his hands is trouble waiting to happen. He could come regular, keep the lawn tidy." He stirred his coffee. "You'd be doing me a favor, Miss Susan."

She didn't know what to say. He took a sip of coffee. "Mind if I take a look?" He walked into the living room, stopping every once in while to squat, scratch at some paint. "Planks still tight, that's good." He stood up, reaching for the mantle to keep his balance. "Your family?"

"What?"

He pointed to the pictures in the frame. "This your family?"

"No."

He paused, expecting more. Nothing came. "I got time to help with the strippin' if you'd like, while Little Charlie's doing the lawn."

***

It had been a long day. They stripped two thirds of the kitchen, Charlie working with the chemicals, while she managed the hand sander. Even with the air conditioner going full blast, sweat rolled down her face, trapping grit and wood dust on her cheeks, forehead and arms. The feeling was too familiar.

They were moving the refrigerator when Jackson showed up to spray. He offered to help. She said they were fine. "So glad the check cleared," she added. Not sure why she needed to be snotty.

"You and me both," he answered. Stalemate. He went outside and they got the refrigerator pulled out. Thick grease and dust like fur on the floor beneath it. She was suddenly exhausted, fatigue sweeping through her like a wave. She wasn't sure when she'd last slept. "Mr. Lyman, Charlie…I'm…"

"You're ready to drop, I can see that. We can finish this another day."

Little Charlie had worked his way around to the back, the rider mower taking out the tall grass with little effort. He was half done. The grass around the decks and steps were neatly mowed. Jackson was spraying at the far corner of the front porch, heading towards the back. Susan wondered where the cat would hide now.

It seemed to take forever before the mower was loaded and they were on their way. She waited, awkward and exhausted by all the goodbyes and thank you's. She hated it, all of it. She craved loneliness the way other people did company.

Patrick had insisted on a wake, took charge for her, in spite of her. So many people, she was sure they couldn't have all known him. Every funeral was a hot ticket to the biggest thing that had ever happened in the city. Hellos, good-byes, hugs, thank you for the flowers. *And this is Sean's wife, Susan. This is Susan, Sean's wife. That's nice of you. I appreciate it. Thank you. You're Sean's wife, aren't you? Susan?*

"Susan?"

Curled in the cardboard chair, her eyes flew open. Jackson stood in the archway to the dining room. "I'm sorry, I didn't mean to wake you."

"I wasn't asleep."

"Right. I'll be back in the morning to finish. Then I'll come back in about week, give it another shot."

"Fine." She wrapped her arms around her middle. He hesitated.

"Look, I didn't mean to offend you the other day."

"You didn't." Clearly waiting for him to go. He turned without another word.

Why didn't he just leave her alone? She'd asked herself that question a million times. If he had just left her alone. It would have been different. She wouldn't have done it on her own. She wouldn't.

Always playing the victim, aren't you, Suz? Sometimes people are victims, she'd said. Sean didn't believe her. He might now.

She picked up the frame and gazed at the two photographs, tracing the shape of the dark haired man. He should be the one she hated, but he wasn't. It was the other one. The other one was a liar. "Liar, liar, liar," she repeated, louder each time, backing into the dining room. The pathetic table. Rubbermaid chairs. She leaned her forehead against the wall, hit it with her fist. "Are you happy now!" She hit the wall again, harder now. "Look at me, are you happy now!" She kicked the wall, a satisfying dent. "Just. Leave. Me. A. Lone!" Punctuating each word with fists and feet. The drywall buckled, bruises to dents to holes. Suddenly aware, panting, what was she doing!

She fled to the porch, the dark so smooth, fireflies dancing in the night. The smell of cut grass was delicious. She sat on the front steps, looking out over the yard. It felt different, a lawn instead of field. She wasn't sure she liked it.

There were flower beds around the porch, edged in crumbling brick. A tangle of weeds and wildflowers, some roses. Yellow daisies, cosmos, fragrant pink and purple phlox coming back year after year even when no one tended to them. Strangling but struggling to stay alive. Why she didn't know. She squatted on the grass. Even with the recent rain, the soil was hard, Carolina clay. Some weeds came out easy, others fought, root and prickle. She yanked on a baby pine tree, falling backwards when it finally gave.

Meow. The cat daintily rubbed its chin against Susan's knee.

"Callie." She could see the bulges moving in its belly. She stroked her fur, scratching along the throat to the jaw line. A purr to rival the rider mower. Susan lay back on the grass, stars sprinkled across the sky like sugar on cookies. Callie Ann batting at the fireflies, jumping, her belly wreaking havoc with her balance. Susan rolled over, spread her arms wide, running her fingers over the silky lawn. Face to the ground, she drew a deep breath. Earth and grass. The cat leapt on her back, kneading, claws digging in.

"Ow!" The cat fled, ducking into a hole in the lattice and disappearing under the porch. "Great! Callie, come on." Susan went to the hole, caught a whiff of something strong and nasty. The termite spray. The cat was pregnant. "Here kitty, kitty." Susan peered in the hole. Golden eyes looked back from the far corner, way beyond her reach. "Come on Callie. Come out of there."

It would kill her. The termite stuff would kill her or the kittens would be born dead or deformed. Panic sucked the moisture from her mouth. She stuck her arm in the hole, blocked at the shoulder. She had to get her out! The cat couldn't know what was going to happen. She was just doing what she always did. Going to work, the Wall Street Journal tucked under arm, riding the elevator, just like any other day.

Susan pulled at the lattice with both hands. It wiggled but wouldn't give. She lifted a leg and kicked. The wood snapped like toothpicks. Kicked again, blood oozing from a scrape along her shin, she yanked a piece free and crawled in. The cat arched, hissed, backed into the corner. Susan lunged for her, claws lashing out, raking the side of her cheek. "Ouch!" She yelped, slamming her head into a crossbeam as the cat leaped past her and bounded out the hole.

***

There was only so much a person could do. It was funny that no one understood that. Those people who called on the phone, asking for their money, it wasn't any different for them. Outside their little cubicles, off the telephone, they were just folks trying the best they could. That's all a person can do.

Jolene picked a stray leaf from the headstone, a brushed pine needles from the top. "How are you, darling?" She smiled, tracing the small angel carved in the top of the stone. "Your brother called today, he's doing so good. I still can't believe he's in college, wouldn't say that to him, of course, I am so proud of him. First one in the family. You'd have gone too, smart as you are, your daddy always used to say that you learned things so quick he'd have to start reading books just to keep up.

That'd be something, your daddy reading anything other than a cereal box."

She stretched out next to the grave. The grass was thin, brown from the heat. Scratchy under her cheek. "I miss you, Darlene. We think about you a lot, me and your daddy. Did I tell you your grandma set her apron on fire last week? Still not quite sure how she done it, but then the curtains in the kitchen caught, it was a big to-do. She's fine though," Jolene added with a sigh. "I miss you baby girl."

She loved coming here. Some folks might not understand the pull a cemetery holds. It was the only place on this earth where life was truly simple. All its difficulties stripped away, burdens exchanged for everlasting peace. Tears welled in her eyes. Sometimes she got so tired. She hated to say so, wasn't a whiner or a crybaby, it was just that the bills never stopped coming and she couldn't get caught up, it was always something, the pump on the well, Mickey's books, Billy's heart pills. The pressure was like a Mac truck sitting on her chest. Slowly crushing her to death. She hated the nasty letters, the phone calls, hard-edged voices lobbying or bullying. As if she had enough to go around. It shamed her, them thinking that she wouldn't pay if she could.

Jolene took a deep breath, let it out. "I'm gonna go now, honey." She patted the ground and straightened the pot of plastic tulips leaning against the stone. "You take care and tell Jesus I said hey. Love you, sugar."

Jolene stood up, ran her sleeve over her cheek. This too shall pass, she knew that was true. But how did a person survive until it did? That's the part she wasn't so clear on.

Chapter 10: August 4, 2006

Four hundred thousand dollars. That's how much it took, give or take a hundred grand. Less than a half a million dollars to bring America to its knees. A defense budget in the trillions suckered by nineteen men. She'd printed their pictures off the Internet, passport photos, their eyes meeting the camera without concern. She had them blown up at Kinko's. Nineteen life-size faces. Some of them looked scary, most of them were young. There were at least two she would have let buy her a drink in a bar. She'd taped the pictures on the wall in their bedroom back in New York. Arranged the men by plane.

Waleed Alshehri was one of the five on American Flight 11, Sean's plane. His face was rounder than the rest, like a college kid, baby fat, a momma's boy. No evil showing. Not like Atta, the pilot, with his thin lips and lined eyes, Florida tan. They mostly showed Atta's picture on the news. He looked the way everyone needed him to be.

There was something about Waleed. She couldn't put her finger on it. The week before she left New York, she took all the pictures down. But when it came time to throw Waleed away she couldn't do it. Couldn't take another loss.

If she had to pinpoint it, that might be when she first knew she was nuts. With Waleed. She talked to him at night. His face played in her head like a song you can't stop humming. Annoying. Obsessive. The name of it always on the tip of the tongue. Who did he remind her of, she couldn't figure it out. Danny Carliosi, the Italian kid who had lived down the block from Maggie? Maybe the guy from Ray's Pizza, not the one uptown but the one on the corner. Original Ray's. No, it wasn't him.

When it came time to go, she couldn't leave him. That's when she got the frame. Put him there, side by side with a picture of Tom, smiling, back in another time.

At midnight, she was back in the yard weeding. She'd made quick trip to Wal-Mart for light bulbs, digging tools and a hose. On impulse, she got a fleece pillow she thought the cat might like and two white plastic chairs for the porch. She stood on one to put a bulb in the porch light, dumping out an inch of dead bugs before she put globe back on.

She didn't know anything about gardening, but pulling weeds was strangely satisfying, like scrubbing floors. She worked steadily, thinning out all of the shorter bed, pleased by the neat brown swatches of dirt in between the flowers. Her fingernails were black, a French manicure gone wrong. She got a beer and sat in one of the new chairs, fanning herself. Even the nights were hot here, over seventy-five degrees. August already. Thirty-eight days to go.

"Let's try the hose, Callie," she said. The cat didn't look up. Didn't bother with the fleece pillow either, curled instead on the other plastic chair.

Susan dragged the hose from the car, unraveling the kinks. She couldn't find a spigot, back into the kitchen for the flashlight. She finally found it on the driveway side, buried in thistles and some clingy spiky vine that climbed up the side of the house. She yanked them away, yipping as the thorns drew blood.

She caught a flash of gold out of the corner of her eye. A deer this close? There was nothing in the yard. Just jungle noises and quivering leaves on a huge hydrangea bush. She'd heard stories of rabid foxes and raccoons, she used to watch the Discovery Channel back when she watched TV. They came right up to people, too crazy to be afraid. She waited for a minute, debated whether to look.

"Don't get spooked," she told herself. She turned the faucet. The pipes groaned, knocked once or twice, spit. The hose twitched and plumped. Victory.

She hadn't gotten any type of nozzle, so she sprayed water with her thumb until it ached under the pressure. Then she laid the hose in the flower bed and went back to her chair, getting up every ten minutes or so to change the water flow. It felt good to have a garden. Wet dirt, mown grass, flowers and fireflies. Not home, but a nice place to be until she had to go.

***

Jolene's Nextel crackled on her belt. "This is Jolene, over."

Susan's voice was garbled, panicked. "Suz, hey, slow down, having trouble hearing you." The squawk was louder, even more shrill. "Okay, Suz, you gotta shut up and listen cuz I can't understand a word you're saying. I'm coming over, okay? I'll be right there." She clicked the phone off. "Best make that two coffees, Dottie and throw in a couple pieces of cake."

"Catering to a Yankee, never thought I'd see the day," Dottie muttered. Betty Jane nodded. "You want me to add Billy's tab on this?"

"Pay it Friday if that's okay with you?" Jolene took the coffee and cake and headed for the truck. She'd been planning to stop at Susan's later anyway, take a look at the sunroom, see if it could get shored up some. Money from heaven, she had to cater. She needed the work.

When she pulled into the driveway, Susan was standing in front of the porch. There was something sticking out of the lattice, didn't make sense to her eye. It wasn't until she got out of the car that she realized what it was. "Chair's supposed to go on the porch."

"Oh my god, Jolene, I hit a dog!"

"What?"

"I thought it was the cat but it's not the cat and I was just going to get some cake so we could have some when you came and last night I thought it was a fox, you know with rabies and I was backing up and..." Her chest was heaving.

"Hey, hey, hey, take a breath, sugar. It's okay. Calm down now, tell me slow."

She was going to the Coffee Cart, backing down the driveway when she saw it, out of the corner of her eye. Just like the night before. A small gold something. "It came out of nowhere, I didn't see it until I was already backing up and then..."

"Okay, all right. Did you hit it?" Jolene asked. "Did you feel a thump?"

"Oh my god!" Susan bent double. "It went in there."

Jolene peered in between the chair legs. Back in the corner, she could see two eyes, a panting tongue. A small mound of golden fur.

64

"Well, it's breathing, so you didn't kill it. Sorry," Jolene added when Susan gasped. "Can't tell from here if it's hurt."

"There's termite stuff in there!"

"Let's take one disaster at a time, okay." She bent and looked again. "Why don't you get some water and we'll see if we can get him to come to us."

Susan hurried into the house, came back with a small bowl and paper plate of Meow Mix. "It's cat food. It won't hurt him, will it?"

Jolene laughed. "You do crack me up, honey." She yanked the chair free, lay on her belly to push the food and water inside. "Come on, boy. Come on."

"Is it moving?"

"I told you it's not dead." Jolene's voice was muffled. "That's right, come on, here you go." She backed out, butt in the air. "Seems to be fine. Come on, see for yourself."

Susan crouched down and looked. The puppy lay on its belly, all four legs splayed out, little nose buried in the cat food, grunting like a pig. "He's hungry," she reported. "I better get some more."

The puppy ate himself to a stupor, Jolene shaking her head, Susan insistent that it was probably starving. They put the chair back and the puppy, blissfully full, feel asleep on its side, tummy rounded.

"Damn near as fat as the cat," Jolene said, sitting on the porch steps. "You still got the cat right?"

"Have you got something in the truck to cover the hole?" Susan asked. "I don't think the chair will stay."

"How'd the lattice get ripped up anyway?"

"I was trying to get Callie. The cat," she explained.

"At least I'm not totally out of the loop."

"Jackson said people dump animals out here, on the side of the road."

"Beats drowning."

"That's what he said. Do you think he belongs to anybody?" Jolene smirked over her coffee cup. "No," Susan insisted hotly. "Absolutely not."

"Hey, I didn't say nothing. So. You and Jackson hitting it off?"

"If you mean is he killing my termites, yes."

"He's a looker, that one. Good guy too. You can tell a lot by the way a man treats his momma. Your momma in New York?"

"She lives in Florida. She got remarried after my dad died. Cancer," she added.

"Me too. Isn't that funny how it all goes around? Jackson's momma, your daddy. Us being friends. God works in circles more than straight lines, that's what I think. Makes you wonder about those crop circles though, doesn't it?" She paused, considering. "Always thought it was aliens, like most folks, but I suppose you can't really know."

"You lost me."

Jolene laughed. "Sorry. I was talking about the cancer. You probably didn't hear about Jackson's momma, being new here and all. She's real sick, on the chemo. Been twelve years for me." She knuckled her head. "Knock wood."

"I didn't know." Not sure what to say.

"Don't be getting all serious," Jolene warned. "It's not like I ever had much on top anyway." Susan couldn't stop her eyes from looking. "Nothing to see. If I had fake boobies, trust me, they'd be bigger than this, Billy'd make sure of that," she said. "Back then, the insurance company didn't have to pay, not for that. Cosmetic surgery, that's what they called it. We had way more bills than we could manage, no money for that." She snapped a bra strap. "A little extra padding and it all looks the same."

"I'm so sorry."

"Don't be, geez Louise. If I see one more pink ribbon, I'll be taking a chain saw to somebody. That's the trouble with cancer, you tell folks about it and they get all sad and piteous, like you're dying or something. As if I'd give Billy the satisfaction," she added. "It's just my story. That's all life is, the chance to have a tale to tell."

Susan got up and stood at the railing, looking out over the yard. "When Sean died, everybody wanted to help me, but nobody even

66

asked what I needed. They just did things. Nice things, but nobody asked. You know?" She turned around.

"I do." Jolene slapped her thighs and stood. "All right, enough of this maudlin crybaby crap. Let's get us some cake and I'll give you a price on that sunroom. Course now that I got ya feeling sorry for me, you being a rich Yankee and all, I might have to gouge you a little."

"Bring it on, Dixie chick."

***

"Yep, we gotta find a new sponsor for next year, now that the Winn-Dixie got shut down," Bubba drawled, a wink.

"Got anybody in mind," Big Jim replied, playing his part.

They glanced at Skeeter. "I been thinking... don't know, maybe but...hey!" As if it just came to him. "How 'bout Gutter Balls!"

"Look good on a bowling shirt," Big Jim bellowed, delivering the punch line.

"Assholes," Skeeter muttered. "I gotta better idea anyway."

"Blue balls?" Somebody yelled, everyone laughing their ass off.

"Can't find nobody in this town who ain't ignorant," Skeeter snapped. "You just wait. Came to me last night, got it right here." He slapped a small yellow pad that sat on the counter. "Not talking about it, not with the likes of y'all."

"Hey," Bobby called from the coffee machine. "You hear the plant might be hiring on for an extra shift?"

The possibility of work caught everyone's ear. Discussion went from that to rising property taxes, then on to something juicier. Midnight last night, Abigail Caine had thrown her husband's clothes out the window and tried to set them on fire.

"Man can't have a few drinks with his friends," griped Duke.

"Jerry's been known to have more than a few," Ben noted.

"Still, burning a man's own clothes," Bubba protested. "Heard she tried to block the driveway so the fire truck couldn't pull in."

"Somebody oughta slap some sense into that woman," Big Jim said.

Billy got up to refill his coffee. Skeeter sulked behind the counter, scribbling on the yellow pad. Billy peered at the paper, lots of lines and drawings, arrows going every which way. Skeeter glanced up, look right and then left. "It's a moose trap," he whispered. "See, you got your pulleys right here..."

***

She woke, disoriented in the dark. Someone was crying. "Sean?" She got up from the chair, followed the sound to the front door. It was the dog. The whimpers getting louder and longer. She got the flashlight and went outside, crouching at the screen they'd stuck in the hole instead of the chair. "Hey, settle down."

It rushed to the sound of her voice, nose to the screen. A puppy for sure, gold snout, brown eyes, ears that were way too big for its head. He huddled close to the ground, submissive, tail wagging, frightened of being alone. "You're okay," Susan soothed, her fingers on the screen. He licked them, on his feet now, dancing with hope. "You want out, is that it?" He whined again, anxious eyes, and pawed at the screen.

"Okay, but you have to stay here," she said. The puppy flew from the hole, jumped against her knees, licked at her face, then raced into the yard, ecstatic, round and round, always circling back to her. Puppy crazy. Susan laughed out loud. "Come here, you goof." He raced to her, skidded to a stop, planted his front feet, rear end in the air. She reached for him, he darted away, back to the circles, running for the sheer joy of it.

She chased him. He loved it. She did too, couldn't believe how good it felt to race around the yard, feinting and dodging and sliding in the grass until she finally went down, breathing hard. The puppy was on her in a second, no mercy, little wet tongue and sharp white teeth, at her hair, her face, like a million mouths, everywhere all at once.

"I got you," she said, grabbing him and pulling him squirming to her chest. He licked her face, struggled to find his feet. "Oh no you don't." She staggered to hers, the dog in her arms. Off the ground, he went still, sitting in her arms like a baby. He was a baby. She glanced at the speckled pink tummy. "She. You're a little girl, aren't you." Susan climbed the steps. "Let's get you something to eat."

She put down a bowl of milk and a paper plate of stew in the kitchen. The puppy couldn't get it down fast enough, tail working like a corkscrew, its head jumping from milk to meat and back. Snorting. "What a little piggy." Tail thumping but not to be distracted. Pushing the empty plate around the floor. Susan filled another. Same routine, just as fast, licked it clean.

On to her now, the puppy planted herself at Susan's feet, looking up, tongue lolling. "No more." The puppy tilted its head, barked. "The kitchen is closed," Susan said firmly. The dog cocked her head, as if she understood, snuffled the plate one last time then trotted from the room.

She toured the house, Susan behind her, sniffing every corner. She circled the cardboard chair, barked at the fireplace, legs stiff, ruff rising on her neck, ferocious. Once the enemy was properly cowed, she squatted and peed on the living room floor. "That's just great," Susan said, going for the paper towels. The puppy sat and watched her mop it up then continued to explore, discovering a pair of flip flops in the bathroom. Nearly half her size, she dragged one around, shaking it and growling.

"That's my shoe, you know." The puppy glanced up, returned to her mission.

Susan sat on the floor, arms around her knees. No lights, just the glow from the porch globe. She felt little, memories stirring of nights as a child, alone in her room, brushing her baby doll's hair. She had always wanted a little sister. When she'd ask, her parents would laugh, their friends would chuckle. She didn't know why. She named her baby Zoey and pretended, crooning to her soft plastic skin, cuddling the doll to her chest. Someone to love. Even then she was looking.

"Zoey," she called. The puppy looked up, cocked its head. "Zoey, come here." The puppy bounded toward her. She scooped it up in her arms. "Baby Zoe."

Chapter 11: August 6, 2006

"Jolene, there's something wrong with the dog. You have to come over."

"You mean the dog you weren't gonna keep, that dog?"

"Just come, okay?"

They'd fallen asleep on the floor. Susan had woken up alone. Two fresh puddles of pee and a trail of puppy poop. Diarrhea. Undigested carrots clearly visible. "Zoey?" The puppy raced from the bathroom, flip flop in tow, its strap flopping loose. Shivering with delight, she yelped and leapt until Susan squatted and let her face be licked. "Don't try and make up," she scolded.

She had it cleaned by the time Jolene arrived, though the smell lingered. The puppy barked madly, planting itself between Susan and the door, running behind her legs when Jolene walked in. "Doesn't look sick to me."

"This is Zoey."

Jolene squatted, held out a hand. The puppy ran to her, wiggling with delight, on her back, legs pumping the air. "What's wrong with her?"

"There's something growing on her back."

Jolene flipped the puppy over, holding it by the scruff of its neck.

"See, right there." It was the size and shape of a large corn kernel, gray in color, puffy and wrinkled. "It's a growth, a tumor or something, there's another one behind her ear."

Jolene burst out laughing. "It's not funny!"

"It's a tick, the dog is covered with 'em."

"A tick. You mean a bug?" Susan took a step back. "That's a bug?"

"Been on her for a while, the sucker's close to bursting." Jolene lifted it with her finger, letting it flop back on the dog's fur.

"I think I'm going to be sick."

"We need tweezers."

"I don't have any." In a box somewhere, buy more at Wal-Mart

"Thread then?"

"Dental floss."

"Good enough."

Ticks thrived in North Carolina, clinging to long wet grass until they could catch a ride on unsuspecting skin. Dog, raccoon, human, they had no preference. There were lots of types and sizes, all blood suckers that burrowed into the skin and latched on. Lyme disease, Rocky Mountain Spotted Fever. "If you're not careful pulling 'em, you can take out a chunk of skin," Jolene said. "You can try putting Vaseline on 'em so they have to pull out their head, but...Zoey, settle down. Susan, you're going to have to hold her."

"Don't hurt her."

"Hold her still." Jolene looped the dental floss and slid the noose around the bug, close to the skin, pulling tight. "Just one more second, got it!" She popped the tick off. It fell on the floor on its back, too bloated with blood to right itself. Susan gagged. Jolene scooped it up, flushed it down the toilet. "Let's get the other one."

The puppy was covered with them. Some still crawling, others recently burrowed, two more like the first. Fleas too, having a field day on her belly and legs. "We're gonna have to dip her," Jolene decided, ten ticks later.

"Dip her in what?"

"Chocolate sauce and sprinkles, whaddya think? Flea dip." She patted the puppy and stood up. "We can run over to Wal-Mart."

It was a little before two in the afternoon. Hundreds of happy shoppers. "No." Quick, too definite. Jolene caught it. "I...I wanna try and shop in town, when I can."

"We can go to the hardware store." The puppy raised madly around the room, chasing after a fly. "You eat lunch yet, you're looking a little peaked?"

"I'm fine."

"You sure, because you look..."

"I said I'm fine," Susan snapped.

"Okay then." Folded lips. "Guess I better wash my hands." Jolene went in the bathroom, looked at the duct taped mirror and decided it was not the day to ask.

"I can't handle the people," Susan said, standing in the door.

Jolene wiped her hands on her jeans. "We all got our stuff."

"Don't tell me it's okay, okay?"

"And don't take me for an idiot. Who cares if it's okay." She shrugged. "It's what it is." Zoey cried at the door when they left. Jolene drove. Susan hung on.

They had it all at the hardware store. Flea dip, collars and leashes, a little bowl with paw prints in the bottom, puppy toys. "Look at this," Susan exclaimed, holding up a stuffed hippo. "It squeaks." She demonstrated.

"That'll be making you crazy in a week. How about this?" Jolene held up a dog training book.

"Jolene, Miss Susan. Help you find anything?"

"Hey Charlie. We're gonna need a sack of that puppy food."

"Billy got himself another hunting dog?"

"Not if he wants to live," Jolene replied. "Nope, Susan's found herself a puppy."

"Her name is Zoey," Susan added. "She's got ticks."

"Well, we can take care of that."

She bought one of everything they had. She was happy in the truck home, actually happy. "She poops in the house, you know," Susan said.

"Ain't that just like a new momma, always talking about the poop!" Susan laughed. "You never had no kids?"

"No." She looked out the window.

"You got all the right instincts, that's for sure." Susan didn't answer. Jolene kept her eyes on the road. "Must be hard on you now."

"Why would you say that?" No more happy. Angry, suddenly angry.

They pulled into the driveway. "I just thought, with losing him, it mighta been..."

Susan jumped from the car as soon as it slowed. "Look, I know you're trying to be nice, but I can't do this. I don't want to. Just leave me alone, okay?"

"Suz…"

"Don't call me that! It's Susan. I'm Susan. Sean's wife. Susan." She grabbed her bags and slammed the door.

***

Sean had taken her to the Grand Cayman as a surprise for their fifth anniversary. She was touched. They had gotten so distant, caught up in the operations of their life. Who would get the dry cleaning, mail the bills, buy the groceries. Almost like roommates instead of lovers. Did you remember to pick up toothpaste, can you stop at Barney's, did you talk to the super about the leak below the sink? Marriage quicksand. Love suffocated in honor of errands and tasks. How did it all become so important.

They spent lazy days, snorkeling and dancing, sex in the morning. She began to remember why she loved him. He had always loved her. Or so he said. It was only women who were never sure, always asking, always needing to know. I could tell you a hundred times a day, he said. A minute later, you wouldn't be sure. She argued the point, secretly knowing he was right. After they made love, she lay awake, wondering if he was really the one. Would she be so uncertain if he was?

There was a balcony off their room. The moonlight lush across the ocean. How do you know that you love someone? Once the chemistry had settled and the romance had stilled. She turned and looked at him, sleeping. He worked so hard. Too hard she thought, never letting him forget it. They needed more of this, more time together. He rolled over, an arm flung across her pillow. It didn't wake him, her being gone.

***

He'd wanted kids. When they'd talked about waiting, Sean never meant forever. She ruined it, just like Jolene, she ruined everything. *Susan can be quite the bitch at times.* Jolene wasn't coming back. She sat at the cardboard table and stared at the holes she'd put in the dining room wall. Jolene could have fixed them. Susan could have taken down the wallpaper, got a light and a real table. But she ruined it. She always did. There was some comfort in that, a constant that no one could take away.

She had a sliver in her foot from when they did the floor. It was bulging now, pus building, inflammation starting to trail up the toward the ankle. She scratched at it, but couldn't break the skin. She didn't have a needle but she'd bought razors at Wal-Mart to shave her legs in the shower. She pushed the bathroom door open slowly. The puppy was asleep in the corner, a favorite warm spot between the dryer and the wall. Quietly, she reached around the shower curtain, feeling for the soap dish. Baby blue plastic razors, buy them by the bag. It took a few minutes to pry the blade free.

She lanced the skin and squeezed. The pus and the sliver oozed out, just a tiny piece of wood. Innocuous. Foreign to the body. Foreign countries, foreign men. While she and Sean were snorkeling with the sting rays, they were making their plan. Living in caves, machines guns slung across their chests like Girl Scout sashes, bullet clips instead of badges. She squeezed again, weeping clear liquid, no more pus or blood.

She was cross-legged on the floor, her foot sole up, resting just above the knee. Her thighs were getting fat. No, not fat, loose. Like those mushy pillows, U-shaped to wrap around the neck. Wobbly sacks of flesh and muscle. It was repulsive.

Without thinking, she ran the razor blade along her inner thigh. It didn't hurt. The opposite in fact. She'd done it before. A thin line of blood. Neat and straight. She lay another line, below the first, longer this time, blood coming faster, just behind the blade. It was mesmerizing, like invisible ink, suddenly exposed. She cut another, pressing a bit too hard. Blood dribbled down her leg.

"This little piggy went to market, this little piggy stayed home. This little piggy had roast beef." She studied her bloody thigh. "And this little piggy..." She made a deliberate slice. "This little piggy had none."

74

Chapter 12: August 7, 2006

Becky was on the morning news now. When Jack walked into Dottie's, there she was, smiling on cue. Not an anchor yet, but on her way. Just had to figure out who to screw, he thought. "Hey." Pretending it was no big deal. "You're looking fine this morning, Miss Dottie."

"Don't start something you can't finish, boy," she advised, handing Jack a coffee. The TV was muted, if he just didn't watch... He turned and looked. She had an earnest expression, brows slightly knit, serious without losing the pretty. Her hair was touched up, red, or maybe it was the lights. She finished her bit, big smile for the camera. Back to you to, Larry. He swallowed without thinking, nearly choked on the steaming hot coffee.

"Careful, shug."

"You trying to kill me?" His eyes watered, a patch on the roof of his mouth raw.

"If I was, you wouldn't be standing there."

Conversation turned to the Pilot volunteer fire department's annual pig pickin'. Dottie had been in charge of donations since as long as he could remember. A sugar-coated bully, holding cake and biscuits for ransom. Dutifully, he signed up for the silent auction. "Sad when all a man's got to offer is dead bugs," Dottie noted, taking the list back. "Better buy yourself some tickets for the fifty-fifty raffle. Two dollars a piece, three for five," she added.

"By the you finish gouging me, I'll have to start a tab."

"Think again, bug boy," she said, pointing to the yellowed sign above the grill. NO CREDIT, NOBODY, DON'T ASK. Ignored anytime anybody couldn't afford to pay.

The door opened and his father came in. "Dad, help me out, I'm taking a beatin' here," Jack called.

"I'm sure Miz Dottie knows what she's doing."

"That's right. Got sausage biscuits today, Ben, sit down and I'll plate one up."

Ben shook his head. "Just coffee, if you don't mind." She didn't challenge him like she should, like she always did. Jack's stomach tightened. His father seemed smaller. He didn't want to see it, didn't like that others did.

"Hey dad, I was wondering if you could come over and take a look at the bike, it's back-firing like crazy," he said.

"Can't today." Ben shook his head.

"Why not," Jack pushed.

Ben turned, eyes cool. "Must be busy."

Jack flushed, as if he was ten. "I didn't mean to..."

"Thank you, Miz Dottie," Ben interrupted, taking the coffee and dropping money on the counter. He clapped his son on the shoulder. "You bring it by tomorrow or the next day, I'll take a look." Ben went out the door into the heat. His truck was parked down the block a bit. He climbed in the driver's seat, fumbled the keys in the ignition.

He was a private man, old school, not one to wear his feelings on his sleeve. He had to be strong, for his family, for Cordelia most of all. He knew that. But his insides, they wouldn't stop shaking, that sense of impending doom, building with every passing day. A volcano ready to blow. He was going to lose her. He was going to watch her die, a little bit at a time. A tremor shook him and he grabbed the steering wheel with both hands. Leaned his forehead on the knuckles, eyes closed, wet behind the lids. He sat like that for a minute, then took a deep breath and started the truck.

***

"Sit."

Zoey rolled over on her belly, wriggling like a fish.

"No, sit." Susan squatted, took her by the collar, planted her rear and lifted her head. "Sit." She let go. The puppy stayed in position, watching Susan's face. "Good girl," she beamed.

Zoey leapt up and raced around the house. Empty house. Jolene hadn't called. No new messages.

***

The girl was a mental case, that's all there was to it. "Hey Mike," Jolene called to the lumber guy at Lowes. "Any idiot can see that," Jolene muttered

"What?"

"Not talking to you," she said, tossing a pile of flashing into the back of the truck.

"Don't see anyone else here."

"I'm here," she snapped. "So don't be listening to private conversations."

Mike smirked, started loading the wood while Jolene went to the cash register. "Hey Tina. It'd help if I could put some of this off until next month," she said.

"We gotta ask Miss Donna, you know, after the last time," Tina replied.

"I paid that," Jolene said. "Can't we just..."

"Gotta ask Miss Donna," the girl repeated.

Jolene knew what Miss Donna would say. "Never mind, don't have time right now."

Money, money, money, running round and round in her head like a trapped squirrel. Living on a shoestring, one day to the next, she'd pinned her hopes on the Garrett place, enough work to get her by and then some, but that was done now. Another door closed. Her momma liked to believe that when one door closes, another door opens. Her daddy would always wink and add that the time in between weren't no picnic. Jolene could attest to that.

She hadn't meant to set Susan off and to be fair, the girl was a time bomb, so set to explode you could almost hear the ticking. Still what was she thinking, bringing up a dead man and the kids they never had. Dumb, dumb, dumb, Jolene thought, Miss Big Mouth, spouting off without thinking, whatever came into her head coming out of her mouth, Billy told her all time. And now she'd pay the piper, no sunroom, no plumbing, no electric, no money. No Yankee anything.

Jolene hated to admit it, she didn't need another nut job, lord knows she'd married into a family full of them, but she was going to miss Susan. Weren't too many girls round town to be friends with, except the ladies at church and Jolene felt out of place with them more often than not. For the most part, they took care of homes and kids, their husbands provided. Some of them worked a bit here and there, but they didn't carry the load. Susan carried more than her share, whatever the burden, it was eating her alive.

Her grandma used to say when a person feels guilty, they usually have something to be guilty about. But that wasn't always true. Life was full of things you'd change in second once you knew how they turned out. A person could get stuck, reliving things over and over, watching a little girl run out the door after her Paw-Paw, hear herself calling, "Be good now." Nothing more than that, becomes one of those boa constrictors, slithering up from your heart to your neck and choking you to death.

"Jolene?" Tina repeated the total.

"Sorry." She wrote the check, carefully noting the amount in the register, not letting herself look at the balance. She spent so many nights at the kitchen table, Billy dead to the world, while she sat making lists of numbers, writing them this way and that, looking for the right combination, robbing Peter to pay Paul. All the work that house needed, she coulda got most of Mickey's tuition money for next year. Gone. All because she couldn't hold her tongue. It was no consolation that Susan wasn't any better.

***

The flea bath wasn't pretty. Susan went through a bag of Pupperoni treats trying to coax her in the shower before she finally wised up, filled the kitchen sink. "Who's the mother here," she scolded, scooping the puppy up. Zoey nipped at her chin, licked her ear. "Stop that." Susan held her up and out, hands under her front legs. The puppy dangled there, one ear flopped over. "It's for your own good."

Zoey fought like a trouper, then subsided in abject misery. Susan worked the shampoo through her fur, feeling the bumps and working the lather into attached bugs. The puppy whimpered. "It's okay, baby.

It's okay," she murmured, pouring a cup of water over the dog's head. It was not okay.

Zoey gave a sharp bark. Jackson stood at the side door, hand raised to knock. Susan turned to look and Zoey took her shot. Up onto the counter, down to the floor, running as fast as her little wet feet could manage. No traction on the wood, the puppy careened around the corner, slid into the wall. Susan heard him laughing. "Not funny," she yelled, giving chase. "Help me!"

They trapped her in the bathroom, almost had her, but the suds were too slippery. By now, it was a game, Zoey in the lead, dodging in and around boxes, claws skittering across the floor. Jackson slid in her soapy trail, down on one knee.

"Get Mr. Hippo," Susan called, chasing the puppy around the chair.

"Mr. What?"

"Her toy. In the bathroom."

One squeak was all it took to get Zoey's attention. She raced to the dining room, ripping the toy from his hand. Her toy. Hers! She growled, bit it, squeaking for mercy, as Susan threw a towel over her. Zoey was enthralled by the new game, kept a grip on Mr. Hippo while Susan rolled her back and forth. At first chance, she jumped free, dropped the toy for the towel and dragged it across the floor.

"I give up," Susan said, looking down at her soaked shirt. "At least one of us won't have fleas."

"You should have called," he said. She looked at him, uncertain. "The bug doctor?"

"Ha-ha."

"How long have you had her?"

"She just showed up in the yard. Wouldn't leave," Susan added.

"Uh-huh. What does the cat have to say?"

"I haven't seen her. I put food out and it's gone, but..." Susan plucked her wet shirt loose and fanned it up and down. "You don't think that stuff that you sprayed, that it could have hurt her?"

"No, I'm sure she's fine. It's probably time."

She glanced up. "Time for what?"

Jackson laughed. "Kittens, hello."

She followed him out to the barn. Little Charlie had cut the grass halfway back, after that you were on your own, grass and weeds thigh high. "You have to watch out for ticks," she said, following the path he broke.

"You can't watch for 'em, gotta check yourself after."

"They're disgusting," she said. "And they look like corn, really old corn."

He chuckled. "That's Yankee talk for sure. Watch your step, there's a hole."

Barely more than a lean-to, the barn still smelled faintly of horse, though Jackson said there hadn't been any for years. There were two stalls off the back, a broken shovel, rusty pitchfork, steps to a loft. A huge plastic bucket, cracked along the rim, sat near the door, cruddy, with rotting straw and dried manure. "Callie, here kitty, kitty." Susan brushed at a cobweb. It stuck to her fingers. "Yuck."

"Callie?" Eyebrows raised, as he started up the stairs.

"Just be careful," she said, ignoring him, gingerly placing each foot on each step.

"Found her," he called. In the bottom of a bin, lying on dried oak shards and moldy grain, Callie lay on her side. Four kittens suckled off her belly like the ticks on the dog. "Don't get too close. If you spook her, she'll move them somewhere."

"They're so tiny." Callie's eyes glowed serene. The kittens squirmed against her, little blind mice. They watched for a minute or two, Susan touching his arm to point to one or the other. Smiling, real smiles. "I should get her some food," she whispered. "Thank you for finding her."

"You're welcome." He helped her down the steps, she didn't stiffen at the touch. Back at the house, he headed for the car to get his sprayer. When he heard her shriek, he ran for the kitchen door.

It was a blizzard, white everywhere. Wal-Mart sold toilet paper in packs of twelve rolls, no room in pantry, she'd left it on the floor against the wall. There was paper everywhere, draped and dragged and shredded covering the kitchen floor, trailing into the dining room and beyond. Zoey curled in a nest of it, paper stuck to her ears and chin and nose, a square fluttering with each snore.

***

He carried food out to the cat before he left while Susan swept. Zoey followed her like a shadow, nipping at her ankles, barking at the broom. "Back off you little monster," she threatened. The puppy wasn't scared.

"So, you're all set. Termite-free."

"Another home saved." She walked him to the car.

"Shucks, ma'am, all in a day's work."

"Thanks again. See you around." She patted the giant bug on the head.

"How does a girl like you end up here anyway," he asked, closing the trunk.

"Girl like what?" Irritated, sharp as scissors.

"Here we go, what pissed you off about that?"

"Is it really so hard to mind your own business?"

"What exactly is your problem?"

"Is it really so shocking that I'll pass on the redneck charm."

He stared at her. "Unbelievable." He climbed into the car, muttering under his breath. Susan can be quite the bitch.

"Why don't you just leave me alone!"

"No problem," he snapped, starting the engine. "But you know you might wanna take care. Sometime you're gonna need something and there won't be anybody left who gives a damn."

***

He was a salesman for DKNY. Blonde, like her, tall and tan, looking a bit like the model he once aspired to be. He and her boss at Macy's went way back.

"This is my assistant, Susan Kearney. "

"Tom Hollaway." He had a good hand shake. "Irish?"

81

"By marriage."

His eyes darted to her left hand. "Nice to meet you, Susan. Bill, we've got a great line of suits I want you to see." The two men walked away. Cute, she thought, watching them go. Nice view from behind. Bill probably thought so too.

An hour later, she was hot gluing fake leaves to a fake tree. "Susan?"

She looked up, surprised to see him standing in the door. "Hey," she said. "You looking for Bill?"

"No, just thought I'd say good bye." His smile was long and lazy.

"Okay. See you around."

"That you will." Again the smile. "I've got to know what a girl like you is doing in a place like this."

Susan rolled her eyes. He laughed and was gone. She found herself smiling most of the rest of the day.

***

"What time is it," Maggie mumbled into the phone. Susan could hear Eric murmur. "It's just Susan," Maggie explained. "Hold on, let me go downstairs."

"I'm sorry, is it late, it's late, go back to…"

"No, it's fine. I thought you might call. Are you okay?"

"My puppy has ticks, they're gross and disgusting and I don't know if the cat has them because she's in the barn with the kittens now and you can't touch them, you can't even get to close or she'll move them and they're really little and I don't know what the ticks will do to them because they're horrible and I don't want Callie to get hurt but there's no one to ask because I…" Susan's voice cracked, her breath catching in her throat. "I make everyone mad, Maggie, no one likes me. I don't mean to be that way, but it's that's what happens and I…"

"Susan! Stop, just slow down for a minute," she said. "What happened today was bound to bring things up."

Something happened? "What happened?"

The New York City subway system had been shut down for six hours. Suicide bombers, a credible threat like in London in years past, men, little more than boys really, carrying their backpacks onto crowded trains. Credible. Everyone paid attention now. Not like before, when Al Qaeda was just a topic in government conference rooms, the Bin Laden team from the CIA on the agenda, trying to make their case. But even they had been caught by surprise by 9/11. In fairness, who would have thought that airplanes weren't just a way to get from here to there, to visit your grandmother or close a business deal. Weapons of mass destruction. There were hangars full of them.

"It's been all over the news," Maggie said. "They didn't find anything, but people were stuck on the trains all day. I guess they had dogs going through everybody's stuff."

"My dog has ticks."

"Susan," Maggie said carefully. "Look, maybe I should come."

"Here?"

"Yeah, I want to see your house."

No she didn't. Susan was quite familiar with the tone. She frowned. "I'm sorry I called so late, Maggie. I'm sorry about the subway, I'm sorry about everything." She laughed. "Sorry Susan."

"I can come, Susan."

"Go back to sleep."

She hung up the phone and stared at the wall. There were three holes and two dents, the drywall cracked, wallpaper tattered and brittle. Jolene could have fixed it. She didn't want to think about Jolene. She got the flashlight and shined it in the holes. Stripes of molding and plaster beneath, not brick. Their old apartment in Chelsea charged extra for a wall of exposed brick. Sean loved it, so New York.

Susan grabbed the edge of a hole and tugged. The drywall shuddered but held. She peeled off a strip of wallpaper, found a taped seam. She ripped open a bag of plastic silverware from Wal-Mart and used a knife to try and pry the tape free. She gouged the drywall, not much more before the knife snapped in two.

She had a hammer, the broken hammer from upstairs, stuck on a shelf in the pantry. A little bit of duct tape and it was set, heavy and solid, she took a sample swing. It should work. Over and over she pounded the wall, making holes, pulling off hunks, choking on the dust. Zoey interested at first, but soon bored, back to sleep, her rounded belly rising and falling.

It was dawn before all the drywall finally came down, a good bit of the plaster too. No more holes to peer in, only the mess underneath.

Chapter 13: August 8, 2006

"I'm telling you, there is something wrong with this girl," Jack said.

"Seems to have gotten under your skin," his father observed, squatting next to the motorcycle.

"I'm a bitch magnet."

"Jackson," Ben warned, glancing toward the house. As if his momma could hear them from the driveway.

"Who does she think she is anyway? It's Doctor Jekyll and Mrs. Hyde, one minute we're talking like normal people, then her head does everything but spin around."

"Hand me that socket wrench, will ya?" Ben grimaced, fighting with the motor.

"She called me a redneck."

"Son." Ben nodded toward the tool.

"Sorry." He handed the wrench to his father. "Is it leaking oil?"

"Let me just get this tightened up." They tinkered with the bike for a while, women on the back burner, finally firing it up. The engine roared, spit, back-fired. "Darn it!" Ben shook his head, Jack cut the engine and they heard a new knocking. Cordelia was tapping on the window, a pretty blue scarf on her head, gesturing them to come and eat.

"What's she doing up, she shouldn't be up," Jack said.

Ben waved, wiping his hands on a rag. "She can't lie in bed all day, that's not her nature."

"But she's..."

"Be careful, Jack, with fussing over her. Don't need to make her feel any sicker than she already is."

Cordelia made BLT's on white toast with tomatoes from the garden. Lots of Miracle Whip. On the side, some bread and butter pickles that she'd put up last year. "Make sure you wash your hands," she said, even as they went to the sink. "And don't even think about sitting on one of my chairs in those pants," she added, banishing her husband to the bedroom to change.

"How you feeling, mom?"

"Good today. Takes a day or so after a treatment, but I'm feeling better."

"Have they scheduled the surgery yet?"

"Eat now, don't wait for your daddy." He started to speak, she held up a hand. "Get's tiresome, honey, talking about it all the time." She handed him a napkin. "How was your week?"

He launched into the Susan story. Cordelia got up to get him a coca-cola, watching him, ice crackling as the soda hit the glass. He was such a good boy, a good man. He'd been loved his whole life, nothing had prepared him for betrayal. To find himself with a faithless wife, that selfish girl, so shockingly cruel that he could see no logic in it, except to find himself lacking. "...leave her alone," he finished.

"Got under your skin," she said, echoing her husband. "I hear she's pretty." He sputtered rudely. "Jolene Mayes says she's had a hard time of it."

"Who hasn't?"

"Jackson, I hate what that girl's done to you."

"I know, she's..." He stopped, suspicious. "What are you talking about?"

"There is nothing wrong with you, Jack, you're a wonderful son and a wonderful man. Becky was not..."

"Mom," he interrupted. "This is not about her!"

"Too much is about her."

"He still talking about that girl?" Ben came back into the kitchen, clean hands, clean pants. "She really got under his skin," he said, reaching over his wife to grab a pickle.

"I can see that."

"Enough with the skin already," Jack groaned.

"I think he likes her," Ben added.

"I can see that too."

***

The Wendell Animal Hospital was just outside of town. There was a large waiting room, all windows, with scuffed linoleum floors. A woman sat behind a desk in the center. She was round, body, glasses, hair, all round. A sign on the counter said payment was due at the time of service. A huge long haired white cat sat on the other end, incredible turquoise eyes, a twitching tail. Zoey went crazy. The cat looked down its nose, scornful and secure.

"Well, who's this," asked the round woman.

"Zoey," Susan said. "Zoey, be quiet. We have an appointment. Zoey!"

The round woman came around the desk, bending with an outstretched hand. Zoey stopped barking long enough to sniff, let her ears be scratched, then turned back to the cat. "She's a cutie. How old?"

"I don't know. Someone dumped her near my house."

"Horrible, the things people do. You're sure she wasn't lost?" She asked. "There's a board over there, people put up flyers." She pointed to the corner of the room. Susan followed her finger. Lots of flyers, most with pictures, tacked on the wall. All the missing faces. She bent and scooped up the puppy, surprised by the fierce rush of possessiveness.

"I put an ad in the paper," she lied. Zoey struggled in Susan's arms, closer to the cat than the ground. The cat licked a paw and leapt gracefully to the floor, sauntering down a corridor behind the desk. Susan could hear dogs barking. "Sorry about the cat."

"Don't you worry, takes more than little Zoey to get a rise out of Snowball. Let's get some information so we can get you in to see Doctor Cross."

Doctor Cross was a small man, wispy hair circling a large bald spot, with glasses he wore pushed up on his head. He held Zoey firmly by the scruff of her neck, not put off by her squirming. Susan watched him, unexpectedly anxious.

"Weight's good, heart beat's steady. She hasn't had any of her shots?"

"I don't think so, no."

"We can take care of that, can't we, girl." He rubbed Zoey's tummy. She threw back her head, nibbled his sleeve. "We need to do something about these ear mites and she's got some ticks."

"I gave her a flea bath," Susan said.

"You're doing fine, don't worry." He let go of the puppy and pulled a large metal tweezers from a drawer. "Worst season for ticks I've seen in a while, winter was too warm this year." Susan chewed her thumbnail. "I can take her in the back, if you don't want to watch."

She shook her head. "I want to be with her." He nodded kindly, slid his glasses down on his nose and took up the tweezers. "Dr. Cross, what's an ear mite?"

Two hundred and forty three dollars later, Zoey pranced out to the car. She had to come back in three weeks, and then again in a month. Puppies needed smaller doses of whatever was in the shots they gave. Susan had instructions for everything, the antibiotics for the tick bites, the drops to kill worms. She couldn't even think about the worms. She would need to buy Q-tips for the gunk that killed the ear mites, little bugs that looked like coffee grounds. Dr. Cross had shown her how to do it. Squirt the stuff, massage it in, swab it out. It wasn't Zoey's shining moment, peeing on the counter and his hand.

"I'm so sorry," Susan gasped.

"Just pee," he replied, turning toward the sink. "That's what puppies do."

"How do you make them stop?"

He was still laughing as he walked her to the front desk. She paid her bill and got the dog in the car, feeling surprisingly proud. She stopped at the Food Lion to buy Q-tips and puppy treats, left the car running, air conditioner full blast. When she came out, Zoey was standing up, paws on the window, tail waving wildly. So glad to see her. She opened the door and Zoey flung herself forward, ecstatic at Susan's return. She had pooped on the floor mat in the passenger side of the car.

***

A customer was a customer, Jolene told herself, nobody said you had to like them, hell, if that was the case half the jobs she had would be gone. Course how they felt about her, now could make a mess of things. Just had to suck it up and give it go. Pulling into the driveway, Jolene was a little nervous. Hard to tell with Suz, what she'd do. Could be nothing, could be something and if it was something, it would be something big. But pride wasn't gonna pay the bills, she figured that out last night. So now, here she was.

She went up and knocked. Waited. Nothing. She could hear the puppy whimpering, shut in somewhere or it would be at the door. She knocked again. The SUV was there. Susan had to be home. Nobody answered. Jolene started pulling lathe and screen off the back of the truck.

"She hired you, this is work," she told herself. If she didn't want it done, she was gonna hafta pay for the materials. And her time. Her time was no less valuable than anybody else's. Jolene went around to the side, got her sawhorses set and looked for a place to plug in the saw. She'd just gotten started making her cuts when she saw Susan coming across the back yard, walking toward the house. She bent over the saw, buzz ripping through the air. The puppy howled. Susan changed routes, came toward her, stopping a few feet back.

"Hey," Jolene said, glancing up from the table saw, set on plywood between two sawhorses. "Can I do something for you," she asked politely, pulling a pencil from behind her ear to mark a piece of lathe.

"No. I just didn't know...I wasn't sure you'd be coming."

"I figured you still wanted the work done."

"I did, I do."

Jolene turned back to cutting. Susan stood and watched. It went that way for close to half an hour. Zoey whined the whole time, howling to crescendo each time Jolene ran the saw.

"Okay, goddammit, this is stupid!" Jolene yanked off her baseball cap, slapped it against her thigh. "I told myself I wasn't coming back here and here I am, just like a fool, thinkin' maybe you were sorry but..." She shook her head. "You're not the only one who's had troubles in her life and you don't get to run around being mean to people because of it."

"I'm sorry, I'm really sorry. I just didn't know how to..."

"You just do it, that's how. You don't sit around and think about it, you just do it."

"I'm sorry, Jolene. I acted like jerk."

"That's for sure." She turned back to the wood.

Susan hesitated. "I'll let you get back to work."

"Expecting me to work after that without no extra compensation," Jolene replied. "I don't think so, gonna take some cake, maybe even a brownie." She glanced over her shoulder, wiggling her eyebrows.

Susan let out her breath. "I can go get some."

"Bout time," Jolene replied, pretending to scowl. "And do something about that dog, she's like to drive me nuts."

Susan came back from Dottie's with every thing possible, brownies, cake, cinnamon buns. Frozen moccachinos, cups squirted with chocolate, filled with ice cream and coffee, whipped cream out the top of the caps, melting in the heat. Zoey bounded from the car, whipped around the lawn.

"I was shitty to Jackson too," Susan admitted, sitting on the plastic chair on the porch. Cake and coffee break. The puppy played in the yard, chasing bugs and chewing sticks.

Jolene licked icing from her fingers. "Turning an asshole into an art form, ain't ya? Why are you so mad all the time?"

"I'm not mad all the time."

"Just anytime somebody tries to get to know ya." Her straw made a loud slurpy sound. "These are so good!" She shook the cup, hoping for more. "Most folks are lonely by circumstance, you know," she said. "Not by choice."

"I'm not lonely. I just like being by myself."

"That's what I mean," Jolene replied. "How long ago did he die?" Susan didn't answer. "Come on now. It's just a question."

"It's coming up on five years." She waited for the criticism, how long it had been and how far she hadn't come.

"You were awful young," she replied. "A lot to handle. How'd it happen?"

They always asked. "An accident."

"Car?"

"No." Her throat tightened. "He fell."

"Bless your heart," she exclaimed. "I can't imagine. He must have been a young man himself."

"Thirty seven. His father was...he was the only boy. Six sisters and Sean."

"Hard to lose a child," she murmured.

"How did you do it? How do you wear the picture, talk about it like it happened to someone else?"

Jolene paused. "You did that to your leg, didn't you?" She pointed to red scratches on her thigh.

Susan yanked at her shorts. "Of course not."

Jolene held out her arm, pushed up her sleeve. Just above the elbow and in the crease were faint round scars. Burned into the skin. "I used to smoke," she said, raising her eyes to Susan's. "Can't explain why it feels so right, hurting yourself. But it was the only thing that made the pain stop. Crazy." She shook her head.

Susan bit her lip, looked away. Jolene continued softly. "Billy was like to divorce me after a while, I couldn't stop crying. Wouldn't tend to Mickey, lord how I neglected that child. It felt like he was doing something wrong by being there...when she wasn't. I still feel bad about that."

"I don't like to talk to his dad, he tries to stay in touch, you know, calls me, but I just..." Susan shook her head. "And I still can't sleep. Even after all this time."

"Time is overrated. It takes what it takes."

"Did you worry about not being a good mother and..." She stopped, suddenly realizing. "Jolene, I'm sorry. I didn't mean ..."

"Trust me, you can't say nothing that I haven't already chewed to the bone. Course I did. 'Bout killed me."

The puppy suddenly wriggled its backside and leapt into the air, intent on a dragonfly that drifted safely away. Both women laughed. "I missed you, Jolene."

"Right back at you, Suz. Susan," she corrected herself.

"No, it's okay." It suddenly was. "Suz is fine."

***

No one could have stopped it. Freedom was too strong a weak spot. People were allowed to get on airplanes in America. Immigration was a paper tiger, buried in its own bureaucracy, the FBI, the CIA, just glamorous, secretive versions of the same.

Still the government had known things, that was certain. The U.S. embassies in Kenya and Tanzania had been bombed back in 1998 when Clinton was in office. Susan could barely remember hearing about it. Hadn't seemed important then, not compared to Monica Lewinski's dress or the second season of Ally McBeal.

Looking back there was half a decade of clues, arrows all pointing, like a flashing neon sign. Just a month before, there had been a presidential briefing on the sixth of August, warning of an impending strike in the United States.

"They knew enough," Patrick argued. *"Bush knew."*

You know I don't like Bush," she said. *She hadn't voted for him the first time, didn't vote at all the second. "But how can you believe he knew and did nothing? Who would do nothing if they knew?"*

"He might not have known what he knew," Patrick conceded. *"But he still knew."*

Everyone knew Bin Laden had agents in the country, there were 70 field investigations already underway. There had been talk, chatter they called it, of taking an airplane. But he'd been talking for so long, the video-taped prophesies of a fanatic intent on destroying the most powerful nation in the world. Who could have known it would be so easy?

Susan flipped the calendar back to August. The sixth was two days ago. Five years and two days ago. She had no idea what she and Sean were doing. He'd most likely worked late, she was reading or running errands or meeting a friend. Better to call it that. She drew a cross over August 6th and 7th. Thirty four days to go.

That night at Wal-Mart, she bought a bigger broom and a larger garbage can for the drywall on the floor in the dining room. Zoey was dragging the junk all over the house. She got a light cotton blanket, a blue bandana, more Excedrin Migraine and Tylenol PM. A bag of puppy treats, milk, four bowls and four plates. A package of real silverware, service for four. She got a squeaky rubber bone, an adorable stuffed cowboy rhinoceros and debated over a heavy braided rope with a ring on one end. The training book discouraged tug of war. Zoey loved it. Susan put the rope in the cart.

"Thought you had a cat," the checkout lady said, sliding the chew toy over the scanner.

"I did. I do," Susan replied, looking up, actually seeing the face. "She had kittens. Four of them."

"You see the price on this?" A bag of rawhide strips.

"Six ninety five, I think."

"Good enough," she said, punching the register. "One thirteen thirty nine."

Susan paid and gathered up her bags. "Thanks for shopping at Wal-Mart," the woman repeated mechanically.

"Have a nice day," Susan responded, just as rote. Then she stopped. "Hey, thanks for remembering my cat."

The cashier shifted, eyes down, compliments not a normal part of her day, maybe her life. "See you again soon."

***

Her perfume preceded her, subtly floral with an undercurrent of something darker. More provocative. He smelled it the second he came through Skeeter's door.

"Hello, Ben," she called. She rose and held out her hand. "It's good to see you."

A gentleman had to take it. "Becky," he replied, with a nod. She waited, as if he would ask why she was here. He didn't, heading to the coffee pot to fill his cup.

"I was so sorry to hear about Cordelia." She moved, as if to touch his arm.

He turned, jaw set. There was a limit to chivalry. Her hand paused in mid-air, turned to smooth her perfect hair. "Well," she said brightly, "how has everybody been?"

Like dogs to meat, the men responded. One or two of them a bit sheepish, knowing her in ways they shouldn't, knowing that Ben knew. They didn't look his way. All eyes on her, just the way she liked it.

"So I got this idea for a moose trap, you know? It's a beauty, you got a minute I could show it to ya, worth a story if..."

"A mouse trap?" She winked at the men. "Darlin', I think that's been done."

"Moose," Skeeter said loudly. "A moose trap."

"I do have a story and I'm hoping y'all will help. The anniversary of September 11th, is coming up, five years, can you believe it? Doesn't seem possible." She frowned prettily, perfect mix of sadness and pride.

"And they still ain't found that son of a bitch!"

"Hiding in some cave somewhere, while we twiddle our thumbs." Big Jim spit chew juice into an empty coffee can on the floor. "Making a fool outta this country, that's what."

"Ought to blow the whole place off the map, all them damn camel jockeys."

"Get the homo's outta the army, then they'd find him."

"Gentlemen, please." She held up a hand. "I was hoping you could help me. You remember George?" Blank stares "George Patter," she prompted. Now they knew, heads nodding. Becky smiled, pleased. She was only one at the station who had known of a local connection. One of their own. It was her shot, she knew it, more air time, become a presence. "He was a hero, on those stairs, helping folks down. I'm

94

looking to tell his story." She glanced around the circle, eye contact with all. "His momma and daddy have passed, so I'm here hoping you can tell me more about him, how he was."

"Used to volunteer at Pilot fire department, you should talk to the boys over there," Skeeter said. "But let me tell ya this, see the moose comes in and…"

"Did anybody know him? Dutch? Ben?"

"He worked out at farm one summer," Dutch answered. "I remember that…"

"Big opportunity for you," Ben drawled. "Being on TV and all."

"Yes it is," she replied. Not the least bit fazed. "But this isn't about me, Ben. It's about our country. And the extraordinary men and women who died for it." Sweet smile, eyes bright with challenge. "Surely you don't have a problem with that?"

"No, I suppose I don't," he said slowly, as if processing what she'd said. "What about the terrorists? You gonna report on them too?"

"Of course."

"That's good. I always heard a person should stick with what they know." He set his coffee on the counter, nodded to Skeeter and walked out the door.

Chapter 14: August 10, 2006

"What exactly is a pig picking?"

"Sugar, you've led a sheltered life."

"Because I don't need any more animals and..."

Jolene hooted. "You don't get a pig, you pick at a pig."

"Sounds disgusting."

"So good. They cook the pig for half a day or so, meat's just falling off the bone." She smacked her lips. "Then folks pick at it."

"Definitely disgusting."

"Listen up, I got a man-free zone and we're not gonna blow it. Billy's going to Blowing Rock with a bunch of his no-account friends, be gone for two whole days. I gotta take advantage, he's bound to come back surly, can't his handle his liquor any better than a girl but that never keeps him from trying. I say, you and me, we're gonna get fired up and find us some boys that like to dance."

"You're crazy."

"Pick you up at three and no excuses."

"I'm driving my own car."

"Fine by me."

"And I'm bringing the dog."

Jolene had already hung up the phone.

She didn't have an iron. At least one that was unpacked. Her clothes were mostly in Wal-Mart bags. She tried to brush the wrinkles from a khaki skirt. Found a white tank top. "Where are my shoes," she asked the dog. Zoey wagged her tail. "I know you know, so don't try and be cute."

There was one blue flip flop next to the dryer, pieces of its mate in the shower stall. Zoey had taken to attacking the shower curtain, jumping in and out, pulling so hard she'd bent the hollow metal rod. The laces on both sneakers had been chewed clean through. She dug through the bags until she found more flip flops. Green.

"Sit." Susan fastened the lease to the puppy's collar. "Now you have to behave today, we're gonna be around a bunch of people. And there is going to be a pig." Jolene's horn sounded in the yard. "I don't believe I'm doing this."

"Come on, let's get going." Jolene was drinking a beer. "You ready for some fun?"

"Are you trying to get arrested?"

"Now you're talking!" She threw the truck in reverse and spun her tires in the dirt.

"Holy crap," Susan muttered. Zoey stood on the seat, paws on the dash, barking.

Pilot was a tiny place, not big enough to have a town proper. The volunteer fire department was a source of pride. Otherwise, it was just a few houses and a trailer park, a crossroad with Privette's gas station, Marvella's Beauty Salon and Don's Detail Shop. Jarvis Gas and Groceries catty corner across the way. Not much more than that. But folks from all around turned out for the party.

Susan followed Jolene into a field that served as the parking lot. Lots of pickup trucks, people clustered in groups, laughing and backslapping. Susan took a deep breath. She hadn't been to a party in years. She didn't go to parties. Parties were for people. Zoey whined.

"Whatcha waiting for? Let's go."

"Jolene..."

"Come on," Jolene insisted, opening the car door. Zoey jumped out, pranced around, then bent nose to ground, sniffing furiously. "Come on," she repeated, following the dog.

There was a line of picnic tables near the double doors of the firehouse. Two heavy set women sat behind the one in the middle, collecting cash for the pig. Another table was for the bake sale, loaded down with cookies and cakes, homemade bread. A bunch of men and boys stood around the third, looking at the new ATV next to it, bright yellow and deep blue with lots of shiny chrome. A special raffle, tickets were five dollars each.

"Jolene Mayes, it's so good to see you," said one of the ticket-taking women. "How y'all doing?"

"Doing just fine, Miz Merry. How's Duke and the store?"

"He's just fine. He's real sorry about Mrs. Mayes and the shotgun," she added, lowering her voice. "I swear, sometimes that man ain't got a lick a sense."

"Ole woman will be the death of me," Jolene replied. "Darned if she wasn't hiding birdshot in the Raisin Bran." She handed over a twenty. "Take out for two." She nodded over her shoulder. Susan stood a few steps away, Zoey straining at the leash. "Miz Merry, this is my friend Susan."

"Hello." Susan cleared her throat. Stupid to be this nervous.

"Bought the Garrett place, didn't ya?" Wide friendly smile. "Well we're glad to have you. Take some of that upside cake home, the peach is mine." Jolene took her change and asked after the beer keg. "Down the hill to the right of tent. Near the port-a-potties this year," she added with a nod.

"Thank goodness for that." Jolene took Susan's arm. "Don't be such a Yankee," she whispered, "folks are friendly down here."

"I should go home."

"Zoey's having too good a time." The puppy was beside herself. "Let's have ourselves a beer and some pig and then we'll see what's what."

***

Jack had come early to help set up the tables and carry beers to Bubba who was in charge of the pig. A bunch of men clustered at the big iron smoker, standing around, nobody doing much but having fun doing it.

There were two fire trucks parked on the grass just off the tarmac on the crest of a small hill. Balloons and kids all over them. One of the firemen was ringing the bell, the kids begging him to run the siren. Jack waved at Big Jim Harrigan, his wife trailing behind him, trying to ride herd on a little girl that couldn't be more than five.

His dad had told him, of course. It was all such bullshit, like Becky ever gave a thought to George Patter. A career move, that's all it was, using a dead man to build her own name. When he saw the big news van trundle down the gravel road, the anger took his breathe away, sharp, like a knife between the ribs.

He heard a shout, turned, a puppy running loose, trailing its lease. Her puppy. He saw Susan chasing after it, Jolene wandering behind. Great, bitches two for one.

"Hey Jack, hotter than blazes, ain't it," Dick Liddle called. He held out a fistful of pens, inscribed with the bank's name. "Gotcha a pen? Is that Becky Howe over there? I can't believe that girl's…" Bubba jerked his head toward Jack. None too subtle. Dick stuttered to a stop. "Geez, I didn't mean to…"

"Don't worry," Jack interrupted. "It's fine." Lying through tight teeth, his eyes never leaving her.

Folks followed her like the pied piper, or at least followed the camera. She made her way toward the fire trucks, like goddamn Princess Diana, waving to the crowds. He didn't have to go anywhere near her, just ignore her, that's what he told himself even as his feet started moving. Bubba called after him, but he didn't turn around.

George Patter had been born in Bunn, just a few miles up the road. He'd been on the high school football team, hoping for a scholarship, but a small town boy is only a big fish in a little pond. He was a few years ahead, Jack never really knew him. He'd joined the army, did his stint and fell in love with a nurse from New Jersey. George became a firefighter up there, had a son and a new baby girl, born just eight months before it happened.

Firefighters had made it to the fifty-fourth floor in the North Tower. The seventy-eighth in the South, where George was. Up, up, up, equipment weighing hundreds of pounds. So many people comforted by the sight of them. Saviors. When the building fell, George's body was part of the five hundred thousand tons that crashed down.

Pilot's volunteer fire department was one of hundreds around the country that raised money after the fact. Everyone desperate to do something, a pandemic of helplessness across the nation. Fire trucks didn't come cheap, and there were so many lost, fire stations emptied of men and equipment. Jack could see Becky was making her way to the display, her new red hair shining copper in the sun. The table held a portrait of George in his uniform, a letter from his battalion in New Jersey. Pictures of the day, the towers, the plane, the smoke. The people running.

"Do you remember where you were, when you heard?" Becky was asking, microphone tilted forward. Her head cocked at just the right angle, always aware of the camera, looking out for her best side. Like she has one, he thought. Annie Lyman had just started to answer when the puppy burst through the crowd, Susan and Jolene not far behind. The dog had run through the water spout, hose set up for the kids to play. Muddy paws and damp fur, she darted among the legs, wet leash whipping in her wake, slapping the cameraman across the back of his knees.

"Hey!" He turned, camera swinging away.

"Zoey! Sorry," Susan added, reaching for the dog.

"What the hell," Becky snapped at the cameraman as Jolene pushed through the crowd stepped on the end of Zoey's leash, bringing the dog up short. "Get that mutt out of here!"

Jolene looked her up and down. "Funny, I was just thinking the same thing." She scooped the puppy up in her arms. Susan was frozen in front of the table, color draining away. The menacing cloud of ash, the firefighters raising the flag over the rubble.

"Spare me, okay, we're trying to work here, if..."

Someone shrieked as Susan crumbled to the ground. People gathered around, Jolene pushing through. "Suz? Suz, wake up." Jolene was on her knees, Zoey pushing into to sniff. "Somebody hold the dog."

"What's going on? What happened?" Becky stood on tiptoes, grabbed the cameraman's arm. "Get over there, come on."

Jack stepped in front of them. "No."

"Get out of my way, Jack. Shoot it," she hissed.

"Hate to see something happen to that camera," Jack warned. The cameraman paused, looking to Becky.

"I need some water over here," Jolene called. Susan was trying to sit up. "Easy now, take it slow," she warned. "Okay everybody, it's done, let's give her some room."

"Darn, you missed it, what a shame," Jack drawled.

"Still a sucker for a damsel in distress, Jack." Becky tossed her hair. "Fine, I'll leave your little girlfriend alone."

"She's not my girlfriend."

"Poor thing, you know it really is time to move on," she murmured sweetly, jerking her head at the cameraman. "Shame you can't let go, shug." Off she swayed, camera in her wake. He tried not to watch, hands shaking but he did and she knew it, pausing to turn and toss him a wink and smile.

"Jack, grab that damn dog!" Jolene yelled.

Zoey was on the move, he grabbed her collar, pulling her up short. "Is she all right?" He asked, squatting next to Jolene.

"I think the heat's got to her."

"Where's Zoey," Susan murmured.

"She's right here," Jolene said. "We gotta get you outta this sun."

"I can drive," she said, trying to get up. Dizzy.

"Like hell you can."

"I'll take her home," Jack said.

***

She woke up on the mattress. It was dark out. She never slept up here, had no idea of the time. Where was the dog? Her head throbbed. Unsteady on her feet, she went to the top of the stairway. "Zoey? Baby Zoe?" She heard a faint whelp, a yip, a volley of barking. She got down the stairs, a hand on each wall to steady herself.

"You're up." Jack was sitting on the porch in a white chair, bare feet on the rail, boots on the floor. He'd brought her home. Her head ached so bad.

She peered through the screen door. "Where's Zoey?"

"Doing battle with the fireflies."

She went to the bathroom, swallowed three Excedrin dry. What was he still doing here. She took a deep breath and went back to the door.

"Your friend Maggie called."

"You answered my phone?"

"Nope. She left a message."

Roaring in her ears. He was listening to her messages. Zoey burst from under the hydrangea, flung herself into the air at an invisible foe, flipped over and landed on her back. Up in a flash, barking at the night like it had jerked her around. He laughed.

"Zoey," she called, stepping out on the porch. "Zoey!" Louder, the puppy stopped in mid stride, ears cocked. "Come here baby." The puppy raced to the steps, so glad to see her. The dog was always so glad to see her. An hour away, fifteen minutes, half a day. Always thrilled at her return.

"Knows her momma, that's for sure. Jolene brought some food, pig and the like, in the refrigerator."

"She didn't have to do that."

"She had to drop off your car."

"I could have driven myself."

"You're welcome," he replied.

"You can go home now."

"Maybe you were brought up thinking it was all right to be rude, but just so you know, it doesn't cut much mustard down here."

"I wasn't trying to be rude. Thank you for the ride."

"Apology accepted."

"I wasn't apolo..."

"Why's your friend Maggie worried about you?"

"You eavesdrop on my phone calls and think I'm going to discuss them with you?"

"Who else you got?" He looked around. "Not exactly beating folks off with a stick. "

"What part of no don't you get," she snapped. He grinned. It was infuriating. She picked up one of his boots, flung it into the yard. Zoey jumped off the steps and chased it like a stick.

"Impressive, how old are you anyway?" He picked up the other boot and walking out into the yard. He grabbed the puppy by the scruff of her neck, tugged the boot from her teeth. "Poor little fella," he added, scratching Zoey's ear. "Picked the wrong house, didn't you?" He got to the car door, stopped for one last look. "And to think I was surprised you aren't married. Guess you cleared that up."

She visibly flinched, then turned on her heel and headed for the door, the dog following in her wake. She got inside, tears burning her eyelids, and went to the cell phone. No new messages. Maggie's was on the machine.

"I need you to call me back," Maggie said. "You're not calling anyone back, your mother has called me twice, thanks for that, by the way. I'm coming to see you. I already told Eric and he's fine with watching the boys, so I'm coming. I miss you." A long pause. "Okay, I'll see you soon."

***

He knew she'd come. There something between them, passion ignited by fight, pulling them together. He waited on the back deck, listening for her. It was somewhere around eight when she finally pulled in. Jack heard the car door shut, anticipation, apprehension, hard to tell, his insides shaking.

Becky came around the corner of the house, carrying her sandals in one hand, a bottle of wine in the other. She'd changed her clothes, reporter's suit replaced by a bright cotton dress that tied behind the neck. She smelled sweet. She stopped at the steps, looking up at him.

"You gonna get me a glass?" He looked at her, slowly reached beneath the chair. Held up a paper cup. She was pleased that he'd expected her. Liked to keep him hoping. "That'll work." She came up on the deck, setting off the motion light, shining through the sheer little dress. "We have to find a way to co-exist, darlin'," she said. Handing him the wine, waiting as he poured. She circled behind him, leaned close to whisper. "You didn't always hate me, you know."

"What do you want?" Holding up her wine.

Becky laughed. "What do you want?" Coming around the front of the chair, taking the cup, hair tumbling free. So beautiful. She tipped her glass up, swallowed, a dribble down her chin. She laughed again and gracefully straddled his legs, skirt billowing up, nothing underneath. "What do you want, Jack?"

His lips were on her neck. She arched against him. He groaned, grabbed her, not enough of her, but whatever he could get. Becky smiled and reached behind her neck to untie her dress.

***

"I'm not trying to gossip, you know that, but I thought you'd want to know, Cordelia," Georgia Childress said.

"Are you sure it was her?"

"Saw her plain as day. Vernon likes his chocolate ice cream, you know, and we were watching Survivor, that's his favorite show," she added. "So anyway, I got up on the commercial to get him a bowl and you know my kitchen window looks straight across the street. There she was, slinking through the grass, barefoot, carrying a bottle of liquor around the back of the house."

"Did she..."

"Car was still there at eleven o'clock when I put the cat out."

Cordelia sighed. "Georgia, I appreciate you calling and..."

"I'm not looking to spread gossip, you know that."

"I do, thank you for that and I..."

"Bless his heart, that boy's got it bad. Can't imagine what he's thinking, everything she done when they was married."

"Yes. Thank you for calling."

"I figured you'd want to know."

Chapter 15: August 12, 2006

"Maggie's coming," Susan told Waleed, drink in hand, her third. Nothing like a pity party with an open bar. She'd always preferred vodka, on the rocks with a twist of lemon or a splash of juice, sipped one at night, waiting for Sean to come to bed. Come to bed, she'd call, lighting candles and smoothing out the sheets. In a minute, he'd reply. It was never a minute. The ice would melt in her glass and the candles flicker out. She'd turn on the light and read paperback mysteries, John Sanford and Lawrence Block. Waiting for him. After a while she looked forward to her time with John and Larry, Robert Parker, Peter Robinson, took them to bed more often than her husband.

"I didn't invite her, but she's coming anyway. Like she has the right to just show up," she bitched, another swallow. "I called and told her not to but she didn't answer. And she was there, too, I know she was," Susan griped, oblivious to the taste of her own medicine. She took a swallow, glanced at Waleed. "You probably don't drink, right?"

The other half, he definitely drank. Gin and tonics. He liked Bombay, Sapphire especially, and used lemon instead of line. He was special like that.

"A man wants to attract a beautiful woman, he's gotta stand out," Tom said

"Really," she replied archly. "Is that how it works."

"Case in point," he said, waving at her like she was door number three.

"So I'm beautiful now?"

"Noooo." Drawing it out, his eyes meeting hers. "You're beautiful always."

She should just go. Pack up and leave before Maggie got here. "Nobody's home," she said out loud, a tipsy chuckle at imagining Maggie on the porch, peering in the windows. But she had the stupid cat and the stupid kittens, stuck up in that dumb barn. The kittens would fry in the heat, like the mouse under the eaves, tiny, furry bodies dried like raisins. A kitten killer. That's what she'd become.

She carried Waleed into the kitchen, folded over so Tom didn't show, and poured herself another drink. The puppy padded around the corner, sleepy, ears flat. She sat, half awake, opened wide in a big yawn. "What are you looking at!" Zoey wagged her tail.

"A toast," Susan announced, raising her glass. "To all the assholes with all the answers." She took a gulp, tucked the bottle under one arm and started for the living room, missed the door and walked into the wall, nose first. It hurt. She staggered back, and stepped on the puppy's tail. The dog yelped, startled, she tried to compensate, turn, couldn't quite get it right, balance abandoned. She threw out a hand to save herself, the bottle crashing to the floor, twisting almost on one knee, all in the second. The drink dropping breaking, shards of glass, vodka splattering, then Tom and Waleed, falling, falling, falling, jumpers jumping, always hitting the ground. Even as she righted herself, horrified, Zoey pushed in to sniff the remains.

"You stupid mutt!" Susan shrieked. The dog froze, a little pee leaking out on the floor. "Get out of here!" Her foot lashed out. Contact made. Zoey whimpered and ran. "You better run! Shit and pee all over the house," she screamed. "My goddamn house! Fucking dog!"

She picked up the frame, afraid to look. One of the corners were dented, and a long crack crisscrossed Tom's face, splintering out at the end like fireworks. Waleed was okay, she held him to her cheek, eyes closed, willing herself calm. It was okay, he was okay. Her penance, to share her life with Waleed. Never with Tom.

"Oh god." She bent for the bottle, unharmed, coming up too quick. Dizzy, she took a swallow, still unbalanced, trying to find her footing, she stepped on a squeaky toy. The sound like a match to gasoline, she exploded. Where the fuck was the goddamn dog!

The puppy cowered behind the cardboard chair. "Get over here! Now!" She went around, the puppy ran the opposite way, catching the wire of the charger, dragging the cell phone to the floor. "Oh my god, my god," she screamed, grabbing up the phone, flipping it open. "You little bitch, get over here!" Frantic, the puppy dodged around her, running through the broken glass to the bathroom. "Gotcha," Susan muttered, stepping inside and slamming the door. Missing the smears of red on the linoleum floor.

The puppy trembled between the dryer and the wall. Small as it could make itself, Zoey watched her advance with pleading eyes. Quivering, cowering, desperate to please, trying to show submission. Susan's teeth were clenched, rage all consuming, she reached for the dog. Zoey cringed against the wall, whimpering.

Maybe it was the sound. Susan blinked. Afraid. Zoey was afraid of her.

Her stomach heaved and she went to her knees in front of the toilet, vomiting booze and pile, no food to purge. Finally done, she wiped her mouth and sank to the floor, curled in a ball. Weeping. The puppy inched forward on its belly, blood oozing from her paw, nudging it's nose under her hand. "I'm sorry," Susan repeated, over and over and over, the cell phone clutched to her chest. "I'm so sorry, baby, I'm so sorry."

Chapter 16: August 14, 2006

"So she's all right?"

"She's fine," Dr. Cross said. "There's a little cut on the pad, already starting to heal." He patted the puppy's head, pulled a treat from his pocket. Zoey gobbled it down. "You're doing a good job with the ear mites."

"Thank you." Eyes downcast.

"Dogs are like children, Miz Kearney, things happen." Dr. Cross patted her shoulder. "Don't worry so much. You're doing fine."

"Shouldn't she have a band-aid, you know to keep the dirt out?

He smiled. "Puppy might not be partial to that."

She wasn't convinced. "What if she gets infected?"

"You get worried you give me a call, but it's looking good. Just a scratch, that's all." He shook her hand, steering her toward the door. "Take care of your momma, girl," he added, tugging on Zoey's ear.

She was doing a window on 34th Street when he knocked on the glass. She turned, he smiled and waved. Tom pointed at a mannequin, made the okay sign with his fingers. Looking good, he mouthed. Thanks, she said back, pleased. Then he pointed at her. You too, he said. She waved it away, shaking her head. He made a figure eight with his hands, winked and walked on.

She and Sean met friends for dinner that night. They ate Tex-Mex and debated the mayor's latest crime initiative, the men dished about sports, the women about shoes. A tall blonde man at the bar caught Susan's eye. She thought at first it was Tom and rose in her seat for a better look.

"Better watch out, man," Sean's friend said, a nod toward Susan. "The wife is trolling the bar."

"Who you looking at?" His girlfriend asked.

"I am not looking at anybody."

"The husband's always the last to know," Sean's friend warned.

"Really" said his girlfriend. "I wouldn't limit that to husbands." She tossed her hair and winked.

Sean laughed. "Looks like you got trouble of your own, bud." He smiled at Susan. "I'm not worried. I mean, look at me, she couldn't do any better." Susan pelted him with sugar packets and everyone laughed. He squeezed her hand, whispered. "You and me, forever, Suz."

Forever wasn't really very long. It was just a word people used to make themselves safe. Establish a constant in a constantly changing world. Susan didn't count on people for that anymore. She built her own fortress where nobody could get hurt. Until now.

She set the puppy on the front seat, walked around to the other side. Zoey had already leaped to the driver's side, paws on the door, nose smearing the window. Tail going round and round and round and round. Susan touched her fingers to the glass. No matter what she did, no matter how horrid she was, Zoey loved her anyway.

She had to get rid of the dog.

Chapter 17: August 15, 2006

"So I'm telling Billy for the ten thousandth time that his momma can't be driving without a license and he needs to sell that damn rattletrap she's got in the yard. Even while I'm talking doesn't the old fool come barreling down the road and takes out the mailbox! I mean, sends it flying and doesn't bat an eye, just pulls in and parks pleased as punch." Jolene stapled down the length of screen. "I'm telling ya. And then Billy says to me, 'See, she's driving.' I mean, what I am supposed to do with that." She wiped sweat from her forehead.

Susan had pulled a plastic chair to the side yard, watching Jolene work. Zoey slept like a rock beneath the chair. "You want a Coke or something?"

"Let me finish this side." She held up a piece of lathe, lining up the cut. "So I bumped into Jackson the other day." Susan didn't answer. "Had another go round, huh?"

"Thinks he's god's gift to women."

"You think so? I wouldn't have thought that myself. But I been married so long I might as well be dead."

"Why he isn't married?"

"You remember that reporter? At the pig pickin'?"

"Kind of."

"That's her."

"Who?"

"Who he married. Divorced now," she added. "They got one of those love-hate things, you know, he wants her, she uses him. Walked out on him a couple years back."

"There you go." As if her point was proven.

"Not what you think. Girl couldn't keep her pants on for more than ten minutes," Jolene said. "Cheated on him all over town."

"I need a soda." Susan got up abruptly, coming back with two. She handed one over to Jolene. "Have you ever…?"

Jolene took the Coke, running it across her forward. "Whew, it's hot. Ever what? Cheat on Billy? Please girl, who the heck with?"

110

"You love him, don't you."

Jolene sputtered. "The man couldn't survive alone, too helpless to do much more than clean his guns and open a beer. Course his momma'd be happy if I was run off, move right in with her darlin' baby boy." She took a long drink. "That's good and cold."

"Do you know anyone who's looking for a dog?"

"A dog? You find another one?" Jolene asked. Susan shook her head, eyes averted. "You mean Zoey?" Her voice went up high. She put down the staple gun. "That puppy's the light of your life."

"I just think she might be better off in a family. Kids maybe. I mean, I don't even know if I'm going to stay here."

"That's crazy. Be like tearing a child from her momma's arms." Jolene squinted at her. "What's this really about, shug?"

"Nothing. Just thinking, that's all."

"Well you're thinking crazy. You love that dog and she loves you." She turned back to the screen. "Don't take that lightly, ain't so easy to find."

She worked for a while, Susan watched. Zoey wandered, finally flopping in the grass chewing on a stick half her size. "What did you mean, about moving?"

"What?"

"Might not stay here, that's what you said. That why you don't unpack?"

"Kind of."

"Well," she said, sticking the pencil behind her ear, "I'd be sorry to see you go." She stapled down the length of screen, one after the other, bam, bam, bam. "Leaving won't change it, you know, it goes right along with ya."

"Wherever you go, there you are," Susan mocked.

"That's why you wanna get rid of Zoey, cuz you're starting to care." The last staple landed. "There, that looks good, don't you think? Nice and straight." She fanned herself. "You know, I got some drywall on the truck, we could get that wall fixed in the dining room. Don't

111

know what possessed ya to start doing demo, but, hey I'm not asking for an explanation."

"I put holes in it, so I took it down." She was watching the dog, wandering too far. "Zoey, come back here." The puppy looked up, went back to sniffing. "Zoey!"

"And the holes were because…?"

"It's fine. Really, it's okay."

"Hate to call you a liar and all, but I seen the wall. It's not okay."

"That's what I used to tell the shrinks. It's not okay."

"What'd they say?"

"That it was normal."

They looked at each other, a heartbeat passed, then both burst out laughing.

"Gotta love it." Jolene wiped her eyes, chuckling. "C'mon, help me get the drywall.

Zoey trotted behind them into the house.

***

The sex was good, beyond good, great. Reckless abandon. In bed, they were always in synch. The things she'd whisper in his ear. It drove him crazy. The way her skin smelled. His hair stood on end at her touch. It should have been enough.

She'd left around three, the bedroom gone cool, as if the AC had suddenly cranked into gear. Jack wanted her to stay, but didn't ask. She'd just do the opposite. Acting as if he didn't care was more likely to peak her interest. She needed a challenge, something to conquer. In her arms, her skin on his skin, he would do anything to stay there. Breathless, complete, the only time he felt that way since falling in love. Afterwards, he was shamed by his need for her. Grateful that no one knew.

They had been lying in bed, the wine almost gone when she'd asked about Susan. Tone so casual it perked up his ears. Worthy of notice. She smelled competition and Becky Lee Howe wasn't one to share the crown.

112

"She moved here a few months ago. Jolene's friendly with her."

"That psycho. Speaks for itself. " She'd turned on her side, breasts tumbling forward. He felt a rush of heat. "She was mean to me, you know." Pouting with a purpose. She ran her finger around his ear.

"You two never really did get along."

"Back in the day, you'd have come to my defense."

"You can take care of yourself, Beck."

"Even so, every girl likes a white knight." Leaning closer, warm breath. "But you were off rescuing another princess." Tongue in place of touch. "You like her more than me?" Barely a whisper. Goosebumps on his arms.

"I don't even know her."

"Didn't look that way." She'd swung up and over him, mouth moving down to his neck, his chest.

"I sprayed her house," he murmured. Body tingling. A moan.

She lifted her head and whispered, "Wanna play bug doctor."

Afterwards, she was gone, no regret or lingering kisses. Up and out, places to go, people to see. He couldn't sleep, sweaty and sticky. He didn't want to shower and lose the scent of her that stuck to his skin.

He made some coffee and sat down at the computer. He tried to read news on CNN but couldn't focus. He clicked over to the station's website, found Becky's picture, read her bio. No mention of the marriage. As if it never happened. Maybe for her it didn't. She barely gave him a thought. He thought about her all the time, wanted her back so bad it made him angry. At her, at himself.

The jealousy was good. Over Susan of all people, how ridiculous was that. The mystery bitch behind door number two. What the hell was her problem.

He clicked on Google, typed in Susan Carney NY, all kinds of links, none of them her. He wasn't sure what he had expected to find but now he was on a mission. He tried spelling her name with "K," no better, then remembered the cancelled check with her name on it. Kearney, with an "e" before the "a." NYC + Susan + Kearney.

He blinked. There were hundreds of pages of links. The Google ads on the side all about 9/11. Images across the top, thumbnails, no less recognizable for their size. The plane hitting the building, the rolling cloud of ash, the anguished firefighters. President Clinton walking a fence papered with flyers of the missing. Susan at his side, a young Susan, haunted and haunting. He remembered it now that he saw it again. Couldn't believe it was her. He clicked the first link. Time Magazine. "Her husband's name was Sean," it read.

***

Sean used to work to on the 87th floor, in a cloistered cubicle at the end of a row. Then he was promoted to a real office, with real walls and shelves, a mahogany desk up on 101. The stairwells had been impassable above the 91st floor. He'd gotten his own secretary. She died too.

So much of his company, their New York branch, was just suddenly gone, like everyone above the impact zone. Thirteen floors, no one left alive, except for a group having a video conference down on the sixty-eighth floor. The equipment in their own conference room hadn't been working that morning. They griped to maintenance, annoyed that they had to move. Such important men, such important business. They made six figure salaries. The service guy who responded didn't make half that. No one knew if he had finished before he died. How long could it take?

Susan set the microwave timer for 102 minutes. Stirring a pan of Cream of Wheat, she dumped in a handful of raisins. It was funny how she found herself thinking that she might be able to tell Jolene. She'd never told anyone and she couldn't explain how she was because she couldn't tell why. Round and round and round. She had never considered telling Maggie. Maggie knew some of it, of course, they had talked all during the before. But not after. How could they, Maggie knowing what she knew. Jolene was...a stranger. Someone who never knew him.

She poured the Cream of Wheat in a bowl, stirred in some sugar and sat at the dining room table. Zoey waited to the right of her feet, ever hopeful, her eyes following the spoon from bowl to mouth. "Chow hound," Susan said. Zoey thumped her tail. She dropped a spoonful on the floor. "It's got raisins," she warned. The puppy didn't care. They ate and played, tug of war with Mr. Hippo, slowly leaking stuffing as his stitches lost ground. Bits of fluff, white guts and gore, floating to the floor.

Ding, ding, ding. She stopped, as always surprised at how little time it took. From the first plane to the final falling tower. Terrorists, two, World Trade Center, nothing.

***

She'd always liked the span of his chest, big and broad, furry with soft, light brown hair slowly peppering with gray. Jolene snuggled against him, his arm firm around her shoulders. She loved him. Never had a doubt. From the first time she'd seen him, back when they were just kids, Jolene was certain he was the man to share her life.

He wasn't the handsomest man, though she always liked his nose and especially his smile. He had his problems of course, even without counting his momma. He wasn't the brightest bulb in the box and not particularly partial to work. Still, for all his faults, he'd always been there, through it all, steady and solid and the same. Darlene, the cancer, the death of her momma, then her daddy. Like the pines in the back yard, old and solid with deep roots, bending in the wind when the storms came. Never cracking.

He stayed calm about things. Sometimes when she sat in the kitchen in the middle of the night, it made her angry. Looking from one bill to the other, worrying over the car note, the mortgage, later the second mortgage. Why wasn't he upset? She was upset, with good reason too. Why didn't he understand! If he understood, he'd be out here too, making list after list of what was going out and coming in.

A few years back, they'd had to put a stint in his heart. It scared her half to death, the chest pains, his face going white, sitting down hard on the front steps. That's when she really took on the business, no more pretense. He never tried to take it back. The insurance company canceled their policy eight months later, a professionally passive-aggressive letter to explain that cancer and heart disease just too big a burden for their company to bear. She had paid them on time, every time, no matter what. It was a slow, steady tumbling downhill from there.

But in his arms, in bed before he fell asleep and left her alone with her thoughts, she felt safe. For all their faults and trials, together still. It was a blessing, to lean your cheek on another's heart, hear it beat, feel your own change to match the rhythm. To belong to someone.

"I tell you Becky Howe showed up at the pig-pickin?"

He listened as she chattered, wasn't much for talking, never had been. He'd always say she talked enough for the whole family. The whole town. Not one for romantic speeches, she could count on one hand the times he'd said he loved her.

"I never liked that girl," she added, "even before what she did to Jack."

"What I hear, she's still doing Jack."

"What!"

Carlene Duckett had talked to Mary Jean Houser, who had bumped into Elwood Droves, who had fixed the brakes on Jimmy Nichol's car, whose sister Georgia had told him that Becky spent the night at Jackson's. "Carlene told Charlie's wife at the Food Lion."

"I can't believe it. What's he thinking!"

"Not with his head, least ways not the one on his shoulders."

She gave him a slap, pretending to be shocked by such talk, then settled back down on his chest. "How does somebody do that? Cheat like that." He didn't answer. "I don't understand it but I'll tell you this, I ever caught you messing around, I'd take your momma's shotgun and blast your particulars all over the lawn." He grunted. Jolene snaked a hand beneath the covers. "Be a shame to waste all that potential."

***

"So how much did we waste on these?" He dangled the shopping bag at her.

Six months past the Caymans, the beach was long gone. "This isn't about my shoes, Sean."

"No, just about how to pay for them."

"That's not fair. I don't care about money." He snorted. "Just once, I'd like to talk about this without you getting mad."

"Just once I'd like to come home and not talk about it at all."

"We never talk, you're either working or watching TV. We don't spend anytime together."

"Ever wonder why?"

"Oh it's my fault!"

"I work my ass off, come home and all you do is bitch, bit..."

"Come home," she interrupted. "You live at the office."

He threw his hands up in the air. "It's my job, for Christ sakes! Work! You should try it some time," he muttered.

"Oh, so now I don't work?!" Raising her voice. "This is about our marriage!"

"You can have it,," he snapped, grabbing his coat before slamming the door.

He wouldn't answer his cell phone, she called over and over. The house was empty without him. She felt sick and scared and wondered where he was. If he was ever coming back.

When he finally did, it was very late. She was in the bedroom. He didn't come in. She didn't come out. The television on low. She read the same paragraph in the same book over and over. Finally she snapped it shut and went to face him.

He was asleep, sprawled on the couch, one arm hanging, the other across his chest. He still wore his shoes. There were lines in his face, she realized. Even in sleep, lines crisscrossing his forehead, drawing down from nose to lips. Long dark lashes over pale purple shadows. She watched his chest go up and down.

His briefcase was bulging on the coffee table. A copy of the Wall Street Journal on the floor. That was his life, that's what was important.

It should have been her. *You're expectations are out of whack, Maggie had said. He can't be thinking about you 24/7.* Why not? She hated to think herself as needy. He said all the time that she was. She'd planned to be so many things. That wasn't one of them.

Sean was always busy, busy. He ran on the weekends, played softball with friends in the park. He liked video games online and read Tom Clancy novels, so thick and dry they choked the throat. He loved them. There was a monthly poker game with the guys from the office, an annual trip to Vegas with his old college pals. He did things, things other than her.

I do things too, she thought defensively. She worked, twenty hours a week. She picked up his shirts. She shopped, for groceries too, not just shoes. Got her hair cut, did her nails. She cooked. She read. *Filling the time until he came home...*

She was suddenly aghast. A hopeless hapless housewife, heart on her sleeve. No! She didn't need a man to make her happy. *Still what was the point of having one if he wasn't even going to try? God, where did that come from?*

It wasn't possible. Was he right? She had been yelling at him for years and he was right. She had nothing of her own. No dreams, no passion, no work, no close friends. Just him. Waiting for him to make her life complete.

Sean opened his eyes. "Suz," he mumbled, lifting a hand to her hair. She caught it, kissed it. "I'm sorry."

"No, no." She leaned her head against his fingers and started to cry. "I love you, Sean, I do. I'll be different, I promise. I won't bitch and nag at..."

"Hey, hey. It's all right. We're okay." He kissed her mouth. A tentative tongue. She pulled his head to hers, fierce. He came down to the floor and they made love right there, the hardwood hard beneath her back.

"I love you, Suz," he said. "You have to know that."

"I do, I really do." He rested his head on her breast, eyes closing. "I love you too."

118

She got him into bed, stroked his hair as he slept. She finally got up, almost dawn, sat at the computer and checked her email. Expecting a note from a friend.

Chapter 18: August 17, 2006

Maggie showed up on Thursday.

Susan and Zoey were at the Coffee Cart. It had become the start to their day. Zoey loved the cinnamon biscuits. Susan fluctuated between red velvet and coconut cake, got brownies for Jolene. At first, she left the puppy in the car, not sure that Dottie would appreciate her baked goods becoming dog biscuits. But Betty Jane had ratted her out, watching from her window like spider in her web.

"You feeding my food to that dog?" Dottie demanded.

"What? No. She's just a puppy. Her name is Zoey."

"Betty Jane tells me you're feeding my food to that dog."

Betty Jane nodded. Susan shot her a dirty look. "Okay, look, she's crazy for the cinnamon biscuits. Whines and cries if she even smells them. It drives me nuts. If I buy them, she has to have them."

"Hmmp," Dottie snorted. "At least the dog's got some sense."

When Susan got home, there was an extra biscuit in the bag.

Now Zoey was a regular, a favorite actually, more so than her. Susan would set her on a stool and she'd put both paws on the counter, trying to lick Dottie's hand. "Stop that now, you're a bad dog," the old woman would croon, scratching her ears. Zoey would sit pretty and wait. Sometimes it was a hot dog, but mostly it was biscuits. Dottie had taken to putting broken ones in a bag, gruffly pushing them across the counter. "Dog needs some meat on its bones," she'd grumble.

"Say thank you to Miz Dottie," Susan ordered, shaking the bag. Zoey would bark, wiggling ecstatically, anticipation unbearable. Dottie beamed and Betty Jane almost smiled.

The trip home was always a tussle with the biscuit bag. Susan dispensed them at intervals, the puppy never satisfied. They were still at it when they got home, Susan opened the door and dropped the bag.

"Surprise!" Open arms. Zoey went for on the biscuit bag without so much as a look.

"Maggie! What are you doing here?" From within the hug.

"I told you I was coming. And who's this," she asked, bending down. The puppy growled, shaking the bag. "Are you Zoey?"

Susan yanked the bag back, the puppy indignant, carrying it and the cake box into the kitchen. Maggie's suitcase sat on the floor. Not an overnight bag.

"This place is darling, Susan. I love it."

"You do?"

"It's adorable. I mean, it needs to be fixed up, but it's gonna be gorgeous when it's done."

"That's what I thought too," Susan lied.

"I'm so glad you finally found a place."

"Do you like coconut cake?"

"Look at these hips, do I like cake." With each baby, Maggie had added pounds. More Happy Meals than salad bars contributed a few more. She was softer, a little rounder, less defined. It suited her, Susan thought. Brown hair, hazel eyes, dimples in each cheek. A sweet smile. "You on the other hand could be a super model, you're so thin."

"Stop."

"It wasn't a compliment."

"Stop," Susan repeated, putting a slice to each plate. "I've already got a mother I don't talk to. And if you start with this crap, I will let you have one bite of this cake and then eat the rest in front of you."

"I'm scared," Maggie replied, snagging a mouthful. "Oh my god, what's in this!"

"Uh-huh." Zoey barked. Susan threw her a piece of biscuit.

They made a trip to Mr. Lyman's hardware store. Maggie bought a small Weber grill and some charcoal, citronella candles and one of those coils you burn to keep mosquitoes at bay. Another pit stop at the Food Lion for chicken and barbecue sauce and potato salad. Susan waited in the car. They had green plastic Adirondack chairs for sale outside, with matching plastic tables. Maggie bought two. A house warming present, she insisted.

They sat in the chairs now, outside the kitchen on the lawn at the bottom of the steps. Zoey slept at Susan's feet, the roses in the side yard coloring the air spicy sweet, bugs in full symphonic tone. The charcoal was slowly turning to ash, throwing off a red glow. The peace of it. She felt almost normal.

"So when is your furniture coming?"

Almost. "What furniture?"

"A couch, chairs, you know, regular furniture stuff."

"I want to get the place fixed up first." Maggie didn't answer. "I do.

"I didn't say anything." She got up. "You want another beer?"

"No thanks."

She came back with one for herself. "You remember the time we went to that party over in Paramus? You were so hot for Carl Oszinski that we took your father's car without asking?"

"You were hot for Carl Oszinski and I got grounded for a month."

"Yeah, yeah, but remember that girl, Debbie something, got so trashed she took her shirt off? All the boys were falling down and she didn't care a whit, just danced around the yard in her underwear." Maggie smiled. "That's what I feel like doing right now."

"There's deer. They come at night, out in the back, near the barn. When you walk out there, you can see the nests in the grass where they sleep."

"It's beautiful here. Hot though."

"You get used to it."

"Not if you're fat."

"You're not fat."

"I am fat and I don't care. I'm fat," she yelled, "and I want to dance around in my underwear." She looked at Susan. "It's a blues song. I'm so fat, a roly poly moo," she sang.

"Stop it." Susan giggled.

"Plump and chubby, baby, through and through."

"Where is BB King when you need him."

"Dancing in my undies, bra and panties big too," she sang. "Thank you, thank you very much," she added trying to sound like Elvis. Susan clapped limply. "It's good to hear you laugh. Been a long time."

122

Susan sighed. "Here we go."

"Look, I love you. You're my best friend. Are you telling me that if I was living in a falling down shack with cardboard furniture you wouldn't be worried?"

"First its adorable, now it's a shack."

"And what's with the mirror? Duct tape?"

"It's broken."

"Yeah, right, funny how that always happens. So you'd be okay with it?"

"If you told me you were all right, I'd respect your decision."

She rolled her eyes. "Like hell you would." Night noises filled the silence. "What's that?"

"A bullfrog."

"Creepy," she said. "This place would have made Sean crazy." Susan tensed. "Can you imagine him about that wallpaper?" Maggie laughed. "Remember that time he was out to our house and…"

"Will you stop!"

"We can talk about him, he was a real person."

"Just say it, Maggie, okay! 'It's been five years, Susan, you should be over it, Susan,'" she mocked. "Maybe I just need to accept it, right? Let go, get on with my life. Or there's the ever popular, Sean wouldn't have wanted this for you. Any other bullshit you care to add?"

"No, you're full of enough shit for both of us," Maggie replied.

***

She went up to bed, came back down to dig through the boxes for a set of sheets. Susan stayed up, wandered the house. It wasn't a shack. At least there wasn't any ugly shag green carpeting like Maggie had in her TV room. Her floors were clean. She had to finish the stripping, okay, but she would. She had all the stuff.

The new dry wall in the dining room did look a little out of place. The absence of eagles and flags and water stains, it was flashy in its simplicity. The wallpaper next to the dining room window was pulling away, ripped. Susan tugged at it. It came loose more easily than she expected, glue brittle with age. Underneath, there was more paper, a different pattern, roses it looked like. She couldn't get her fingernails under the edge, suddenly needing to see what lay beneath. She pulled at another strip of eagles. It peeled away and exposed a seam on the roses. She dug, faded yellow flowers revealed, beneath that, sprawling vines, a claustrophobic chokehold. Who picks this stuff? She worked the vines free and finally reached the dry wall. Masks stripped away, nothing left but lifeless beige.

Once it was light she took food out to the barn for the cat. She was surprised to find Callie at the barn door, keeping a watchful eye on the kittens as they tumbled in the grass.

Susan put the bowl down and sat, watching them. Three of the babies rolled en masse, separating occasionally, to arch, to spit, to leap back into the fray. One sat to the side, the calico, little tail curled around her haunches, watching the others play.

"What's the matter, sweetie?" Susan wiggled her finger in the grass. The kitten's eyes followed. The kitten crouched, head in motion, targeting the finger. Susan twitched, fast, changed direction. The kitten wriggled and charged. It reached the finger in two bounds, batting with both paws. Susan batted in turn and it leaped away, back arched, hair straight up, hissing, tiny and ferocious. Callie growled low in her throat. She leapt gracefully over the squirming pile and took the calico kitten by the scruff of its neck and carried it into the barn. She glared at Susan on the return trip, grabbing up another kitten, soundly cuffed when it resisted stopping play.

"Okay, I'm going."

Maggie was up, in the plastic chair, sipping coffee. "Hunting deer?"

"Feeding the cat."

"Did you sleep at all?"

"So when do you have to go home?"

"Very subtle. So, I was thinking there must be a place to buy a couch around here and we..." Maggie started

"I don't need a couch and if I do, I'll go get one. Okay, Mommy?"

"You don't have to be such a bitch. I thought it would be fun."

"Sure you did. A little shopping, a little therapy, a quick jaunt to the loony bin."

"Get over yourself, okay? I'm sick of it. We're all sick of it."

"Oh, there's a group now? The save-Susan-from-herself club?"

"Not a lot of members left," Maggie snapped back. "The late night teleconferences take their toll."

"You know, you didn't used to be like this."

Maggie hooted. "Look who's talking!" She looked away, then back. "Fine, okay, stick with the cardboard, look crazy. Feel sorry for yourself all day long."

"Fuck you."

"Snappy comeback," Maggie said, getting up. "I need more coffee. You want some?"

"No."

"Wah, wah, wah."

***

"Maybe it ain't the trap, it's the moose," Skeeter pondered. He pulled a couple of long-necked Budweisers from a case on the floor, handed one to Billy. "I got to thinking last night, I mean, how many mooses are folks really trying to catch, you know?" Billy nodded. "Gonna make us some money, we gotta think."

He sat down on a crate, took a swallow, thinking hard. Billy drank beer and thought about whether he should turn off his phone before Jolene called trying to find him. "That's it, that's what we gotta do. A trap ain't worth a damn, no matter how good it works, if it don't catch something that folks want caught. That's what we gotta figure on, what do folks want caught." Billy nodded again. They sat for a while, finished their beers. Skeeter got up, got two more. "Yep, that's the way to go all right." He scratched his chin, looking at the pile of pulleys and rope on the floor. "Anything come to ya?" Billy shook his head. Skeeter sat down and sighed. "Guess it's gonna take time."

"Better'n taking money."

"Ain't that the truth," Skeeter replied.

***

Cordelia barely made it to the bathroom, the nausea coming so fast, her body too tired. So hard to move. There was a bucket in the bedroom, but pride prevailed. Not for much longer. They'd warned her the chemo would get harder. This last treatment proved them right.

She could feel the cancer inside her now. Like a fetus, growing, changing, moving. Getting bigger. Behind her careful smiles and bright promises, she knew. She was so tired. If it wasn't for them, she'd have let it come. Have its way unimpeded. Eat her alive. Like it was doing to Ben. That was killing her too.

They had married young, both below twenty, confident in happily ever after. Thirty years later, it had proven true, for the most part. But it had taken a while. She was grateful that divorce hadn't been so easy then. It was shameful in those days, a failure. Such a popular option now, it was almost a badge of courage, an epiphany in the search for true love, no one thinking anything of taking multiple trips down the aisle.

Neither of them were fighters, but both were quietly stubborn. Each with their own ideas of how a marriage should be. What it should offer, how it should feel. They disappointed each other more often than either cared to admit. Both of them wondering, her more so than him, women inclined to worry over matters of love more so than men. There were so many times that walking away would have been easy.

It was after the first miscarriage that the real marriage began. No pretty white dress or cake. No fancy ring. Just a dull pain in the small of her back most of the morning. She was cleaning the refrigerator when it unexpectedly stabbed her. She thought at first she'd wet her pants. How strange. Embarrassing. Blood. So much blood.

He'd raced home from work. He'd called her momma before he left the shop, she was already at the house. Too late for the baby. Cordelia was hysterical. Nothing helped. No comfort to be had. Ben had exiled himself to the garage, awkward, unneeded. This was for the women to handle. He fiddled around, trying not to think about what had happened, what was happening. He wanted a child, a son he hoped, though a daughter would have been fine too. Cordelia would have had six children, ten. God would see fit to give her only one.

He wasn't sure what to do, garage time stretching from minutes to hours. Her mother came out just around supper time, said Cordelia was resting. She was going home to make dinner for his father-in-law. "Please careful with her," she'd said, touching his arm. He nodded, not sure what that meant. Decided that she needed time to rest, he shouldn't bother her. In truth, seeing her cry drained him. He'd vowed to protect her. No man chooses to be seen helpless in front of the woman he loves. He took apart an old vacuum that hadn't worked in years. He couldn't fix that either.

"Why?" Barely a whisper.

She surprised him, his back to the door, bent over the work bench. "What are you doing out here, you need to be in bed." He moved toward her, she sidestepped, an arm up to hold him off. Face chalky white, eyes so big. Dry now, rimmed in red.

"Why?" A raggedy voice, on the edge of angry.

"Honey, I...we can't understand God's..."

"I'm talking about you! Why are you out here?"

Ben fumbled, not sure how to answer. "I thought that..."

"You hate me," she whispered. His eyes widened. "I killed him and you hate me and you can't stand the sight of me." Voice cracking, rising to a wail, she fell apart. Broken, messy, pieces everywhere. Not Cordelia at all. Her very soul screaming. And he'd left her alone. He'd left her to face it alone.

She crumbled to the floor, on her knees, white cotton nightgown sprinkled with tiny roses, her robe a pink puddle. Pain so dense it held shape and mass. He sank beside her, no attempt to raise her up, wrapped her in his arms, gripping his own wrist to lock her in. "I killed him," she said, over and over and over and over again.

It was a long time before they went in. He led her gently up the back steps, across the deck and to the kitchen door, to the half-clean refrigerator. She suddenly balked, panicked, fingers digging into his arm. "I can't," she sobbed. "I can't." Covering her eyes, cowering against him.

This time he picked her up, carried her down the stairs, around to the front door. He brought her to their bedroom, sat by her side. Listened to her ramble, not trying to change her mind, stroking her hair while she emptied the poison out of her head. Love is in the showing, not telling. She finally let him give her two of the pills her mother had brought. Sometime after three, she fell asleep.

Her mother had cleaned the blood spatters from the floor. The kitchen was bright and shiny. White walls and snappy green trim, a border of apples halfway up, circling the room. Magnets on the refrigerator. A list of baby names. A calendar counting down the days. It was a place for coffee, where bacon sizzled and biscuits were pulled from the oven, swiped with burning fingers and playful slaps. Nothing more. So much more.

He went to the garage, got the ladder, the brushes and rollers. A tarp. A dolly. He started taking the border down, scraping it with a knife. He unloaded the refrigerator, stuck the dolly underneath. Found a shoe box, carefully packing the calendar and magnets and the baby names. The rattle on the counter, a tiny pair of shoes she couldn't wait to buy.

At seven, Ben called Charlie, no more than a minute on the phone. Charlie opened the store. It didn't take long, paint and spackle, neither saying much. When Ben got home, she was still asleep. He called in to work, called her momma. Then he painted the kitchen a soft yellow with fresh white trim. No more apples. Nothing red. A little after ten, Charlie came with his brother-in-law and Cole Jarvis. They brought a refrigerator up the backstairs, chocolate brown instead of white. They took the other one away.

He was waiting at the table when she finally woke up. Heard her coming down the hall, stopping at the bathroom. She called his name.

"I'm here," he answered.

Her steps were tentative, halting. Same nightgown, no robe, no slippers. Fragile little feet. Her hands were shaking, as she turned the corner to face the kitchen. The cheery, homey kitchen where her baby died.

He would never forget her face. She would never forget his. Marriage vows that before had been merely spoken, now were lived. They reached for each other and would never let go. For any reason. It was two weeks before she bought another calendar. Sunflowers. Added a magnet to the refrigerator, a small cross at the top above the words.

"Love bears all things, believes all things, hopes all things, endures all things. Love never ends." Corinthians 13:7-8

They went through it one more time before Jack was born. And two times after.

***

Maggie hung up the phone. "Eric says hi." Brightly. "I thought maybe we could work on that wallpaper. You started ripping it and if we get it down then we could go look at paint."

"I don't want to paint." Petulant. Maggie started to speak, closed her lips. "It's my house."

"Fine." She turned, went upstairs. Susan paced around, tripping over Zoey, nervous now. Maggie came back down, carrying her suitcase. "What's that?"

"What does it look like. Could you call me a cab?"

"For what?" No answer. "I can take you to the airport."

"No thanks. I'll wait on the porch." Screen door slapping behind her.

Oh god, she hated this, hated people, hated all of it. Susan made herself go outside. "Maggie, don't, okay?"

"Don't what? Don't worry, don't care, don't try and get back to sleep after one of your phone calls? Don't wonder if tonight's the night you're going to kill yourself. Sure, okay, no problem."

"I won't call anymore, I promise."

"That will fix it. Asshole," she muttered. "Did you call the cab?" Susan was mute. "How thoughtful." Maggie got up.

"Don't, please." Susan stepped in front of her.

"You wanted me to leave, I'm going."

"Not like this."

"It's always on your terms, isn't it, Susan? Do you even care that you stopped being my friend?" Maggie pushed past her into the house.

"I am your friend!" Following her.

"No you're not. When was the last time you gave a shit about anything other than yourself? Maybe the dog, I thought it might..." She shook her head. "It doesn't matter."

"I know I'm messed..."

"How old are my children," Maggie interrupted. Susan blinked. "You remember my children," she added sarcastically.

"Matthew is four," Susan stammered.

"Zach is four, Matthew is eight. You're his godmother and you don't even know how old he is." She picked up the phone, dialed. "Wendell, North Carolina. I need the number for a taxi. No, I don't have a name. Could just you look it up, please!" She waited. "Thank you." She dialed again. "I need a cab to the airport. As soon as possible. Uh-huh, hold on." She put the phone against her shoulder. "What's the address again?"

Susan opened her mouth, closed it.

"You don't even know your own flipping address!" Maggie slammed the phone down. "What is the matter with you!" She raised her hands, shook them. "Why won't you talk to me!"

"I don't know," Susan managed. "I don't know." She did know. She turned her head, away from Maggie's eyes. "I'm sorry. I'm sorry about Matt, I didn't mean to...I'm sorry. I won't call anymore, please, Maggie. I can't...." Her chest heaved, struggling for a breath.

Maggie led her up to bed, tucking her in like a child, real sheets, pillowcases smelling of face cream. Zoey curling on the covers, in the crook of her knees, she slept and dreamed. Not of towers and planes, but a clear mountain lake. Swimming, her and Tom and Maggie, all of

130

them laughing. Sean standing on the shore, something in his hand. A kitten. He had a calico kitten, heading for the water's edge. Sean, Susan called, what are you doing? He didn't answer, flung the cat into the air. Flying, little legs spread, blue eyes wide, sailing over the water. Susan tried to run, fighting muck and lake, yelling for someone. Jolene, she screamed, Jolene. The kitten hit the water, sank like a stone.

Susan sat up, heart pounding. Zoey was gone. It was dark outside. She went downstairs. Maggie was in the dining room, piles of wallpaper on the floor at her feet. She held a flat plastic square to the wall, a bandana around her hair, wisps curling out in the steam. "Oh good, you're awake." She set the steamer down. The wallpaper had bubbled. She stuck her finger underneath and pulled the sheet free. "Wal-Mart," she explained. "These things work like a charm." The flags and eagles were mostly gone, the room was down to roses, patches of those peeled away too, with green vines peeking through. "Coming along, don't you think?" She stood back to survey her work.

"How long have I been sleeping?"

"A while. You hungry?" She asked. "I got pizza. I can heat it up."

"In a minute."

The white chairs from the porch were inside. Susan sat, head fuzzy. Maggie went back to the steamer, adding to the pile of dingy strips curling on the floor. "I'm gonna head out tomorrow. You mind giving me a ride?"

"No, of course not. Where's Zoey?"

"She's in the kitchen sleeping. Too much pizza," she added. "Susan?" Maggie glanced over her shoulder, steamer on the wall. "Just don't die, okay? It would really mess me up. If you die."

Chapter 19: August 20, 2006

He hadn't planned to tell her that he knew. He'd talked it over with his mother, because he had to tell someone. It was too much to keep to himself. In a weird way, it was like meeting a movie star, in mufti among mortals. He was a bit embarrassed to find tragedy so titillating. But this was 9/11, the Kennedy assassination of his generation. A day locked in memory, no one unaffected, a bond forged that would be forever shared and now to be so close to an inside view. It was hard to put out of his mind.

She was in the garden when he drove up, the puppy running toward the car. Almost dark, she had the porch light on. She rose from her knees, both capped in red dirt, not happy to see him. Bracing herself. You shouldn't be here, he told himself, climbing out of the truck. "Hey."

"What do you want?"

He held up both hands in surrender. "Look, I know we got off to a bad start and I wanted to tell you that I'm sorry. For the things I said. No right to be talking like that."

"You didn't have to drive all the way over here for that."

"I just figured, you know, apologize in person, you know. Start over." He held out a hand. "Jackson Wyle, ma'am" She didn't take it, holding up dirty hands in way of explanation. "Okay, well, then..." he hesitated. "I guess I'll see you around then." He started for the truck, was almost there. She was already back on her knees when he turned. "Susan?" She looked over her shoulder, caught off guard, just for a second, he got a glimpse of that girl, that face frozen in the photograph. Damaged. Defenseless. He wasn't going to say it, then he did. "I know."

"Know what?"

"You know, I know. About New York." He didn't want to say her husband's name. "What happened." He wasn't sure what he had expected, despair, a tantrum, nervous break down. She just looked at him for a long minute, her chin lifting. A twist of her lips, she took a deep breath and sat back on her heels.

"Zoey," she called. The puppy's head popped into view, from behind his truck. Sure of the dog's whereabouts, she went back to the weeds, leaving him standing there. Feeling stupid. Always feeling stupid.

"I can't imagine what it was like for you. I was in Dottie's, you know, just like always and it came on the TV and nobody thought…I mean, we thought it was an accident, you know and then…" He stopped, watching her fight a pine seedling with stubborn roots.

"Go ahead," she said. Strangely detached.

"I'll never forget the second plane, it was like watching a movie, it didn't seem real, all the people running, the cloud of smoke behind…"

"Ash."

"What?"

"It was ash. It was gritty."

"It must have been horrible for you."

"Uh-huh."

"I can't even imagine."

"I know." Kindly.

"We just couldn't leave the TV," he said, needing to tell her. "They kept showing the same pictures over and over but you were afraid to leave in case there was something else. It was…" he groped for the right words. "I don't know, it was… I just wanted to get in my car and go help and…" He stopped.

She was still at the weeds, scraping at the dirt with bare fingers. "Do you know what this is," she asked, pointing to a plant with long leaves. He squatted to look.

"Looks like a cone flower."

"I thought it was a weed." She patted the dirt down around the roots.

"It's Echinacea, you know, the stuff for colds. Gets a flower in the summer," he added. Absurd, this conversation. He remembered the

133

black specs in the sky, the moment that he'd realized they were people. Jumping. "I don't know why…I guess I just wanted to…"

"To tell me. I know."

"I'm so sorry. I can't imagine," he repeated.

"I know." The puppy raced over to them, stick in mouth. She planted her front feet, butt in the air, wiggling. Susan smiled, reached for the stick. Tussling with the puppy, she finally yanked it free and threw it out into the yard, Zoey in joyful pursuit.

"Do you want to tell me about it," he asked. Sorry the second the words came out of his mouth. "I'm sorry, I didn't mean…to pry, you know. I just thought…oh crap. I'm a total jerk, okay." He stood up, running his hands through his hair.

"You did give me a heads up on the cake," she said. Surprising him.

"Always count on Dottie to save my ass."

"How'd you find out?" She didn't need to clarify.

"Google."

"So what are you going to do?" She looked up at him.

"You mean, am I gonna tell anyone? No, no, of course not, but…" He hesitated.

"You wonder why I don't."

"Well, I mean it's none of my business." She shot him a look. "Okay, I already said I was a jerk, but I guess, if it was me, I guess…"

She actually laughed. It was the first time he'd seen that. She asked him if he wanted a drink, got him a beer and herself a soda. She threw the puppy a piece of a cinnamon biscuit. Zoey gobbled it down, had to check every hand and pocket before she was convinced there were no more. "Go play," Susan told her.

"No one can imagine but everybody knows what they'd do. It's funny, isn't it?"

"Yeah," he said sheepishly. "I guess we all felt a part of it, it happened us too, in a different way. I mean, compared to you, it's…but…I remember when the Pentagon …"

134

"That's why," she interrupted. "Do you know how many times I've heard the stories? How many times I've been expected to listen? As if it's my duty." She shook her head. "I married a man. Not a hero. And he died. What more is there to know?"

"Susan, you don't ..." Jackson said, eyes dark.

"All those people, pouring out their memories, as if I'm some kind of bucket. It's too much, it's too…it swallows you and suddenly you're not real anymore, just Sean's wife and 9/11 and ..." She stopped.

"I'm sorry," he murmured.

"That too," she said, shaking her head. "Memo to the world, you're sorry, I get it." She rolled her neck. "I know that sounds mean, it's…it's just…everyone says to move on but no one does, not around me. It's everywhere. God, even at that pig-pull Jolene made me…what?" He was trying not to smile. "What!"

"It's a pig-picking. Tractor-pull, pig-picking," he added. She stared at him, then started to laugh. Both of them, on the steps, laughing so hard. Zoey ran over, barking. Jack scooped her up, a baby in his arms, rubbing her belly. "Is that what happened in Pilot?"

"I hate that flag picture, it always freaks me out. But I was really hot and I didn't wanna go in the first place. Too much," she added.

"And if people knew…"

"Exactly. There'd be a ceremony, they'd want me to talk, recognize my sacrifice. He's the one who died. Then there's lots of pictures, me and somebody, then somebody else and somebody else and they all need to tell me," she said. She took a swallow and looked away. The weight was tangible.

A bucket can only hold so much until it slops over the sides, he thought. Cardboard furniture and mismatched shoes. Duct tape on the mirror. It wasn't the mirror that was broken. And just like on that day, there was nothing anyone could do, just watch, try to comprehend. Helpless to change it. He took a pull on his beer, set the bottle on the steps.

"The garden is coming along," he said.

"It's a mess."

"Go faster with some help." He got up, knelt down next to the steps. She sat for a second longer, then got up and went to the further end and started pulling. They didn't talk, just worked.

"Are you going to tell?" She asked quite a bit later.

"No." He tossed some weeds out on the lawn. "Don't pull that," he warned. "It's bee balm."

***

"The bug doctor," Jolene exclaimed. "Making a house call! Boo-ha!"

"This is the nosiest town I have ever seen."

"Come on now, it's not like his car is hard to spot."

"I'm not exactly on the main drag. And you're the second person who mentioned it."

"Charlie told me."

"That's three. Dottie this morning. You people need to get a life." Jolene hooted. "Coming from you?"

"I've got a dog," Susan said. "And nothing is going on."

"Awful touchy for somebody with nothing going on," she said. "So who's this Maggie?"

"An old friend, from home."

"I would have liked to meet her."

"I couldn't...it was a battle zone," Susan sighed. "She wants to save me. Ever since Sean, she won't let up."

"Cares about ya, that's all. Shoot, I pray for ya every night, you wanna fight with me?"

"No. Your mother-in-law's got a gun."

"Was that a joke? Did you just tell a joke?"

"Shut up."

"So did I tell you 'bout Billy's trip up to the mountains? Be damned if those idiots didn't take potshots at a moose. Or so he says, for all I know they coulda been chasing a Winnebago. Now even if it was a moose, which you aren't supposed to be hunting now in the first place, it's damn stupid to shoot at something that big when you're

136

drunk as a pig. Which is probably the only reason they were shooting at it at all." Jolene leaned back in her chair. "Men. What did we ever do to deserve 'em."

"Boo ha!"

"You don't say it right, a little more boo and a little less ha."

"Boooo-ha."

"Well now, that was bad, just plain bad."

They sat in the Adirondack chairs on the back deck, the citronella candles smoking. Thunder clouds were building in the sky, smoky cotton candy, growing higher and higher. The air was still and heavy. Zoey panted in the yard, Mr. Hippo trapped under one paw. "Have you ever done anything really bad?'

Jolene thought for a minute. "I've done my share, I guess. I stole once, not kid stuff like a candy bar, took money from a house I was working on. It was just sitting there, a nice neat little pile. Don't know what came over me, but I scooped it up quick as a flash. The people, they thought it was the Mexicans, you know? Made an awful stink, one of 'em ended up getting sent back," she added. "I felt pretty bad about that."

"Did you ever tell?"

"Hell no!" Jolene tossed a pretzel at Zoey. It bounced off the puppy's nose. "That dog has no catch reflex at all."

"Did you wanna tell?"

"And go to jail, no thank you! Billy was just getting over his heart problems back then, we were behind every which way but loose. Don't make it right, but that's how it was. I had to make my amends to the Lord, though. No secrets from him."

"There isn't any God, Jolene, it's made up," Susan said.

"Not for you to decide."

"People want to think something can save them. It's so stupid. Somebody left a bunch of pamphlets here last week. Coming to my house, leaving crap on my porch.

"There's an old saying, 'For those who believe, no proof is needed. For those who don't, no proof is possible.'"

"As if anything you do can just be wiped away. In Jesus name, see ya!" Scornful smirk. "I mean, you can't take things back just because you feel bad that you did them." Susan shot Jolene a glance. Waited. Jolene waited too. "I did something once. I've never told anyone."

"And now you're thinking about telling me?" Jolene watched her hesitate. "Take your time with it, Suz. Don't be spilling milk you aren't ready to mop up."

"Maggie says I'm feeling sorry for myself."

"Well, duh! Makes sense, living how you do, sitting a secret like that." She suddenly slapped the arms of the chair. "Now here's a question for ya, why is it that a man cannot use a bathroom without blowing it up? I swear Billy came out of the toilet yesterday morning and I about had to fumigate the house. I mean, we're eating the same food. A mystery of science, that man's bowel." Susan laughed. "Nothing funny about it."

"Boo ha!"

"Not even close, darlin', not even close."

***

"So where were you the other night?"

"When?" The cell phone tucked under his ear as he drove.

"I was out and about, thinking I might drop by…" She let it stretch. "But a little birdie told me you weren't home," Becky purred.

"Didn't know I had my clear my schedule with you. Or your birdie."

"Now, honey, don't get testy."

"I don't call you and ask what you're doing."

"That's cuz you're afraid I'll tell you." Teasing.

Jack's jaw tightened. "Not hard to figure out, Beck. Some things never change." He was this close to calling her a tramp, all the old stuff coming up. But it was what she wanted. To get a rise. "And last time I looked we weren't married anymore."

"My, my, I believe I hit a nerve."

"What do you want?"

"I'm gonna be coming around, talk to folks about George. I just thought you'd wanna know."

"Have at it."

"You know, Jackson, whenever you get testy, it's because there's something you don't want me to know," she said. "But I always find out, don't I, sugar? That never changes too."

Why the hell did he answer the phone? He always answered the phone! He threw it now, bouncing off the dash on to the floor.

***

Susan checked the voice mail on the cell phone. The puppy danced in circles around her, knowing it was time to eat. "No biscuits today," she warned. She poured Puppy Chow into Zoey's silver bowl. "Sit." The puppy quivered until she set it on the floor. Then it was a free for all, kibble tumbling over the sides of the bowl. Zoey ate as if she'd never been fed. Susan used to worry that she wasn't feeding her right or that the worms were back. But it's just how it was. Zoey met each meal with the same crazed excitement. Food falling from the skies, it amazed her. She chowed it down, sniffed the bowl and floor, gobbling up fallen kibble, looking for more.

She was getting bigger, longer legs and longer body. Her tummy was still plump and her ears too big for her head, but she was growing. Susan thought there should be a chart, like for kids, where you could mark the wall at head and tail. Maybe there was, she'd have to look. Zoey was changing right before her eyes. She be gone soon, the puppy she knew, never to be seen again.

Susan surveyed the boxes. She must have a camera. She thought she might have bought one in Oklahoma. So many boxes. So much to sort through. She could get a disposable camera. Send the whole thin in and they send back the pictures. That was better, just picture cameras. She was sure they would have them at Wal-Mart. I little after nine in the morning. Too early for Wal-Mart. herself unwilling to wait.

There was a Walgreens on the corner at the stop light in the center of town, a drive through for prescriptions. It shouldn't be that busy. She could go there, they must have cameras there. Sunglasses too. Zoey had chewed her sunglasses and her flip flops, and everything else within reach. Susan had to stack a pile of boxes high against one wall to keep the cell phone safe. Maybe they had rawhide bones.

Walgreens had everything. Not a lot of people there, a few older ladies, a man checking his blood pressure on a machine. Susan got more flip flops, a hair brush, dental floss in case of ticks. She turned the corner, found herself in the cosmetics aisle. She used to spend so much money on makeup. Not in places like this, but in fine department stores. Fine department stores centered their sales around a skin care regime. Lots more to buy. No Cover Girl or Maybelline, Clinique and Estee Lauder, counters full of pretty bottles and pretty girls dressed in white coats, tote bags bulging with free gifts.

She'd played at being beautiful then, pots of colored shadows, lipsticks from pink to scarlet red. She waxed her legs, her eyebrows, painted her toenails, whitened her teeth. The more he earned the more she spent. The more time it took to use what she bought, running from the manicurist to the hairdresser to the tanning salon. So much work. Sean seemed to like it. She was beautiful, he said. Like the other wives, sophisticated, put together. All the rough edges covered over, like wallpaper layered on a wall.

Now she washed her face with Dawn or whatever dish soap she happened to buy. Same with her hair. Walgreens sold dish soap and aluminum foil and charcoal briquettes. My Dog Lets Me Live Here, proclaimed a small sign, hung with twine, a picture of a chewed up shoe. She bought that too.

They had disposable cameras, but there were a few cheap digitals that caught her eye. No waiting. There were flash sticks for memory, to save the pictures. Susan had left the computers in New York, but she wouldn't need a one. She could take the sticks to Wal-Mart, they had a machine that let you pick your pictures, cut them, crop them, print them or small.

She spent the entire day taking pictures of Zoey. The humidity had miraculously lifted, a glorious day, mid-eighties, all sunshine, pretty, poufy clouds tripping across the sky. She chased the dog through the back fields, in the high grass, over the lawn, round and round and round a tree. She caught the puppy rolling. Chasing butterflies, chasing her tail, purposefully digging in the dirt for god knows what. Susan crawled on her belly to catch the puppy at eye level and was attacked for her efforts, a love mauling. Zoey was overcome with joy. It was hard not to feel alive.

She went to Wal-Mart as early as she dared, just before midnight. She'd taken hundreds of photos, used both memory cards. She needed to get another one while she was there. She spent more than two hours at the machine making pictures. Eight by tens, five by sevens, little three by threes. Zoey leaping toward the sky. Zoey's front paws, and the tip of her nose. Upside down, the speckles on her belly. A close up of Zoey's face, one ear flopped over, her tongue lolling, eyes full of love. Gotta love Wal-Mart. No place like it.

She got a big bottle of Elmer's Glue, thought better of it, put it back and got some putty. Re-stickable. She couldn't resist a better digital camera with a zoom lens and two more memory sticks. She looked until she found her same cashier in a different line.

"This is my dog," Susan said. "Zoey."

"A real cutie pie!" The woman shuffled through the top of the stack. "Took yourself some pictures, didn't ya?"

"I got a little carried away."

"Look at that, almost see the tail wagging. Thought I saw you the other day, at the pig-picking."

"I didn't stay very long." Looking away.

"These came out good," she said, getting the hint. Scanning the putty. "I'd like to get me one of those," she added, taping the box with the digital camera. "Got my granddaughter living with me now. Cute as button, smart too. Can't catch half of it, she moves faster than fish i' pond." A proud smile, missing teeth on the right side. "Had to tak from my girl, you know. She's not right." Her sorrow was cl me this job so I don't have to be on the WIC. Government money, that's no good." She shook her head.

"Ellie," a manager called as she passed, "after you finish with that customer, you can take your break."

"Yes, ma'am. Thank goodness," she said to Susan, rolling her eyes. "My legs are 'bout to bust. Five hundred and twelve dollars and fifty two cents," she added. Susan slid her card. "Debit or credit?"

Dead man money.

***

"Did you hear the one about the blonde who decided to paint her living room?" Tom asked. Susan groaned. "Her husband comes home and finds her in the middle of the room, brush in hand, wearing both her furs. So he says, honey what are you doing? And she says, I'm painting the living room and I have to put on two coats."

"Oh god." Susan rolled her eyes..

"I got one," Bill offered.

"I'm leaving." Susan started to push back her chair.

"Oh no you don't." Tom put his hand on her back.

"How can you tell that a blonde's been using your computer?" He paused. "There's white out on the screen."

"That is so old."

"Why did the blonde dye her hair dark brown?" Tom asked. "Artificial intelligence."

"Insulting," Susan replied. "And why are these jokes always about women? You're blonde."

"Not the same." He shook his head. "What do you do when a blonde throws a hand grenade at you?" Tom waited. Susan met his eyes. Nice eyes.

"What," she sighed.

"Pull the pin and throw it back."

"That's it, I'm going. You guys are pathetic losers and as a blonde, I am embarrassed to be seen with you." She slung her purse over her shoulder and stood. "Do you know why blonde jokes are all

one liners? So men can understand them." She tossed her lunch bag into the trash can.

"Ouch," Bill said, getting up. "Back to work."

"Do you know what has eight arms and an IQ of sixty," Susan continued. "Four men watching a football game."

"Don't make me hurt you," Tom warned.

Susan laughed, walking backwards to face them. "Do you know why doctors slap babies on the bottom when they're born? To knock the penises off the smart ones." She'd shrieked as Tom chased her through Herald Square. Caught her and spun her around, swept off her feet.

Chapter 20: August 21, 2006

"Somebody oughta knock some sense into her," Big Jim griped. "Woman keyed his truck. My old lady tried something like, well..." He shook his head.

"Jerry was crying like a baby," Bubba added.

The boys were having their coffee, discussing the latest chapter of the Caine marriage wars. Skeeter nursed a beer, looking a little rough for wear. The men commiserated over Abigail Caine's temper – "No wonder the man drinks – and discussed the new gas tax coming down the pike.

"Shame, that's what. Gonna put a gallon of gas over two dollars," Randy Teator said.

"How's a working man supposed to get by?"

"Like the government gives a damn about the working man," Big Jim said.

"It's the Yankees, that's what. Got so many of 'em down here, starting to look like New York. Whole state's going crazy," Bubba complained.

"Speaking a which, you hear that Yankee girl passed out at the pig-pickin'?"

"Saw her just before she went down. Skinny little thing."

"Jack took her home," Ben said, his first contribution of the morning. "Guess the heat got to her."

"That's what I'm talking about," Bubba said. "Don't belong here."

"Can't stop 'em from coming," Skeeter snapped. "No point whining about it."

"What's wrong with you?"

"Probably got hisself a case of gutter balls."

***

They came to pray with her at least twice a week, always brought food when they did. All of them excellent cooks. She didn't eat much but it was good to know that Ben was fed. Took a load off her mind.

"...so Carlene had to come to school and pick her up at the principal's office," Louella said. "Poor thing."

"Children can be a challenge," Nancy Parks murmured.

"But such a blessing," Cordelia added.

"The pastor is bringing on a new youth minister, did y'all hear? He's from up north, round Ohio, I think," Queenie Bitton said. Her husband Dean was on the church board.

"Ohio! How did they meet?"

"At that conference last year, remember, in Kentucky? Evidently this young man gave some powerful testimony. Pastor says we're lucky to have him."

"Time will be the judge of that," Louella said, clearly annoyed that she hadn't been first to know.

"And he's not married," Queenie added, not above rubbing it in. "I was thinking that I might have a little supper party, introduce to him to Anne's oldest girl, she...."

"Might let him get here before you marry him off," Louella interrupted.

"Did I tell you we stopped by the Garret place the other day?" Nancy stepped in to keep the peace. "We wanted to pay a call on...goodness, her name's gone right out of my head."

"Susan. Susan Kearney," Cordelia said. Heads turned. "Jack knows her."

"Really." Queenie wiggled on her chair.

"It's not like that, he sprayed the house for her."

"I heard he took her home from the pig pickin'."

"Carried her off right in front of Becky," Louella added.

"It's not like that," Cordelia protested.

"Like it or no, good to see that girl get a come-uppance. Long overdue," Louella said.

"Now it's not our place to judge," Queenie said.

Louella snorted. "Just cuz her momma's brother is your husband's cousin."

"Did you talk to her," Cordelia asked. "Susan, I mean."

"No, the car was there but she didn't come to the door. We left a welcome packet," Nancy said. "I'm hoping we'll see her in church."

"She's had a hard time," Cordelia said. "Lost her husband a few years back."

"Really?"

***

"The old bat must've put this on with Krazy Glue," Jolene griped, working the steamer, the last layer of wallpaper was not inclined to give ground. "Hot as hell in here." Her hair curled in wisps.

"It's the steam." Susan didn't turn around. She stepped back, surveyed her wall.

"When you told me about this, I thought you were nuts but it looks good, real good," Jolene said, stopping to look.

The bare drywall had been a blank canvas. Susan hadn't bothered to prime it. The mosaic was forming now, she'd always had a good eye. A wall of Zoey. Last night, she laid the pictures on the floor, arranging and rearranging, until the puppy had romped through them, carrying one off to tear into pieces. Now they were on the boxes, careful piles by size and shape, before moving to the wall.

There had been no way to avoid them, pictures were everywhere you looked. Frantic families and friends, taping flyers on buildings and telephone poles, on the barriers slapped up to keep the people from the site. There were thousands, flapping like loose shingles, overlapped, taped, tacked and stapled. She'd walked along them so many times, with and without President Clinton, looking at the faces, wondering about their lives.

Some of the pictures were vibrant, a guy holding a child up to Mickey Mouse. A man in front of a Christmas tree, golf clubs at his feet, a bow on his head. A young woman clutching a trophy, one fist in the air. Susan had been saddened by the pictures with forgotten hair styles and out of date glasses. No recent photos. She wondered if their families were ashamed, caught in the act of indifference. Too late now.

146

There were formal shots too, like yearbook photos, of cops and fireman and Port Authority police. The walls had started as a bulletin board. They became a memorial. Twenty-three killed in NYPD, the Port Authority lost thirty-seven. FDNY racked up three hundred and forty-three. Two thousand nine hundred and seventy three people who would never be more than pictures on a wall.

"You've got a good eye."

"It looks okay?" Susan stepped back to look.

"Shoot yeah." Jolene came to stand beside her, looking. A streak of dirt ran across her nose. "That dog is so darn cute . You could make a calendar."

"You've got dirt on your face." Jolene swiped her cheek, smeared the dirt from her hand in the sweat. Susan grimaced. "Worse."

Jolene went to the bathroom, Susan turned back to the wall. Held another picture at the edge of the collage. She cocked her head. Tried it in a different place. Still not right.

"I've been meaning to ask you, what happened to the mirror?" Jolene called.

"What?" She forced her eyes away from the wall. "I'm sorry, what?"

"The mirror, what happened?"

"Nothing." Puzzled.

"It's covered in duct tape."

"Oh, yeah."

Jolene waited. "So what happened."

"I taped it." She held up the picture, trying to find the place.

"It broke?" Susan didn't answer, absorbed. She found perfect spot, pressed the putty to the wall. Perfect. Wait. Maybe an inch lower. She chewed her lip. Thinking.

"It's not even cracked," Jolene called from the bathroom.

"What?"

"The mirror, it's not broke."

"What did you do?" Susan's voice rose.

"Calm down."

"Don't tell me to calm down, what did you do?"

"I took the tape off, at least most of it, it's on pretty…"

"Put it back!"

"But it's not broke," Jolene protested.

"Put it back, right now!" Susan started toward the bathroom, stopped, turned, stopped.

"What is the matter with you?"

"Put it back! Put it back, put it back!" Literally shrieking.

"All right, that's enough! You're two steps away from the funny farm, Suz." Jolene grabbed her arm. "And I'm about over it." She dragged Susan toward the bathroom.

"Let go of me!" Susan struggled. Zoey lifted her head, awakened under the chair. "Let me go!" Jolene pushed her through the door, a knee to the back of her knees. Susan stumbled into the room.

"It's a mirror, just a plain old mirror, that's all," Jolene snapped, closing the door as the puppy reached it. Zoey whined on the other side, scratching, stretching a paw beneath the door.

"Get out of my house." Susan bent over, clutching her stomach, hard to breathe. Don't look, don't look. "Get out," she yelled.

Jolene leaned against the door, shaking, trying to not to show it. "I'm not leaving. And just so you know," she added, "I seen worse hissy fits on a two-year old."

"Get out, just get out!"

"There's been way too much walking on eggshells around you, Suz. Everybody feels so bad for ya, we keep making excuses for all the crazy stuff you do. But it ain't helping, us pretending about you."

"Please," Susan pleaded, changing tact. "Please, just put it back."

"Not gonna. And you ain't either."

"I hate you," Susan hissed.

"That's fine," Jolene replied, folding her arms to hide her trembling hands. "Hate me all you want, but you can't scare me off. I'm no Yankee, honey. Shoot, you can't scare me at all."

***

148

She had gotten old. In five years, ten years older. Where she had been terrified to look, now she couldn't look away. She was still pretty. It shocked her. Not like before, there were lines and creases now, but still pretty. In a worn out kind of way.

She stared at her face, inspecting every lash and pore. Blue eyes with dark flecks near the pupil. Dainty lines to each side, charcoal shadows beneath. Lashes and brows that had a tendency to fade away without pencil and mascara. Her face was more angular, cheekbones too sharp. Too thin. A good nose, freckled from the sun, but still her best feature. Dull teeth, dull skin, dull hair, dull eyes.

The puppy trotted in the bathroom, carting the new favorite toy, Cowboy Rhino, one of its legs hanging by a thread, already going the way of Mr. Hippo, now an empty shell of raggedy gray fur. Susan scooped up the puppy and held her to her cheek, looking at the woman and the dog in the mirror. Zoey barked at the stranger, squirming and scared.

"It's a mirror," Susan explained. The puppy kept barking, the dog in the mirror barked back. "I don't like them either." She set her down. Zoey sniffed around her legs, settled on the towel spread in front of the shower stall, ripping at Cowboy Rhino's head.

Susan pinched her cheeks, watched the color spread. She bit her lips and inspected the results. All made up and no place to go. She hesitated, then slowly pulled the band from her hair. Blonde, a little more brown than before. It swung lower than her shoulders, straight, ends fried to frizz. Still it softened her face. The woman in the mirror was almost familiar. She felt sick.

There was a knock on the door. Zoey ran toward the sound, barking.

"Hello?" An unfamiliar voice. "Anybody home?"

The woman was smiling, as if they knew each other. More church stuff, no doubt.

"Look," Susan said, keeping the screen door between them. "I'm not interested in church and I'd appreciate…"

"Church?" The red-headed woman laughed, perfect white teeth. "My, you do have a sense of humor."

"Do I know you?"

"You know my husband." Susan blinked, her stomach twisting. "I'm Rebecca Howe." She opened the door, Susan stepped back. Reflex as opposed to welcome. Zoey barked like a mad dog.

"Be quiet," Susan told the puppy. The woman was in her house, eyes roaming the room. "I'm afraid I don't..."

"Are you feeling better?" She was beautiful. Like another redhead from long ago. *You know my husband.*

"Is this about Tom?" For the first time, the power shifting, Becky was confused.

"I though his name was Sean?" She frowned.

"What are you doing here?"

"I'm Rebecca Howe, from WRAL, TV," she added. "Mrs. Kearney, our station is doing a piece on 9/11, the fifth anniversary and all. I'd love to have you on. I understand your husband was one of the victims at the World Trade Center. I'm so sor..."

"You've made a mistake." Susan started for the door.

"You are Susan Kearney?" Becky didn't follow. "This is you. In the picture?" The tone was professional, just a hint of smug, holding up a copy of Time Magazine.

"I don't give interviews." Susan opened the door, waiting.

"I can understand how difficult it must be for you." Zoey snuffled around her shoes. She bent, let the puppy sniff her fingers, gave her a pat on the head. "Nice doggie." Becky straightened up, smiled. "But it would mean so much. This is a memorial, a retro..."

"I said I don't do interviews."

"It's a chance to remember your husband and..."

"I remember my husband," Susan snapped, temper flaring. "Please leave."

Becky paused, clearly assessing the situation. "So you are feeling better at least? I know Jack was worried about you."

"What?" Totally thrown off.

150

"We stay in touch," she said, almost flippant. "First love and all. Hard to let go, though between you and me, Jack is a little needy," she confided. Susan stared at her, trying to process. Jolene had told her about his wife. His ex-wife? "Tell me about Sean, was he your first true love?"

Bright white spots exploded in front of Susan's eyes. "Get out of my house."

"Surely we can come to an understanding. Given all we have in common."

She meant Jack, she thought they were... "If you don't leave..."

"Yes?" Smiling. Insolent. Finally, slowly she strolled forward. "I must say, it's quite disappointing. I'd expected a patriot."

"Don't let the door hit you in the ass," Susan said, swinging it shut behind her, too soon, so it would do just that.

***

Jolene stopped at the cemetery after going by CP&L to pay down the electric. She was one step ahead of them, just enough to keep the lights from getting cut off. She'd tried to call Susan, talk her into going to Dottie's but there was no answer. Jolene didn't know why the girl had a phone, much less two. She never answered, most times didn't call back.

"Hey baby girl, how are you today? I miss you," she said, smiling at the stone. "Not much new, though your Nana's been acting up again. Got into a fight in the Food Lion, Queenie Bitton's girl was checking her out, kept insisting that she was being charged for tomatoes, which she was because she had tomatoes. Started yelling and cussing, I swear the woman needs to be in a home. And not mine," Jolene added.

"So how are you, honey? Jesus treating you right? Just kidding," she said, glancing up at the sky. "I know how happy you must be, now that you're with Him, but I gotta say I wish you were still here with me. Your daddy does too." She caressed the name on the headstone. "I tell you got me a new friend? From New York City, can you believe that? Her name is Susan and she's kinda crazy, maybe more than kinda, but I like her. She's funny, even when she isn't trying to be. Been a while since I had a girlfriend to talk with, I mean, I love your daddy and all but he ain't much for conversating."

"Listen, Darlene, I need you to do me a favor. Miss Susan, she's had a hard time of it and she can't get out from under." Jolene pulled a dandelion from the edge of the headstone. "If you could, would you ask Jesus to look in on her? It would ease my mind some. She doesn't have nobody, like I had your daddy and your brother."

"There's something weighing on her, has been for a while. I think she's thinking that she could tell me about it. Makes me kinda nervous, truth be told, how she is, I wouldn't wanna say nothing wrong and make it worse for her, you know?"

"So if you could ask Jesus, when the time comes, let the words come from Him, not from me. Thank you darling. Love you."

***

Susan locked the puppy in the bathroom. He told. He told her! After everything he said, he told, a reporter of all people. She was so stupid. She'd liked him. Even thought that…so stupid! She hit her forehead with her fist. Such a sucker! The paranoia built, taking her back, how they'd tracked her. The poster child, the pretty face of an ugly day. She'd open a paper and see a picture of herself on the street, walking, coffee or groceries in her arms. Caught unaware.

The house had no curtains or blinds. They had long lenses and short ethics. There would be pictures. Breaking news, film at eleven. The fifth anniversary. Good for ratings, paper sales. Are you Susan Kearney? She should have changed her name. Is that you, in the picture? Stupid. Stupid!

She went to the calendar. Nineteen days left. She paced the kitchen. Round and round and round. He told her. He said he wouldn't tell. "And you believed him," she said out loud. Facing the huge window in the kitchen. Wide open.

She had sheets, Maggie'd found the sheets. Susan ran up the stairs, stripped the sheets from the bed, grabbed another pair from the open box. Downstairs, she got the staple gun and started in the kitchen, stapling the sheet to the window frame. Left a space to a peep through, so she could be prepared. For what? For anything.

On to the dining room, smaller windows, two pillowcases each. She covered the picture window in the living room and ran out of sheets. She had to think. Zoey cried from the bathroom, whines at crescendo. Susan picked up Cowboy Rhino and tossed the toy inside as the puppy charged the door. He told. He told her! He said he wouldn't. And now they would come, had already come.

Cardboard! She got a knife from the kitchen, slashed the tape on a box marked MOVIES. She dumped them on the floor, stepped on the carton until it went flat. She put it over the window left in the dining room. Pop, pop, click. No more staples. Plenty of duct tape. She covered the rest of the windows in the living room, brown with silver frames, long overlapping strips, no attempt at symmetry. She closed the inner door, locked it. No chain, no dead bolt. Susan taped it shut, wishing she had nails for the hammer. Ripping the tape with her teeth, like Zoey ripping at Cowboy Rhino.

She dumped boxes as she went, piles of stuff in every room, pens rolling, papers flying, glasses bouncing in their bubble-wrap. Cover the door in the kitchen, the small window where she could see Callie waiting on the rail. Another box broken down. Helter-skelter mounds of forgotten useless things. Saucers and silverware and deodorant and Band-Aids. Tupperware with and without lids.

She slapped the last strip in place. Done. A feeble barricade but the best she could do. She went to the front window, peeked. No satellite vans, no trucks, no cars. But they'd come. She couldn't stop them.

Maybe if she had a gun.

Jolene knew about guns. She could get a gun. A big gun, one with a long barrel that she could use to wave them off her porch. She could see it, liked the way it looked. Standing strong, gun resting on her hip until she raised it up. The fear in their eyes, the scavengers, jackals, trying to feed off Sean's remains. She imagined the sound when she cocked the gun. Get off of my property, she'd say. And they'd run. And if they didn't, she'd fire a shot in the air. Boom! Maybe two, boom, boom! A twenty-one gun salute at Ground Zero. Everyone had a gun. Jolene would know.

"No....in hell ... gun," Jolene said, phone crackling static. "Coming over ...wait for..."

She didn't wait.

***

The bell over the door jangled. Her tic twitched. A man she didn't know was behind the counter, she started checking the aisles.

"Charlie!"

"Miz Susan, how can I help you today?"

"I need some duct tape." He shouldn't have told. He said he wouldn't.

"Right over here." He looked at her. "Little Charlie keeping up with your lawn?"

"Oh sure, he's great. Really great, the lawn is great."

"You feeling okay?"

She resonated like a tuning fork, mouth working, compulsively chewing her lip. "Fine, I'm fine. Do you know where Jackson Wyle lives?"

"Miz Susan, you wanna sit down for a minute? You look a mite flushed."

"I need to find him, Charlie. Right now," she added, close to shrill. He blinked. She backpedaled. "I mean, I was supposed to give him a check, you know, and I forgot all about it and I feel really bad and I just want...to find him."

"Saw him earlier, didn't seem concerned."

"He's probably not, so nice and all, but I won't sleep if I don't take care of it." She rolled her neck, heard it crack. Tried to make herself stay still, fingers fidgeting, toes almost tapping. "I just want to find him. To drop off the check." Smile, Susan. Be a good neighbor.

If only she had a gun.

***

154

It was someone else's pipe dream, not Bid Laden's brainstorm. Khalid Sheik Mohammed. A freelancer, without affiliation, he considered himself an up and comer. Like Sean, full of ideas, looking to make his mark. He'd gone to college here in North Carolina, less than four hours from the house. He was the uncle of Ramzi Yousef, the man who bombed the towers the first time in 1993. Nepotism the same in terror as any other game, he secured his meeting with Bin Laden through his famous nephew's name.

It was the first time the idea had been articulated. No one was sure it would fly. No pun intended. A classic case of male ego, same site, bigger spectacle. Simple one-ups-man-ship. Their meeting was in 1996. Bin Laden didn't bite, not until late 1998 or early '99. Then he gave the green light and the operation was on.

***

Jackson lived just outside of town, farm country. The house was a ranch, with neat shrubs and a red door. She pounded on it. There was no answer. The car was in the driveway. The motorcycle gone. He wasn't home. Just the stupid car. She kicked the bumper as she passed, the bug's legs jiggled. Two more steps and then she stopped, turned. The bug…

It was designed to be taken on and off, she just had to figure out the buckles and snaps. It was heavier than she expected, styrofoam head, body stuffed with plastic pellets. Susan staggered as it came loose, bug legs flopping in her face. She threw it on the asphalt and got the duct tape from the SUV.

She staked it out at the end of the driveway, like a great white hunter on a fire ant hill. It lay on its back, antenna bobbling, duct taped legs and middle, round wiggly eyes begging for mercy. She backed up the car, sighted the target and stepped on the gas.

Up and over, both tires, hit the brakes and shift into reverse. Back and forth, forth and back. Plastic pellets burst from the seams, rolling into the street like a strand of broken pearls. The bug splattered on the asphalt, its head popped off like a squeezed pimple. She picked it up before she left.

Susan drove away blindly without landmark or direction. Enraged, crazy kicking in with a vengeance. She'd thought she could get past it, have friends, a garden, a rocking chair. Stupid! She was stupid! Faster and faster on country roads, twisting and turning, farther away or closer to home, she didn't know. She didn't care. She glanced at the bug, sitting on the passenger seat. "Don't lose your head," she said. Laughing.

Maybe she liked being crazy. Had anyone ever thought of that? No, no one listened to her. It was all about Sean. She was nothing except as the wife of Sean. A walking tombstone, she was a stand-in for the body they never found.

She drove too fast, slipping on the curves, tires spitting gravel, the SUV grinding up the road. She swung a turn, fishtailed wildly and the deer was suddenly there. Just there, in the road, a deer. No headlights, but still it stood, frozen, watching her come. Slender legs, dainty feet and little white spots near the tail. She slammed the brakes and cut the wheel to the left, the rear of the car thrown forward. Spinning, the bug head flung to the windshield, bouncing around the car until the SUV shuddered to a stop.

She pulled over, sat for a minute, then got out, hands trembling and bent to breathe deep. The deer was gone, completely, gladly, gratefully gone. No fur or blood, no body parts scattered along the road. Susan open the passenger door, picked up the bug head and buckled it in the passenger seat, a ping pong ball from the end of an antenna unnoticed in the wheel well.

Carefully, she buckled herself back in, used her to blinker to turn out onto the empty road. She drove for a mile a two, speedometer at thirty five until she reached a stop sign. "I don't know where we are," she said, glancing at the head. "You're the one who's from here." She sat at the stop sign, waiting. "Fine, don't tell me, but no whining if we run out of gas." The car turned left.

156

She ended up near Wal-Mart, driving past the church with the red roof, Jolene's church. Jolene was going to be mad that she didn't wait. "Probably should have waited," she told the head. It didn't disagree.

She pulled into the Wal-Mart parking lot. She needed more staples. Ellie was at her register. Aisle three, twenty items or less, on her feet all night long. Staying off the WIC. She looked up, saw her and waved.

Normal people took it all for granted. Being normal. She was so tired.

Susan turned her cart and found the camera aisle. She picked the best camera they had, two memory sticks and a printer that didn't need a computer. She got three stacks of photo paper, two extra ink cartridges and a frame that said I Love Grandma.

She paid for them at the service desk and left them under Ellie's name. Then she drove herself home, careful not to talk to the bug head on the way.

Chapter 21: August 22, 2006

"Ben been in?" Bubba asked, putting a third spoonful of sugar in his cup.

Billy shook his head the same time Skeeter said, "Not yet."

"Heard somebody messed up Jack's house last night."

"The car, not the house," Randy corrected.

"Damn kids," Skeeter spat.

"Heard that big old bug was smashed flat, all over the place. Mike Taylor said, he got the call."

"Jack called the cops?'

"Didn't hafta, Georgia Childress did. From across the street?"

"Nosy old biddy," Randy griped.

"Too bad she didn't see who done it."

"Don't it just figure, missing the most important part, busybody like that," Big Jim added.

"There's an invention for ya," Bubba called. "BusyBody binoculars, attach 'em right to the window."

"Damn kids," Skeeter replied. Billy nodded.

***

"So I come all the way over here with a bucket of original recipe and you're not even and the place is done up like a bank robber's hideout. Not that I ever seen one, course, 'cept the doublewide that Joey Drake lived in," she said. "He robbed the BB&T over in Knightdale, dumber than a box of rocks, his cousin Phyllis works the drive through. Can you imagine? Caught him before he even had time to buy a pack of gum."

"I'm sorry." Susan sat on the floor with Zoey, gently tugging at Cowboy Rhino. Zoey was furious, feet planted still sliding along the plank floors. She growled, lips curling up from her baby teeth.

"You should be sorry," Jolene said. "You coulda called me, you know."

"I didn't have a phone."

"There's a cell phone right there, ain't never seen it doing nothing but charging."

"Don't touch that!"

Jolene rolled her eyes, picked up the cell phone and waggled it in the air. "Look at me, touching the phone."

"That's not funny."

"Hello, Mr. Phone, how y'all doing today. Fine, Miz Jolene, how's by you." She flipped it open. "I can put my number right in here and..."

Susan scrambled to her feet. "Don't! Please! It's Sean's," she lied.

"Oh shit." Jolene snapped the phone shut, held it out. "I'm sorry, Suz."

She took it, carefully plugged it into the charger. "I just like keeping it, you know. For the voice mail, sometimes I need to hear his voice. Stupid, huh?"

"No, honey, no. I shouldn't be making fun." She settled on a box. "So what's with the cardboard?"

"I don't have any curtains."

"Bless your heart, not the choice most folks make, Suz." She snapped her fingers and the puppy ran to her. "Zoey, your momma is a real nut job." Zoey shook her toy, nudged it under Jolene's hand. "Wanna play, huh? Okay, come on, give it your best shot."

She shook the toy so hard it shook the puppy. Zoey was delighted, fighting back with fierce determination, her body quivering with effort. Susan got the camera as they tussled, Jolene literally lifting the puppy off the ground. Airplane spin, round and round, legs spread and tail straight out behind. "Tough little bugger," Jolene grunted, finally pulling Cowboy Rhino from the puppy's jaws. She flung the toy into the dining room. The puppy scampered after it, back in a flash at Jolene's feet. "You know, I got kids, you'd think I'd know better than to start this."

"C'mon, Zoe, come on, outside." Susan walked to the kitchen door, Zoey and Jolene trailing. "I have to sit out there or she won't pee." Zoey dashed into the yard. Callie arched her back and hissed from the rail. "Jolene, grab that box of cat food."

They settled into the Adirondack chairs. Callie had brought kittens down from the barn, under the deck. Susan wasn't sure when, but she would see them now, tumbling in the yard. Zoey was fascinated by the tiny balls of fur that puffed up and skittered sideways at her approach. Hissing, miniscule claws raised, so fierce. Zoey only wanted to play, but Callie wasn't having any of it. She streaked forward, hair a ridge on her spine, walking with her butt swung forward, growling from deep in her throat. After a couple of warnings and a good scratch across Zoey's nose, it settled into a cold war. Each watching the other. Leaving the kittens alone.

"So, you hear about Jackson? Some kids vandalized his car, right in his driveway. What is the world coming to, can't park your car in front of your own house. Though Billy said with that big bug and all, he was surprised it hadn't happened before. A prank, he says. Prank, hell, destroying people's property, my Mickey knows better, or he'd better cuz I'd take a strap to his butt, college or no. He wants to be called Michael now, did I tell ya?"

"Uh-huh." The bug head was upstairs, sitting on the bed. "Did you know his wife?"

"Whose? Jack's?" Jolene snorted. "Wish I didn't. Why?"

"No reason, just curious. Do they still talk and stuff?"

"I think Jack would do just about anything to get her back. Can't figure it, the girl's a train wreck and everybody knows it but him."

"She's beautiful."

"How do you know?"

"I saw her. On TV." Jolene looked around the room, raised her eyebrows. "At Dottie's."

"Just curious, huh? Come on now, give it up. You like him, don't ya?"

"I don't want anything to do with him," she snapped. Jolene shot her a glance but didn't reply. "I don't!"

"Up to you."

They sat for a few minutes watching the kittens play. The sun golden in a perfect blue sky. So beautiful, the grass mowed, scent of

160

roses on the wind. "She came here," Susan said suddenly. It took Jolene a second to catch up.

"Becky came here? What for?"

Susan hesitated. "I think she thought that Jack and I…"

"Holy crap! That girl, I'm telling ya, she's got herself some balls, excuse my French!" Jolene shook her head. "After all she's done, the nerve to try and mess things up for Jack."

"There's nothing to mess up."

"She already messed him up good."

"Maybe he deserved it."

"Little harsh, shug," Jolene said. Susan didn't answer. "Is that what's up with the cardboard?" Still no reply. "Suz, I know you're antsy around folks, but, shoot, Becky Lee Howe isn't nothing but dressed-up trailer trash."

Another spell of silence. "Have you ever been to New York?"

"Nope. Hey, maybe you and me can go there some day, you can show me around. Shoot!" She sat up straight in her chair. "You been to see the ball drop? I always wanted to do that, watch it on TV every year. You been there?"

"A couple of times."

"Really!" Her eyes shone. "Was it great? Did you love it? How could ya not! That Dick Clark in his tux with a big ole bow tie. They had Regis do it a couple years back, I think Dick was sick or something, remember? I like Regis and all, but just it wasn't quite the same, you know?" She paused for a breath. "Still I love watching all those folks, dressed up so nice, blowing horns, having a good ole time." She smiled. "Billy says I look the fool in them little hats, which I am willing to concede do cut into the chin. He won't wear 'em," she confided. "Even if I promise sex stuff I won't do all the time," she added. "Now that's a man who hates a pointy hat."

Susan laughed. "I think you should be on TV. You could have your own show."

"One of them sitcoms, maybe, or wait, a reality show! Can you imagine all of America watching Billy's momma coming over once a week to wash her teeth in my dishwasher!"

"That is not reality."

"That's what I'm saying. If people knew the life I live, shoot, Suz, you won't look so bad after all."

"Is that supposed to make me feel better?"

"I tell ya what'll make you feel better, getting that damn cardboard down."

"Not today."

"Well we're taking the tape of that door at least. No sass," she warned, "or I touch the phone."

***

"Bill's in a meeting," Susan said, working in the 33rd Street window.

"I just stopped by to see if you guys wanted to have lunch."

"I don't know when he'll be back." She repositioned a hat, supposedly blowing away in the wind. She couldn't get the wire right.

"Here, let me help you," Tom said, stepping into the window. "It's twisted. You hold the hat and I'll straighten it out." He reached above her head, her back almost against his chest. She tingled. "There you go." He stepped back. "So you wanna have lunch?"

"Sure, okay, I suppose so. I don't have a lot of time though."

"We'll have to make the most of it then."

"Are you flirting with me?"

"Maybe." He winked.

"I'm married, you know."

"Keeps us honest, don't you think?"

162

Chapter 22: August 24, 2006

After the first bombing in '93, Port Authority had invested millions. Emergency lighting, training, glow in the dark arrows. Money well spent. So many lost, but so many lived. Sean would come home, complaining about the drills. Floor leaders and safety directors, escape routes, single file, stay calm, stay in line. Like high school, he'd gripe.

It happened on February 26, 1993. Not quite as catchy as "Nine Eleven." Most people didn't even know the date, much less remember where they were when they heard. Only six people died. Only.

Simple concept, a rental van was left in the parking garage with a 1500 pound bomb. Boom. Over a thousand injured. The evacuation took more than four hours. The bomb blew out the public address system, the lighting failed. There was so much smoke in the dark stairwells people were afraid to go down. The NYPD used the heliport to pull people off the roof, the last rescue fifteen hours after the blast. Everyone knew about the roof rescues. Eight years later, it would be hard not to assume the same. With no other options, it was better to believe. Some of the 9-1-1 operators sent people to the roof, but the helicopters never came. It didn't matter, really, there was no other way for them to get down.

That was her life now. Being accountable for what shouldn't have happened to him. Dead from the second he'd pushed the elevator button in the lobby. Not some name in the newspaper. Sean. He had loved her so much.

While he was alive, she never saw it. Now it was a crystal clear. Millions of moments that had never even registered. He bought peanut M&Ms and tucked the bags in her coat pockets. He kept up her computer, her hard drive defragmented and her virus software current. That's where she got her email from Tom. Sean always noticed her shoes. Made her take vitamins. Set up the coffee maker every night so that she would wake to a fresh pot. He was long gone, out by six. When they were first married, she used to get up with him.

He was not a perfect man. He worked way too much. He was overly analytic, not much of brainstormer, had to plan things down to the smallest detail. When she talked, he didn't always listen. Her sloppiness irritated him and he found her liberal tirades tiring. Corruption, conspiracy, injustice, she loved to point it out. Stop whining and do something if you feel that way, he'd say. But she was a backseat driver, living in the cheap seats. She thought he should have known that. He expected her to have a life. It never occurred to him that she didn't know how.

All those years she and Maggie had spent planning their future. Only looking at the destination, never plotting out the route. So many options. She would be a political activist, start a fabulous, chic boutique, lobby against domestic violence. She would be a caterer to the stars, direct documentaries, write children's books. She would learn to play the piano, get her masters, go to Africa, do magic tricks.

None of it. She'd done none of it. She thought about all of it. Ideas raged in her brain, trapped in synapses that didn't know where to send them. She started things, she was good at that. She did research and proudly presented her findings to Sean. He would take her ideas seriously, make suggestions, recommendations. He offered interest. She was looking for affirmation. A week or two later, she would be on to something else, the old idea pushed aside, half done or barely conceived. Off to Barnes and Noble to buy another book, more research, and bring home cookbooks by the armful.

She loved to cook, loved cookbooks but only if they had pictures. There was something comforting about looking through them, even if she never made the food. She was a messy cook, lots of pans and bowls and sauce on the walls, sometimes the ceiling. Sean would shake his head, patiently explaining the benefits of cleaning up as you went along. Susan just laughed. He'd do the dishes every time. In morning when she got up, the kitchen was pristine, hers to mess again.

It frightened her, that she couldn't recognize love when she saw it. The inability to realize she already had what she so frantically sought. Not like the perfect pair of shoes or the right shade of lipstick or the best little black dress. All immediately spotted. Hooted over, talked about, praised, valued. She didn't value Sean. He'd loved her anyway.

In some place, she knew, that he was solid and she was hollow. She started to feel guilty. It made her resentful. And so she nagged, she argued, nothing was enough. Because the more he tried, the guiltier she felt. Cynical, superior, rolling her eyes. Sighing with other self-righteous women, mourning the imperfections of the men who had chosen to share their lives. She was a bitch.

He loved her anyway.

Chapter 23: August 25, 2006

Becky had called twice while he was working, his phone in the car. She expected him to pick up when she called. He always did. The second call only proved what Jack already knew. He was most desirable when she thought he'd lost interest. She valued the things she had to chase. And yet he always answered. Knowing better and doing better were two different things.

There was no voice mail from the first call. But in the second, she showed her hand. She didn't like not knowing. Just a hint of petulance, leaving the number at the station, as if this was a professional call. She was a professional, all right, hooker or hit man, hard to know which.

He wasn't going to call her back. When he wanted her, she didn't care. Hard to get, she was all over him. He knew that. He wasn't sure how that would help him keep her, but it was enough to give him another shot at trying. Let her come to him, keep coming. He knew that was the way to go.

She answered on the third ring. "Back from the woods?"

"Sorry I missed you."

"Are you?" A little too brittle for coy. "Sometimes I wonder."

"You're not the type."

"What type am I?"

"Dangerous," he said.

She laughed. "You are the cutest man!" Pleased. "I just don't know how I let you get away."

His heart contracted. "Who says I did?"

"Well," she teased, "you're not taking my calls..."

"I was working," he protested. Quick to explain. "The phone was in the car." He could almost hear her purr. "What did you want?"

"I need a little favor. And maybe, just maybe I mighta been missing you."

"Is that before or after I do you the favor?"

"Don't be mean, sugar, it doesn't suit you. I need you to talk to your girlfriend for me."

"What girlfriend."

"Please. Jack, it's all right. I'm not a prude. I understand that we haven't been…well, but I can still come to you, can't I? Because I need you sometimes and well, don't make me beg, darlin'."

His heart thumped. "I still don't know what you're talking about."

"I went to see her but she practically threw me out of the house. You knew the story I was working on, Jack. You could have told me, about her husband," she added softly. As if she was hurt.

She knew about Susan. Becky had gone to see Susan. His chest felt tight. She knew about Susan. "When did you talk to her?"

"Are you upset?"

"Just tell me. Was it the day before yesterday?" His tone had sharpened.

"I'd have to check my schedule." Annoyed at being questioned. "I don't know what she told you but I was very sweet with her. I understand what she's been…"

"I gotta go, Beck."

"Wait! Jack, I need you to…"

He snapped the phone shut.

***

The heat had returned with a vengeance, the nights in the high seventies, moist and sticky. "Sit. Good girl." Susan squatted in front of the puppy and held out a hand. "Okay, Zoey, shake." The puppy looked at her quizzically. "Shake."

The books said you shouldn't give the command more than once. Say the dog's name. Be gentle but firm, wait for reaction and reward positive response. Susan wiggled her hand, leaning closer. Zoey grabbed the remains of Cowboy Rhino, one ear cocked, hoping for tug of war.

"No. Shake," Susan repeated. Zoey shook the toy fiercely, racing in circles around the lawn, leaving a trail of fuzz guts. Susan laughed, tossed her a treat and looked up to see his car coming down the drive. Bugless.

"I didn't tell her," he said, as soon as he was out of the car.

"Bullshit." She called the dog and headed for the door.

"I told you I wouldn't and I didn't." He followed her.

"Fuck you."

She opened the door for Zoey. Jack pushed past her into the house. The puppy dashed past him, almost blending into a wall covered in her image. It was new, all the pictures, changes around the room, the wallpaper gone, down to drywall, smooth and blank. But the window was covered by a stapled-on sheet, cardboard furniture still the same.

"We need to talk," he said. "I didn't tell her, you've got to…"

"No, I don't," she interrupted.

"If I could find out, anybody could find out. She's a reporter."

"Who just suddenly decided to Google my name. How'd she even know my name?"

"I don't know. But I didn't tell her."

"Fuck you." She walked to the kitchen. He followed, stopping in the doorway. A calendar on the wall. Set to September, everything after the eleventh blacked out like teeth on a rotting pumpkin.

"Susan, I have no reason to hurt you." She was at the counter, fussing with a mug and a tea bag.

"No," she said coldly, turning to face him. "But from what I understand, you'd do anything for her." Like a punch in his stomach. "Screwed you every which way but loose from what I hear."

His face darkened. "Me and everybody else in town."

"Makes it more pathetic, don't you think?"

"Stop it! If you wanna talk pathetic, how about your little visit to my house the other night? I could call the cops."

She lifted her chin. "Go ahead."

He shook his head, "I know you think I…"

"I know you did!"

"Why won't you just…" He suddenly stopped. "Oh shit. Shit."

"Finally some fake remorse." She went past him, a cup of cold water with a tea bag floating in it.

"She called you my girlfriend. When she called tonight," he added quickly. "She wanted to get me to talk to you."

"And here you are. Go fetch," she mocked.

"Listen, I think she thinks that I...that I like you, you know. That would be enough to run the search and anybody could tell her your name."

"You are so full of shit I don't know..."

"I'm trying to explain," he interrupted. "Why don't you give the benefit of the doubt for fucking second! Is this how you were with Sean, because..."

"Don't you dare say his name!" She stepped toward him, finger outstretched. Eyes blazing. "Sean has nothing to do with this. He would have never..." She choked on the words.

"Well neither did I!"

"I'd like you to go now. And make sure your wife," she emphasized the word sarcastically, "gets the message. I wouldn't spit on you if you were on fire."

He was finally pissed. "Oh because you're such a prize, right? Look at this place," he said, striding into the living room, waving a hand around the room. "Talk about pathetic!" The frame on the mantle caught his eye. He picked it up. "Is this him? The sainted Sean," he snarled, pointing at Tom. She gasped, color draining from her face.

There was a noise, click, click, click, little nails on the stairs. Zoey bounded around the corner, carrying the bug head, black circles jiggling in white oval eyes.

"Well," Jack said. "If I'm an asshole, at least I'm in good company."

***

The first time she'd let Tom kiss her was at a little bar in midtown. He'd taken to showing up when she was getting off work. In the beginning he'd ask her to have a drink in front of Bill, sometime they all went. Later he only asked if she was alone. It was fun, the flirting. Susan was flattered, felt attractive, liked the attention he paid her. Like

Sean had done before they got married, before she became the ball and chain, the bitch, the pain in his ass. Tom listened to her, liked to talk to her, thought she was witty and clever. He told her so. He liked the sound of her voice, the shape of her smile, the way she constantly pushed her fingers through her hair when she talked. It drove Sean crazy.

"You're driving me crazy," Tom groaned.

"It's not hard, just concentrate," she said. "I'll show you again." She stuck out her tongue and curled up the sides until they touched. "See?"

"You're a freak. Betcha can't do this," he said, holding up a hand, spreading fingers to form a V.

"Please," she scoffed, doing the same. "Live long and prosper."

"I should have known." He signaled the bartender. "Two more."

"I really have to get going," she said.

"One more drink won't kill you."

"I'm half trashed as it is." She slid off the stool. "And I need to pee."

She'd known all along. Knew while she looked in the mirror, checked her makeup. It was just a matter of when. Letting the anticipation build, slowly moving pieces of her life around in her head until it was rationalized. This was no different than a yoga class or a pedicure. A harmless adventure, Sean would never know. It was just a way to feel better about herself. And that would help things at home. It would, she thought, touching up her lipstick.

Tom whistled as she walked back to the chair, letting her hips swing a little more than normal.

"What?" She smiled.

"You know you're a knockout."

"Who says?" She started to slip by him to get to her chair. It was all so natural. His hips against hers, his lips coming down, her own spreading in welcome. "Wow," he'd whispered, looking deep in her eyes.

170

***

The first flight school Atta considered was in Oklahoma. Zacarias Moussaoui went there later on, but Atta decided on Florida instead. He could handle the heat. He arrived in June. In September of 2000, he requested a change in visa status, to become a student instead of a tourist. The paper work wasn't processed until 2002. His request was approved. The media had a field day.

But Atta was not one to wait around. Before the application was even filled out, he was already in the Accelerated Pilot Program, had soloed in July, passed the private airman test in August. It was on to a different school, from Venice to Sarasota, learning to fly commercial planes. Big jets with lots of room for lots of people and plenty of fuel. He had no student visa. Back then, no one really cared.

They did care that he was a jerk, arrogant, argumentative, irritating the instructors during training flights. When he failed the test for instrument ratings, he ran, ego tucked between his legs. Back to Venice where things had gone well. By mid-December, he was certified by the FAA. Using their flight simulators to practice the plan. It took less than six months. Atta was an ambitious man.

***

The puppy lay snoring on a towel. Susan stood, staring in the mirror. It was time to go again. Pick up and run. She would be doing it forever. Running forever, locked in time forever. She sighed, pushed the hair off her face and tried to find the strength inside, that place she'd always pulled from when there was no courage left. The place that forces you up and out and makes you move forward, even when there is no forward to be found. Where had it gone?

At what point do the reserves dry up, how long can a person go living on fumes and fear and guilt? Essence slowly draining away, separating life from the body, reconfiguring the mind to bleak endurance. So desperate to escape, yet following the same route every time, knowingly or unknowingly tracing her own footsteps back to

171

same wall, running full tilt into the bricks. So tired. And it was time to start again.

The woman in the mirror had too much time. Death a blessing that she hadn't earned, and would not allow herself to steal. Decades yawning ahead. Her life for his, penance paid, it was the only way. Perhaps she had forgotten. Let this little house lull her into some semblance of hope. It didn't matter how or even why it happened. Jack swore he didn't tell and maybe he didn't, it really only mattered if she was staying. And she never stayed. She couldn't. There was no way.

Jolene.

Why did she think that? It came to her too often. That Jolene would understand. That Susan could tell her everything. And the world would still stand, their friendship remain. How stupid. Jolene didn't even know who she laughed with and told her crazy stories to. She'd be gone, horrified, revolted, Susan's ugliest fears validated. The woman in the mirror was unredeemable. So why did she think about telling Jolene?

Chapter 24: August 28, 2006

The first firefighter was killed when a jumper landed on him.

There was so much falling debris, human and otherwise, that most of the firefighters had to enter the South tower through a walkway from a Marriott Hotel in the Trade Center complex. A command center was set up there, both fire and emergency medical response. It was abandoned when the South Tower fell.

There was no evidence that the buildings would collapse. No one in charge seemed to consider it, perhaps a false sense of security from the earlier bombing. Maybe what they already had on their plate was enough. Around 9:30, a South Tower caller on the 106th floor told a 9-1-1 operator that she'd heard the 90th floor was collapsing. Fifteen minutes later, the message was sent to the battalion chiefs, mistakenly reporting that 106th floor was crumbling. The caller wouldn't survive to clarify.

The fire fighters kept climbing. A group of civilians were trapped in an elevator on the 78th floor in the South Tower. Firemen and security guards freed them at 9:58. They had one minute to live before the building fell. It took ten seconds to come down.

A thousand one, thousand two, thousand three, thousand four, thousand five, thousand six, thousand seven, thousand eight, thousand nine, thousand ten.

***

"I have things to do," Susan said. "I don't have time for this.

"You got nothing but time," Jolene hooted. "Gotta pick something up. Just want some company, that's all."

"Zoey's home by herself."

"She'll survive."

"Where are we going?"

Jolene turned into a neat split level, beige siding, maroon shutters. A separate garage at the end of the drive. "Come on." Jolene got out of the truck and started up the sidewalk. She stopped, turned and flapped her hand. "Come on!"

Susan got out reluctantly and followed. A man opened the door. He was tall, white hair and a strong nose that was bigger now that age had thinned his face. Jackson's nose. "Jolene!" Jackson's smile. "Nice to see you."

"Mr. Wyle, this is my friend Susan."

"Ben Wyle," he said, shaking her hand. "My son Jack has spoken of you," he added. "Come in, Cordelia will be happy for the company."

Susan followed them into a living room, warm with color, cushy chairs and worn couch, newspapers on the floor, coffee on the end table. Family pictures on the walls. A young Ben and a younger Jackson holding up a string of fish. Jack at high school graduation, both parents beaming. A black and white wedding picture of happy newlyweds, in front of a tall cake, their hands entwined on the handle of a knife. His father was handsome, his mother luminous, shining off the film, a pretty girl turned beautiful in the day.

"How's she feeling today?"

"A little tired, but better than last week. Getting some broth down."

He led them down a short hall and up three steps. The bedroom was on the left, not theirs, a room for her now. A single bed, with a tray on a stand that could swing over or be pushed to the side. There was a white painted bureau topped with a TV, bookcase full of books. Pretty curtains with bright red poppies, a matching coverlet, crisp white sheets. On the nightstand, there were yellow flowers in a chipped white pitcher. A bendy straw sat in the half-empty water glass, a bible resting by its side.

"Honey, Jolene stopped by with her friend Susan."

The woman on the bed was ravaged, whiter than the sheets. Red spots on her cheeks, like crayon scribbled on a wall. Her arms were sticks, her head bald, covered by a scarf that didn't quite hide it. Her eyes were brown, her cheeks concave, and her lips a dull plum. She smiled, the same smile as the wedding picture.

174

"Jolene! How nice to see you," she said, a lilting voice of southern sugar.

"You're looking good today, Miz Wyle."

"Hush, I'm a fright and we both know it. I'm sorry, I missed your friend's name?"

"Susan. Susan Kearney. Hello." She stayed back.

"Is this the Susan that Jackson goes on about?" Jolene nodded. Cordelia patted the coverlet. "Sit down here and let me get a look at you, my eyes aren't what they used to be." Susan perched awkwardly on the edge of the bed. She could smell the cancer. "Pretty, just like he said. No, now don't you blush, if a girl's pretty she has to learn to live with it."

"Miz Wyle, I was hoping I could pick up that bag?"

"Of course you can. Ben, there's a bag for Jolene in the closet in the TV room?"

"Be right back," Jolene said, following him out. .

"And Ben," Cordelia called, "can you bring our guests something cold to drink? Lord," she sighed, shaking her head at Susan. "I don't get out of this bed soon folks will wonder if we have any manners left at all." Susan tried not to fidget. "She'll be right back. I won't bite," she added with a smile.

"How long have you been sick," Susan asked.

"Been doin' the chemo for a month or so now."

"My father had it. Cancer."

"I'm sorry." She didn't ask if he had survived. "It's so much harder on the folks who have to watch. When it's yours, you make peace with it. After you stop tussling, it's almost, I don't know, like a get-out-of-jail free card," she said, smiling. "All the silly things you worry about, just not important anymore."

"You're not dying," Susan said. Cordelia didn't answer. "Are you?"

"Remains to be seen, I suppose."

"Jackson never…"

"It's harder for them," she repeated. Susan looked down, toe tracing a diamond on the rug. "What is it?" Cordelia asked. "It's all right," she added.

"I just wondered…are there things you can't forgive yourself for?"

"There used to be."

"How did you…I mean, if they were awful, so awful you can't even tell anyone."

"There's only one way I know. When you can't forgive yourself, you have to let God do it for you."

Susan shook her head. "God hates me. And if people knew…"

"People are people, they will be as they are. But God, He's not the same. He's so much bigger than that it's beyond explaining." Her fingers gently resting on Susan's hand. "Faith is such a comfort, honey, don't deny yourself a place to take the pain."

Jolene's voice floated down the hall, growing louder as she came.

"…about rat poison to kill the rabbits! Old woman's got the damn box sitting on the table, blind as a bat, next thing you know she'll be using it to sweeten the tea."

Susan stood. Mrs. Wyle's hand dropped to the coverlet.

Ben followed Jolene in, carrying a tray with a pitcher, tall glasses filled with ice. Cordelia smiled. "I see you brought some of those sugar cookies," she teased her husband, eyes twinkling. "The man's got a sweet tooth but he just won't admit it," she whispered loudly.

"I brought 'em for the company," Ben protested. On cue, years of practice.

"Of course you did, darlin'." Cordelia winked at Jolene. Men, she mouthed.

"Miz Wyle," Jolene replied, "you are preaching to the choir."

Ben grunted, grabbed a couple of cookies and left the women to talk.

Chapter 25: August 31, 2006

The last day before tomorrow. The countdown begins. Susan shivered, staring at the girl in the mirror, red blossoming on her throat, the first hive forming under her arm.

***

She hid in the bedroom. Alone in the dark. Safe there. Black with shades of gray. No reds or yellows to jump out and startle the living. They were talking about her in the other room. She couldn't hear them but she knew. She wished they would go away. The wake was over. Patrick had invited them back, salads and deli platters lining the counters.

She didn't understand their obsession with companionship. There could be no comfort and that was a state better endured alone. But they wouldn't listen. Too busy talking about Sean.

She had his gym bag open in her lap. Two pairs of socks, a clean jersey, shorts, dingy white jock, all Downey fresh. He left her no sweaty clothes or dirty laundry. Nothing with the smell of him. But at least it was familiar. The neatly creased jeans and ironed T-shirts, ties arranged by color, crisp shirts, cardboard still in the neck. The novel on the night stand, his place carefully marked with a business card. No folded corners, no bent spines. Precise. How like him.

She was a mess. How like her.

If it had been her, Sean would be out there with them. Letting them hug him, listening to all the meaningless crap people say when there is nothing to be said. He'd comfort her mother. She didn't want her mother anywhere near her. He'd have all the right answers, no shrinks for Sean. His voice would crack and he would cry and he would wonder out loud what he would do without her. Everyone would understand. No one would look at him the way they looked at her.

Because she was empty. Of everything, tears, feelings, heart, lungs, liver. No bone or blood, no muscle to propel her forward. Nothing. A bag of skin, if she opened her mouth, she would deflate, softly hissing air. She didn't want to say his name. Not out loud. It was wrong.

She put one shoe on each hand and walked them down the comforter. Palm to sole. She was his soul mate, he said so at their wedding. Everyone said they were so lucky to have found each other. Susan and Sean. Sean and Susan. Almost one word. She would be just Susan now. Plain old Susan. Only, lonely, Susan, no more Suz. Only Susan. Her name played sing song in her brain. She let herself go with it until the words ran themselves out.

She should feel something. Everyone did. She didn't. She didn't know why. No, she knew. She'd cried, she had, only a monster wouldn't cry. She wasn't a monster. Was she? Because she felt nothing. A bottomless pit of nothing, reaching down into the darkness to find nothing more than more. Sean wouldn't have felt like this. He'd have so much to remember, stories to tell. The time they went to Boston and watched the Yankees cream the Sox. The time he fell asleep at the ballet and did pirouettes on the sidewalk outside the theatre to make up. The time they got drunk and tried to have sex in a hotel elevator, and the doors opened and an old lady shrieked. He'd remember everything about her.

"Susan?" The door opened, light creeping in the crack, reaching for her. She inched away. "Honey?" It was Patrick. He was her chief watcher. "Father Downey is getting ready to leave. I thought you might want to say goodbye."

Why would he think that? It amazed her, what they thought. If they would only go away. Leave her alone so that she could find something to feel.

"How are you doing?" He sat on the edge of the bed. She held up a hand in a shoe. "Oh darling girl." His eyes were rimmed in red, his nose a map of little red lines. She could smell the whiskey on his breath. "I know, I know. It's killing me too."

There was an old woman who lived in a shoe. Had so many children she didn't know what to do. Because nobody would leave her *alone. Susan let his arm go around her, let him pull her head to his shoulder.*

"I know you're hurting, Suzie, but I hate to think of you in here all alone." Gently he slid the shoes off her hands. "Your family's here, we want to help you."

Go away. Go away. If you want to help me, go away. What if she just said it?

"I'm worried about you. Sitting here in the dark. Just a little light, huh, darling, let me just..." He leaned across her for Sean's night stand, toward the lamp. Susan grabbed his wrist. Held it tight.

"All right then, it's all right." He dropped his arm and slowly she let go, watching. He didn't listen, none of them did. He'd try again. "Talk to me, honey."

She looked at him, mute. He looked back until she dropped her eyes.

"I remember when Sean told me he was going to marry you, I knew before you did, did you know that? He barely knew you and I tried to make him see sense but he said, 'Da, she's the one. Like you and mom, she's the one.'"

One potato, two potato, three potato, four, five potato, six potato, seven potato more. Shut up, shut up, shut up!

"...prettiest girl he'd ever seen. So smart, that's what he always said. I'm grateful for you, honey. If he had to..." His voice broke. "His life was a story worth telling, and you're a big part of it. The best part, he'd say."

Susan caught her thumbnail between her teeth and pulled at it. Manicure smooth, she gnawed it to roughen an edge then ripped a ragged strip free. She spit it on the bed.

Patrick sighed. "You rest. I'll check on you later." He leaned down and kissed her hair. "I love you, sweetheart."

Thankful beyond belief when the door shut behind him, she set the two sneakers on end, holding them upright between her thighs. She looked at them for a while, then held out her hand, thumb extended,

fingers tight and pointed. Tilted to the side. Making a noise like an
airplane, she drove her hand forward and knocked the sneakers down.
She felt nothing.
She set them up and knocked them down again.

***

Lowes Garden Center was winding down, leftover perennials on
sale, lots of mums in all different shades. Stand-alone plants and
hanging pots for porches and decks. The first flats of pansies were in, a
classic fall garden filler, blooming through the Carolina winter soon to
come. You'd never know it today, Jack thought, wiping sweat from his
forehead.

He'd come for a new ceiling fan but wandered over here. There
were boxes of bulbs, tulips, daffodils and crocus. Planted in the fall,
they came up in the spring. She might like them, he thought, might stay
to see them come.

He had been thinking about her on and off, not as much about the
last night, but that first night he told her he knew. The night in the
garden lingering in his mind.

There had been something mystical about it. He didn't know how
else to describe it, the two of them, weeding in the dark. The puppy
passed out on the porch steps, the cat suddenly separating herself from
the night to rub her nose on his knee. A little after midnight, the moon
had come from behind a cloud, and suddenly everything was bathed in
silver. They barely spoke. It felt like they didn't have to.

Jack knew he was a simple man. Contentment was his prize. Not
so much ambition or drive. Becky hated that about him. She was so
fevered, always in hot pursuit. In the garden with Susan, there was a
calm, taking quiet comfort in the dirt and flowers and moon, digging
side by side, from one end to the other, coming to the middle. No need
for more. Surely a man who has enough in the moment has found what
he seeks.

But not what he chased? How could that be? Acquisition was
Becky's life force. More was her mantra, ferociously consuming,

forever thirsty for what she might have missed. Like a tuning fork, always vibrating, leaving him anxious, inadequate. Nothing he could do to fill her up. Make her happy. He was the dead weight she dragged behind.

So many times he'd played their marriage over in his mind. Trying to find the instance, the moment in time where he could've done something different. Fixed it, made her see how much he loved her, how willing he was to do anything to make her happy. He never noticed that she didn't, perhaps couldn't, offer him the same.

He hated the bare finger on his left hand, had worn that ring until he couldn't stand the embarrassment of leaving it on. As the white line faded to tan, he felt like a piece of him was disappearing. He couldn't articulate it, even to himself, but something essential to him was vanishing right before his eyes. He'd made a commitment, a vow. And he'd failed to fulfill it.

It might have been easier if he hadn't seen what marriage could be. Two people working in tandem, putting themselves behind the other, building a history. It had played out in front of him all of his life. Not a fairy tale, his parents were real people. There had been spats and disagreements and times of trouble but always a return to the core. The two together, caring for one another – even during times when feelings may have faltered, the commitment never did.

He wondered how it had been for Susan. Susan and Sean. It sounded strange to speak of her as one of two - so alone now. Were they happy? They must have been, damaged as she was by the loss, her pain almost tangible, the weight bowing her shoulders. He didn't know if she would ever get passed it. But that night in the garden, in those quiet moments, clearing away the weeds to free the flowers, there was a hint of future. A chance to be content.

He had pursued Becky with blinders on, intent on the marriage, not the partner. She never pretended to be anything she wasn't. Even as he thought it, his heart ached with wanting her. Wishing she would choose him, that he would be enough for her. He wanted it still. But just for a moment, in that garden, there was an inkling of another way.

Jack tossed a box of tulip bulbs in the cart, a trowel, two mesh bags of hyacinth in all different colors. Susan would like all the colors. And hyacinth was fragrant, the scent lovely when it lingered in the air. Some sweetness to cut through the sorrow.

She was an extreme version of himself, so desperate to change the past. Death had left her forever inadequate. Sean was never coming back. Her only way out was blocked like the stairs he couldn't get down. The cardboard furniture, the stapled sheet, the calendar frozen in time. How long before he became the same, running endlessly after what he couldn't have, a hamster in a wheel, never moving forward, convinced of what should be and not what was.

He stopped, looking at the bulbs in the cart. Small brown lumps in frail paper-thin wrappers, no sign of what was to come. No evidence of the pictures that adorned the boxes, the life that lived inside, waiting out the cold to unfurl in a blaze of simple glory.

So easy to misjudge what was possible. Or know when it was time to give up.

***

"Where have you been, girl?" Dottie demanded. "You'd think I got nothing else to do but worry myself sick over you! Betty Jane, lookie who's back without so much as a how do you do." Betty Jane shook her head. "Where's my darlin' girl," Dottie crooned. "Where's my little biscuit?"

Zoey's ears perked at the word. She jumped to stool to counter, planting her feet on Dottie's apron-clad belly, barked twice. "Sit pretty for me." Zoey sat. A biscuit was dispensed. Heaven on earth. "So what do you have to say for yourself?"

"What do you mean?"

"You hear that Betty Jane, what do I mean! I mean that you don't be coming here regular every day and then just not show up no more without letting somebody know, that's what I mean." Betty Jane nodded, folded her lips. "Yankees! Ain't got no manners to speak of, I'm telling ya."

182

"I didn't mean for you to worry."

Dottie snorted, tossed another chunk of biscuit Zoey's way. "Just wondered if you were movin' on, that's all. Heard you had the place all boarded up?" She raised an eyebrow. Susan ignored it.

"Can I get a cappuccino and I need some cake." It felt nice to be missed, another new feeling. "Really bad," she added.

The door jangled and Jackson came in. His eyes went right to her, Susan smiled shyly. Betty Jane didn't miss a thing. Dottie glanced between them, then toward the back of the store. "You want that coffee to go," she asked.

"No. You trying to get rid of me?"

"She means me, I'm sure." Becky said, sauntering down the hallway from the ladies room. "Dottie always thought I was bad for you."

"Folks can't help being what they are," Dottie replied.

"Non-fat latte to go. Please," she added, a pretty smile. She filled the room, using up all the air. "Jack, good morning, darlin'. And Mrs. Kearney, so nice to see you again." Susan's chest got tight.

"Becky," Jack said, stepping between them. "What are you doing here?"

"I told you I'd be around," she purred, eyes never leaving Susan. "Remember, the other night, at your house?" She reached a manicured hand to his arm, sliding down the muscle, an obvious caress. Jack flushed.

"Dottie," Susan said. "I'll just take a coffee. I need to get going and…"

"Already got it started, don't be changing your mind now."

"Actually I was hoping you had changed your mind," Becky interrupted. "About the interview."

"I've gotta go," Susan said. "Come on, Zoey." The puppy ignored her, waiting on a biscuit.

"Becky, this isn't the time."

"So protective, Jack. Isn't that sweet." Everyone was watching now, no pretense in eavesdropping. "It's hard to understand what there is to hide."

"What are you going on about," Dottie snapped. "Ain't gonna be no trouble in my place, missy."

Becky sidestepped Jack and smiled at Susan. "I'm surprised you don't know, though of course Mrs. Kearney isn't exactly forthcoming." Susan skewered by her eyes. "That's why I wanted to interview her."

"Leave her alone, Beck." A warning in Jack's voice.

She laughed. "Or what, Jackson? Everybody finds out?"

"Finds out what," Dottie demanded.

"Do you want to tell her, Mrs. Kearney?" Advancing. Susan backed up. "No?"

"What's she talking about?"

Jack took her arm. She didn't bother to shake him off. "Mrs. Kearney's a widow, a 9/11 widow to be exact."

Susan's stomach contracted as if punched, no less prepared by knowing what was coming. All eyes swung to her. She could feel them. All the stories waiting to be told. She stumbled backwards, bumping into a chair.

"Her husband died in the World Trade Center. Such a tragedy," Becky murmured. "You'd expect a hero's wife would be…"

Susan turned and ran, blind, out the door, desperate.. Had to get away, get away! She heard Jack call after her. She didn't stop. Running, running, running.

***

Jolene had been looking for her since Jack called. Her car was still parked on the street near Dottie's. Her purse on the counter, keys on the floor where they dropped. As much as she wanted to find Susan, Jolene was on the look for Becky Lee Howe. That girl was long overdue for a bitch slapping and Jolene was aching to make it right.

184

This is what Susan wanted to tell her. Jack said how he found her on the Internet. He didn't know how Becky knew, swore he hadn't told her. It didn't matter. The secret was out.

Jolene couldn't imagine what it had been like. As she drove around, she remembered that day, Annie Lyman coming outside, calling her name. Jolene had been putting up a screen porch, cutting planks in the yard. Annie was so upset, kept saying she had to come in, had to see. They stood in front of the TV, reaching for each other's hand, trying to understand what was happening. They watched the second plane. It was surreal, no video of the first but the second caught forever on tape. A speck in the sky, growing darker, bigger, the plane coming around, slamming into the building. The smoke, the screams. Newscasters unable to hide their shock. They played it over and over and over again. Everyone glued to the screen.

"Lord Jesus, please help her," Jolene prayed.

She'd called Billy. "It never even occurred to me, you know? And her from New York and all," she said, fingers tight on the steering wheel.

"Lots of people in New York," he reminded her. "Couldn't have known."

"She wanted to tell me and I shoulda just let her talk," Jolene protested. "But I kept running my mouth."

"Nothing new there," he replied dryly. It forced a half-laugh, half-sob from her. "You be you, that's what's gonna be best for her. That's who she wanted to tell."

For a man who drove her crazy, he could say just the right thing. She got off the phone, swung down a side street, eyes scanning every doorway. No sign of Susan. Why was it a secret, Jolene wondered. It wasn't anybody's business, that's for sure, but it wasn't really. ..*Did you ever do anything bad?* That's what she'd asked. There was more to this, Jolene thought, looking up to see Becky driving past, talking on her cell phone. Business as usual. She spun the truck around.

***

Susan sat on the ground, her back against a tree. She wasn't sure where she was, in a lot behind some place with a loading dock, truck backed up to it. It didn't matter. They knew now, everyone knew. The hero's wife. They didn't even know him, who he was, what he cared about, what made him laugh or get mad. Just a hero, flattened to a label, a picture on a flyer on a fence, all a person had to do was die, in the right way, at the right time to lose their life all over again.

She'd spent days in front of the TV watching it over and over. Not thinking of a hero but of him. She'd counted down floors from the top of the North Tower to find him. The black smoke billowing, the broken shards of building underneath. Did he feel the heat? Did he see the second plane? Was he still breathing when the building fell?

The firemen running the hoses, police screaming into radios, the pieces of the plane falling, the jumpers jumping. Each time, she watched the people streaming from the lobby, up out of her chair, close to the screen, looking among the faces. All shell shocked, some soot covered, others bloody, some looking the same as when they walked in the door that morning. Survivors instead of heroes.

No one that she knew.

***

"Are you crazy!" Becky was out of the car, furious.

Jolene jumped from the truck. "Got your attention, do I?"

"You ran my car off the road. Look at it," she screeched, pointing to the front bumper. "I hope you have insurance because I'm calling the cops and ..."

Jolene slapped her face, hard. The cell phone went flying. Jolene swung again, but Becky dodged, backing up, the hand whistling past her hair. "What is wrong with you! Get away from me!"

On the ground, the cell phone suddenly rang, startling them both. Jolene was faster, her boot coming down, one, twice. The ringing stopped abruptly. Becky's eyes widened in disbelief.

"Listen up, shug, we're gonna have a little talk," Jolene snapped. "I didn't say nothing when you ripped Jack's heart to pieces and I

186

didn't say nothing when you screwed Missy Sykes' husband and made sure everybody knew it. But I'm telling ya now, you leave Suz alone, you hear me?"

"I have no idea what you're…"

"I'm not playing!" Jolene poked a finger toward her. Becky stood her ground. "You've had it easy, twisting these boys around by their wieners, but you don't wanna mess with me, trust me on that.

Becky straightened her suit jacket, spots of hot pink on each cheek. "Oh, so now you're threatening me?"

"Don't see many tramps on TV, least ways not on the news."

"Wow, my feelings are so hurt." She turned headed for the car. "You'll hear from my lawyer."

"Be a shame if word got out, how you screwed everybody but your husband."

Becky glanced over her shoulder. "And wouldn't Jack just love that?"

"He'll survive," Jolene lied. "Not sure we could say the same about your precious new career. Especially if your horizontal talents was what got you the job."

Direct hit. Becky stopped and turned, face dark. "Stay the hell away from me or I'll have you arrested." She whirled, back toward the car, climbed behind the wheel.

"Don't forget your phone." Jolene lifted a boot and kicked it across the road.

***

He finally found her. She didn't resist. Nothing left to fight him. He got her in the car, called Jolene to let her know she was all right, and took her home. Jolene met them there, brought the car, purse and keys, cake and brownies. It wasn't until a few hours later that any of them remembered the dog.

***

"I left her there," Susan whispered. "I just left."

"We'll find her," Jack said. "Don't worry."

"No. We won't."

"We will, I promise."

She shook her head. "They looked so hard, but they didn't find him. They never found him."

"We're gonna find Zoey," Jolene said, shooting a worried glance at Jack..

"He was dead."

"Zoey isn't dead. She has to be somewhere, we'll find her."

"That's what Patrick said. We'll find him, but we didn't." Susan wrapped her arms around herself and rocked.

Jolene motioned to Jack. He followed her to the kitchen. "I'm not sure we can leave her alone."

"I know." He glanced over his shoulder. "I called Dottie's but no one knows what happened." He shook his head, "It was such a mess, Becky and I got into it after she ran out, everybody was caught up in that."

"That puppy lives and breathes for her, probably took off after her first chance it got."

"I'll stay with her," he offered, "if you wanna go look. Zoey might come to you."

"Yeah. I'm gonna swing by the house, got some pills that will make her sleep. If you can get her to take 'em."

They walked back to the living room. Susan hadn't moved, still rocking, faster than before. "Suz, I'm gonna go find Zoey and Jack's gonna..." Jolene started.

"Atta, Suqami, Alomari, Alshehri, Alshehri," she whispered. She knew their names, all their names. "Atta, Suqami, Alomari, Alshehri, Alshehri."

"Honey, you have to..."

"Hanjour, Alhazmi, Mihdhar, Moqed and Alhazmi." Rocking, rocking.

"I'm gonna kill that wife of yours, Jackson, let me just tell you that," Jolene snarled.

"I'm not married," he snapped. "Let's just find the damn dog."

188

Chapter 26: September 1, 2006

So close now. The rash was spreading, both underarms now, the back of her knees. She took the phone off the charger, checked the messages. She shivered in the warm night and slipped the phone in the pocket of her shorts, feeling the weight against her leg. It was time.

***

She should take the pictures down. Start with one, just take one at a time, then the next and the next. Zoey would be gone. Erased, like Sean. As long as she kept moving, he was out of sight, out of mind. Boxed up and packed away. She could do the same with Zoey. Nobody waiting if the puppy found its way home.

She was a bad person, could barely remember when she had been something better. Maybe she had never been better. Maybe she had always been selfish and thoughtless and careless with the people who loved her. Was that really in doubt?

Susan got up and looked for the box. It was smaller than the rest. She'd gotten the box herself from the Korean grocer down the street from their apartment. MISCELLANEOUS, she'd written when she sealed the flaps. Never opened since.

She sat down on the floor and pulled it between her legs. Stroked the sides gently, patted the top. The tape was dry, curling on one end. She pushed her finger underneath and pulled. The cardboard halves met in the middle, stripped to ripples where the tape refused to give. She pulled the flaps apart. The first thing she saw his book. Net Force, the Clancy novel he never finished. The author had published two others since. Sean never knew how it ended. Susan turned to the last page, read the last page out loud. "There. The end," she said, closing the book. She set it aside and reached in the box.

There was the pillowcase from his pillow. A trophy from his softball team. His hairbrush, his razor, a tube of gel that he used on his hair. Tightly capped. There was a T-shirt from a Bare Naked Ladies concert, the cap that he wore when he went out to get bagels on a

Sunday mornings before he'd showered. She used to wait in bed, feeling pampered and spoiled, unless he forgot the honey walnut cream cheese. He didn't forget often. If he did, she let him know. All about letting him know.

She reached in again, her fingers touching velvet. She didn't know when he bought it or why. Too late for her birthday, too early for their anniversary. She'd found it tucked in his underwear drawer. A purple velvet box. No ribbon, no card.

The necklace inside was silver because she didn't care for gold. Delicate strands littered with tiny sapphires that seemed suspended in air. In the center was an opal, flashing pale blue fire in a simple oval setting. Stunning. Sean would have loved the look on her face when she saw it.

Near the bottom of the box there was a copy of the flyer that Patrick had put up on the wall. PLEASE HELP US FIND SEAN! There was a large black square in the center that used to be a picture of him at his sister's wedding. He'd been making a toast, his arm outstretched, so handsome in his tux, hating the bow tie but loving his sister more. Susan had colored over it with black magic marker, filling in the zeros on the phone numbers that no one ever called.

And then finally, there he was, looking up at her from the bottom of the box. A long manila envelope beneath him, flap closed with red string wrapped around a little circle. Her hands trembled reaching for the picture. She'd taken it in their first apartment, before they moved to Chelsea, on a Saturday afternoon. He wore no shirt, elbows on the table, the newspaper and coffee mug that said Real Men Don't Drink Decaf. He'd turned when she called his name, the sweetest smile. The light in his eyes.

She pressed the picture frame to her chest and tried not to weep. He never should have loved her.

She propped the photograph up against the cardboard and picked up the velvet box, gently separated the necklace from its mount. The stones sparkled in her hands. She raised it to her throat and remembered the gold chain. She pulled it over her head, the ring resting on her palm.

190

"I never took it off," she told him. He smiled back from the frame. She tucked the chain in her pocket and raised the necklace to her throat.

The neckline of her T-shirt was too high. Susan pulled it over her head, no bra, the necklace cool against bare skin. The silver strands rested just above her breasts, delicate and lovely. "Do you like it," she asked the picture. He didn't answer. "I love it."

She touched his face through the glass. "I miss you. I know you might not think that, after everything that…and you know, all of this." She gestured to the room. "I'm messed up, Sean. More than normal."

She told him everything. All the details of before and after. She told him about driving, staying with Maggie, Idaho, Kansas, landing in Wendell. "I had a dog," she said. "Zoey. If you were here, you'd find her. I know you would."

She could hear him in her head, as clear as if he was in the room. It's up to you, Suz. He always saw more in her than she believed was there.

She took the chain out of her pocket, undid the clasp and freed the ring. No fanfare, no hesitation after all the years of madness, she slid it on her finger. "I'll be back," she told him, setting the picture on the table. "I gotta get to Wal-Mart." She started for the door, stopped and turned. "I guess I better get a shirt, huh?"

Sean just smiled.

***

"You're out late tonight," Ellie said.

The boxes were so big it was hard to see over the cart. "I'm not sure I can get these on the belt," Susan said.

"I can hand scan 'em, that's fine. Whatcha got? My goodness, a computer. Looks like a nice one too."

"And a printer."

"Lots of paper," Ellie said, scanning ink cartridges. "If you don't mind my asking, what's your name?"

"Susan. Susan Kearney."

"Ellie Harrigan. Nice to meet you." She came around the counter to get the barcode off the printer. "I've been meaning to ask you…please don't take this wrong, but…" She hesitated, uncomfortable. "Somebody made me a gift, a camera and all kinds of stuff, and I couldn't think who might have done it because I ain't got nobody who would be spending that kind of money and well, I …but then I remembered that you …" She glanced down at her register, voice gruff.

"My dog's lost," Susan said. "I'm getting the computer to make some signs."

"I am so sorry, Miss Susan. You bring a flyer, I'll put it up."

"I have to find her."

"You got plenty pictures, that's a blessing. You bring me in a bunch when you're done. There's a board in the front of the store for community events but sometimes folks take stuff down that ain't for church suppers or the like. I'll put it back up everyday."

"Thank you." Susan ran her card. "It's credit."

"You bought that camera, didn't you?" Ellie stuck a paid sticker on the computer and printer. Susan loaded bags in the cart. "Didn't you?"

"I'd like to see a picture of her sometime. Your granddaughter."

Ellie got busy with the receipts and bags. "I can take a flyer to my church and Cissy's preschool too. That's my little girl, Cecilia's her given name, but always called her Cissy. You need somebody to help you out with that?"

"No, thanks, I'm good."

***

There was nothing worse than a phone ringing in the night. Jolene was instantly awake. She said a quick prayer, picked up the phone. "Mickey?"

"I know it's late, I'm sorry."

"It's so late it's early," Jolene whispered. "You know what time it is, Suz?" She didn't wait for an answer. "It's after three, and I'm talking three a.m., not three p.m. in case you don't know the difference."

"What's that noise?"

"Oh just Billy snoring. Hold on, let me get myself outta bed so I don't have to deal with him waking up. Not that he would, take an atom bomb and I'm not even sure about that."

"I'm sorry, Jolene."

"Unless you're dying you darn well should be," she groused. "Scaring me half to death." She stopped. "You aren't dying, are ya?"

"No."

"Then give me a second." Jolene yawned, padding toward the kitchen. She dumped some coffee in the basket. "Did the dog come home?"

"No."

"Hold on, one second." She set the phone down, filled the pot with water and poured it in the machine. "Okay, so what's got your knickers in a knot?"

"I have to get cable." No response. "Hello?"

"Hells bells, did I hear you right? Did I hear you telling me that you woke me up in the middle of the night, out of a sound sleep, which I don't get too much of on account of Billy sounding like a buzz saw, because you decided you wanna watch cable TV?"

"It's the Internet. I need the internet."

"Suz, you are a royal pain in the ass."

"I know, but I have to find Zoey. There are websites with lost dogs, in case somebody finds her, and I can put her picture up. I'm not just gonna sit here and feel sorry for myself, Jolene. I am not gonna do it again and I need the internet, that's all and I don't have anyone to ask so I'm calling you because I need it right now," she insisted. "Right now."

Jolene paused before replying. "Crazy as it sounds, you seem better."

"I have to find my dog."

"I got it, I hear ya. Let me get dressed. I'll come over and we'll figure it out. Okay?"

"I'm not crazy, Jolene, I just need cable."

"You are crazy, like a goddamn loon, but the cable is something we can probably do something about."

***

"Next Tuesday is too late." Susan looked up from the computer as Jolene hung up the phone.

"I know that, can you give me a minute to figure this out?"

"I need the internet."

"Suz, you say that one more time and I swear I'll stick your head in the toilet bowl and flush it down." Jolene paced the dining room, Nextel in one hand, coffee mug in another. "I gotta get a hold of Glenn Nichols and I can't seem to catch him. He does the installing for Time Warner and sometimes I help out if he's stuck. I mean, I can put the lines in, that ain't our problem, but we gotta get the equipment and hook up to the main."

"Why are they saying Tuesday? Why don't they come today?"

"Because the folks in the office don't know that the world revolves around you."

"I'll pay extra."

"We need to find Glenn."

"Where is he?"

"If I knew that I wouldn't be taking this crap from you, now would I!"

Susan hit the print button and sent another next ten copies to the printer. $500 REWARD it read across the top. She'd wanted it to be a thousand but Jolene said no one would take it serious. There was a big picture of Zoey, looking straight into the camera, one ear up, one ear down. Her blue collar showing. No tag. She'd never bothered with a tag, hadn't even thought of getting a tag.

The Nextel rang. "Glenn, thank god, you don't know what you're saving me from. Yep, uh-huh, he's fine. How's Millie? Good."

"Internet," Susan said, standing up.

Jolene waved her away. "Glenn, I'm out at the old Garret place, yeah, I know, yeah, couldn't believe she sold it either but anyway, we need to get some cable installed here, lickety-split and I can't get nothing earlier than Tuesday on the schedule." She stopped to listen. "Well, I know, but you and I both know you could bump someone."

"Give me the phone." Jolene turned her back. "Give me the phone," Susan insisted, reaching for it. Jolene twisted out of reach.

"Hold on a minute, Glenn, will ya?" She covered the mouthpiece. "Cut it out!"

"Give me the phone!" Susan grabbed it from her hand. "Mr. Nichols, this is Susan Kearney. I need cable access today for my computer." She listened for a second then interrupted. "No, I don't think you understand, I need it done today." She listened again. "No, today. What do you need to make it happen?" Squawking from the phone. "I realize you have a schedule, and I'm more than willing to pay for your inconvenience. How much? Will five thousand cover it?"

"Whoa," Jolene exclaimed.

"No, I am not kidding. You get it done by three o'clock and I'll make it six. Uh-huh. Yes, from New York. Right. No, cash is okay. I'll do the five up front. Plus the normal installation costs." She listened. "Okay, good. Thank you. Uh-huh." She held out the Nextel. "He wants to talk to you."

"I bet he does." Jolene walked into the kitchen, her voice low.

Susan picked up the house phone and dialed the accountants in New York.

"Jim, Susan Kearney. Yes, fine, thanks. I need you to wire six thousand dollars actually let's make it ten just in case, and I need it today." She listened. "I'm getting cable." She held the phone away from her ear. "Well, thank you but it's really not your concern and it is my money, so let's make it happen." She worked out the details and hung up the phone. "All set," she said.

Jolene stood in the doorway, holding the picture in her hand. "Is this him?" Susan nodded. "Oh honey," Jolene said. "I'm so sorry. Though I bet you're sick of hearing that."

"A little." Susan sat back down at the computer. "I wasn't the greatest wife. Not doing so hot alone either, obviously. God, Sean would hate all this."

"I see ya put your ring back on. I think that's good."

"I don't know if it's good or not."

"Running only works if you can shake what's chasing ya. I think it's good," she repeated. "Suz," Jolene paused. "While back you said you wanted to tell me something. When I heard about this I figured that was it, but...if there's something more...if you...well, I'll listen if you wanna tell me."

Susan sat quiet for a second. Then she said. "The day it ..." Susan stopped, shook her head. "No, we don't have time."

"Suz..."

"Jolene, I know you don't understand, but right now I have to find Zoey."

"Well, then better get busy. I'll start digging the trench." She stopped at the front door. "Five thousand dollars? I mean, for real? Five thousand dollars?"

***

Within twenty six hours, the last living victim would be pulled from the rubble. No one knew she was the last, but the operation turned from rescue to recovery. A nice way of saying they were looking for corpses now. No more were found alive, not many more found dead. Over forty thousand tons of debris had been delivered to Fresh Kill landfill by the following Monday. How bits of bodies rested there? Freshly killed.

The woman had been an office manager on the 64th floor. When the plane hit, she'd felt the building sway. Nothing more. Many of her co-workers left but a voice over the loudspeaker told people to stay put and wait for emergency personnel. She waited until the second plane hit the second tower before she started down.

She was rounding the 13th floor when the building fell. Ripping a co-worker from her touch, lost forever. It was a miracle, they said, her head wedged between two concrete pillars. A helmet against the tons of broken stone that crushed her leg and pinned her to the rubble. When the silence finally came and the dust finally settled, she waited for the sounds of others. A man cried out for help, once, twice then never again. It wasn't Sean. He was already dead. So was most everyone else. She lay in the mass grave until a fireman found her the following day. It was a miracle, they said. After 26 hours.

Zoey had been missing longer than that.

***

She was supposed to meet him at the Marriott in midtown but she'd chickened out. The flirting at work, the kisses in the dark bar, that was nothing more than romantic fantasy. But a hotel reservation, a room in his name with a king size bed and a mini-bar. Nothing fantastic about that, it was all too real. Cheap and sordid, no way to deny that it wasn't the same as a pedicure or a facial, not the same at all. It was an affair, a woman cheating on her husband. Keeping yourself only unto him, do you, Susan, take Sean?

"Tom, I can't," she'd said when she called. "I'm sorry, I just can't."

"Don't do this, I want to see you. I need to see you," Tom insisted. "Just come and have a drink. We can have a drink at the bar and..."

"I can't," she'd whispered and hung up the phone.

That was the night she wrote the email. Sean worked late like always, came home tired. He was pleasantly surprised by the waiting dinner, clean kitchen and freshly laundered sheets. She'd coddled him and rubbed his neck and shoulders, easing the knots from the muscles. Worrying about what Tom was thinking.

She got Sean off to bed as soon as she could, pretending love and concern. We don't even have to talk, she teased. He'd let her care for him, surprised and grateful, asleep by nine thirty, a book on his chest.

She went online immediately, checked her instant message log. She'd hoped he'd be there. He wasn't. That afternoon she had been panicked, now it was more of the same, just for different reasons.

Would he stop coming by for lunch? Worse yet, would he still come and act as if nothing ever happened? Pleasantly polite, the loss of her of no significance. She opened up her email.

"Dear Tom," she wrote. "I know you must be upset and I want you to know that I am so sorry. I was so looking forward to our...." Susan paused, uncertain what to say. She deleted the line. "You are such a bright spot in my life, I can't even remember how dull my days used to be. I didn't mean to hurt you."

Was she jumping to conclusions? She didn't want to assume, look foolish.

"Maybe it didn't hurt you, maybe it just pissed you off that you went to all the trouble of getting the room and then...This will probably sound funny, but it did hurt me. I wanted to be with you so much but..."

What came after but? She deleted it.

"I wish that we could be together for real. Have dinner, watch movies, lay in bed and listen to the rain. It scares me how I feel. I need some time to think."

She tried to imagine herself on Sunday mornings, bagels in bed with Tom, the paper strewn across the comforter. They'd fight over the book reviews, not like Sean who read the financial pages first. Susan always had time to read what she wanted.

Tom wouldn't work all the time, that was for sure. He liked his fun and he liked her company. He wouldn't take her for granted as if she was a cow tied to a fence. As if she would always be there, waiting. He wanted her.

"I want you," she wrote. "I want to feel your skin, your lips, breathe your breath. Please just give me some time, Tom, time for a second chance."

How to sign it? She typed her name. It looked forlorn, only Susan. Love, Susan? Did she really want to go there? Did she love him or was she just sick of waiting for Sean? If he had only spent more time with her, she wouldn't have to be doing this at all.

"Love, Susan," she typed. Stared at it for a minute then moved the cursor to the end of the first word. "And lust," she added, putting it in

*parenthesis, a colon on one to make a smiley face. Light-hearted. Not
too risky. She clicked Send.*

*The next day, Sean sent her flowers. To my beautiful wife, the card
said. When he found the email, things weren't so beautiful after that.*

***

"…Jack hadn't stepped in, cat fight for sure. Like to have been a
fly on that wall," Bubba said, smacking his lips.

"Already been down that road, ain't ya?" Skeeter cackled. "Least
one side of it"

"Shut your mouth."

"Can't believe Jolene didn't know nothing about it. I thought she
was hanging around over there, Billy?"

Billy grunted.

"Heard Jolene kicked the crap outta Becky," Tommy Lee added.
"Over there in front of Wilson's, right by that new Mexican place."

They veered off into a discussion about the Mexican food, half for,
half against. Big Jim pulled them back, giving Billy the eye. "Women
in this town are getting outta hand. Don't say much about their men."
Looking for a rise, getting none.

"Jolene sucker punched her, that's what I heard from Carl Tilley, a
shot right in the mouth. Becky went down like a load of bricks."

"Jumped right on her, that's what I heard, the two of them were
rolling around in the dirt. Almost got hit by a car, that's what Ginger
Davies said."

"Why's that girl got to hide herself for anyway?" Skeeter asked.
"Every American she meets be proud to shake her hand."

"That's right," Bubba agreed. "Never forget the day it happened. I
was in the drive-through at the bank. Cashing a check, I put it in the
drawer and the girl took it and then she disappeared. I couldn't see
where she was and she didn't come back, even when I pushed the
button. Had to drive around to the front and go inside. They were all
standing in the lobby, staring at the TV. Never forget seeing that plane
come round."

***

Susan pulled on to Main Street, Cowboy Rhino in the passenger seat, looking for a place to park. Everything was parallel, not her best. A spot between a pickup and a Saturn. She pulled up and went back and forth, back and forth, in and out, straighten the wheels, back out, try again, nose in, rear stuck out. "Screw it," she said and turned off the car.

She got out and gathered up the stack of flyers, a staple gun and roll of masking tape in her purse. Cowboy Rhino stared through the windshield. Black sewn-on eyes beseeching her. "Okay," she said, unlocking the door and pulling him out. "She's your dog too."

She tucked him under her arm and walked toward the closest door. A factory outlet store, sweatpants and towels from the Mortel plant. She could see two older ladies inside, crisp white curls and polyester pantsuits. Her throat was dry, but she pushed through the door.

"Good morning." They looked up and smiled.

"How can we help you today?" From the lady in yellow. The one in blue kept folding a huge pile of sweatshirts.

"I lost my dog and I have a flyer. Can I put it up?"

"Well, now, I suppose we can do that. Donna, we can do that, can't we?"

"What?" Donna asked, looking up from the pile of clothes.

"This lady lost her dog, bless her heart." She took a flyer. "So cute, Zoey, that's a sweet name too. How long she been missing?"

"Two days."

"My grandson lost his dog," Donna piped in. "I told him to get a dog tag, write the phone number on his collar, that's what I said, but the boy never listens." She shook her head.

"Can I put up the flyer?"

"Never did find that dog, child was devastated. His momma got him another puppy but it wasn't never the same. I told him, I tried to tell him."

"I'm sure you did your best," the yellow lady said.

"Can I put up the flyer?" Louder than intended.

200

"We aren't supposed to put things up in the windows," Donna replied primly, offense taken.

"We did put up that notice about the craft fair at church," the yellow woman said.

"That was to raise money for the Sunday school," Donna protested.

"But this is an emergency, and it's such a cute little dog."

"She got a tag?"

"Please," Susan said, ignoring the question. "I have to find her."

"We can tape it right here by the register, on the counter. Not on the window," She added, before Donna could protest. "That'll work."

"Thank you," Susan said, taping the flyer to the counter before she could change her mind. "I appreciate your help."

"Does that say five hundred dollars? For a dog," Donna exclaimed. Susan was already half way out the door.

"I hope you find her," the kind woman called.

Susan hurried past the store windows, stopped to lean against a building next door. Cowboy Rhino dangled from her arm. "Did you hear her," Susan asked. "That bitch!"

Stick with dogs, Cowboy Rhino advised.

***

Cordelia was quiet on the way home after meeting with the doctor. The tumor in the left breast had shrunk a little. The right breast not so much. Her lymph nodes had been completely unaffected. Despite the chemo, it was spreading. Neither of them spoke of it, Cordelia barely spoke at all. Ben tried small talk then lapsed into silence.

It was a gorgeous day. Not too hot, the air just starting to take on a tang, the beginnings of fall. Fall was lovely here, not as gaudily adorned by northern leaves, scarlet and yellow and brown, but perfect days all the same. Sun bright, air crisp, nights cool but not cold. She loved the fall, drank it in. Her last.

"Ben, we have to talk to Jack," she said, breaking the silence.

"Whatever you want."

"I need to stop," she said. Ben immediately slowed, looking for a place to pull over. "No, I mean, with the doctors. The treatments." He pulled over anyway and stopped the car. She reached out and touched his arm. "Ben?"

"I know you're tired, but we got this far and we need to keep going. You don't know what's gonna happen."

"Really, Ben? Please don't."

"Cordelia, you're worn out." His hands tight on the steering wheel. He didn't look at her. Couldn't bear to look.

"You know that's not it." She reached across the seat. Hands so thin, almost translucent. "It's selfish, I understand, and I'd do anything to spare you pain, but..."

"Let's get you home." He cranked the engine. Dread spreading like fog.

"They aren't going to work, Ben, this is beyond human power. I don't want to spend my last days in a room with a bucket by the bed."

"These aren't your last days," he snapped. "You're sick, the doctors are taking care of you. Least you can do is show up." He eased the car out on the road, eyes straight ahead. She didn't answer, face turned toward the window. "It will be all right," he said.

"I'm sure you're right."

He cringed, hearing the resignation in her voice. She'd do it for him, for Jackson. Let them have their hope. It wasn't fair and he didn't give a damn. Just a second more of her, if that's all it meant, he would fight her for it.

"Jack and Becky had a go-round, I didn't get a chance to tell you." Because she'd been so sick, sleeping in between attacks of nausea. Pills for the pain. "Guess she was bothering that girl, the one who came to the house with Jolene."

"Susan?"

"Yeah. The TV station's doing a story on September 11th, and I guess her husband died in it. Didn't want anybody to know. Jack got real upset."

202

Cordelia turned to look at him. "How did Becky...?" She stopped abruptly.

"You wanna stop at Dottie's? Have some coffee, maybe a piece of cake? Coconut," he coaxed.

"Not today. I'm tired." Her face back to the window.

"It wasn't a bad thing," he said, glancing her way. "Good to see him standing up to her, least that's what I think." He waited for her to comment. She didn't. He took the cue and drove the rest of the way home in silence.

***

"The internet is up and running."

"Thank you, Jolene."

Black cable snaked across the floors, running from a splitter on a jack in the living room. "Sorry about the lines all over the place, I'll come back later and tack them to the baseboards."

"It's okay."

"I figured we might as well hook up the TV while we were here. I had to find it, opened a couple of boxes, so don't be getting all upset. I closed 'em right back up," Jolene added.

"It's fine."

"Don't know how you been living without TV, been meaning to ask you. Can't imagine not having my soaps. For an extra eight dollars a month, you can get the Soap Opera Network, watch 'em at night."

"You could try TiVo." Susan sat down and booted the computer.

"I don't even know what that is. I mean, I hear talk about it but shoot, we still can't figure out the VCR and the damn thing's already a dinosaur," she said, shaking her head. "Though I do like the sound of the word. TiVo," she repeated. "Remember that band, Devo, remember them? Whip it, whip it good!" Jolene rocked her hips, cracked an imaginary whip.

"They haven't found her," Susan said, staring at the website for the Wake County Humane Society.

"Give it time."

"What if she's dead?"

"She's not dead."

"But what if she is?"

"We're gonna find her, Suz."

"You don't know that."

"Yes I do."

"You do not."

"Yes I do! I'm psychic, got the sight, you know."

"If you had the sight, you'd have known about Billy's mother."

"That woman's the devil, can't be holding me in account for that."

Susan got up and ran her fingertips over the Zoey wall. "Do you believe in the devil?"

"Course I..."

"You think the devil makes people do bad things," Susan interrupted.

"Well, human beings are sinners from the start, that's the truth of it. And God did give us free will."

"How can people be sinners from the start? I mean, how can a baby be bad?"

"Never had to teach a child of mine to lie or steal, but I did have to learn 'em not to."

"Come on," she scoffed.

"Suz, there's no way to convince ya and I'm not about to try. I figure God isn't looking so good from where you're sitting and I'm not about to tell you that I'd feel any different if I were you," she said. "But I believe God has a plan, and just cuz I don't understand it, doesn't mean...."

Susan interrupted, "Yeah, yeah, mysterious ways. At least Bin Laden claimed responsibility."

"No pride in that."

"Depends on where you live, doesn't it? The Palestinians were dancing in the streets." Susan stood up. "Don't you ever want to know," she asked. "Don't you ever want to say, hey, God, what was up with the planes? Why'd you let my little girl die? It never crossed your mind?"

204

"God doesn't account to me."

"Seems like he should account to somebody," she muttered.

"And who would that be, Suz? You? No offense but your resume might be lacking a few credentials."

Susan flushed. "Not everything I think is crazy, Jolene."

"No, but not everything is as bad as you make it."

"Oh right, my pity-party."

"Don't get huffy. You got a right to live your life the way you want, I'm not trying to stop ya." She paused. "Unless you do something really off the wall."

Susan snorted. "Thanks for that."

"Look Suz, you got money out the wazoo and you live in a broken-down house with cardboard furniture, half stripped floors and sheets stapled to the windows." Jolene plopped down on the Rubbermaid container, across the table from the computer. "I practically gotta climb around a refrigerator to get through the kitchen door."

"Use a different door then."

"Still huffy."

"I'm not huffy!" Susan got up, stalked into the kitchen.

Jolene followed, stopping at the calendar. She looked at it, flipped a page or two and sighed. "No matter what, you couldn't have changed it."

"You don't know everything." Picking up a sponge, furiously scrubbing the counter.

"Doesn't matter."

"Yes it does."

Jolene opened the refrigerator and pulled out a soda, watching her for a while. "Ever hear how they trap monkeys? Hunters would weave these cages out of bamboo and leave a little hole in the bottom, just big enough for a paw to slip through. Then they'd bait 'em with some meat, monkey's like meat, did you know that? I woulda thought they'd use bananas, but anyway they'd hang the traps in the trees." She popped the top on a cold Coke. "Those monkeys, they come along and smell the meat and stick their hands up through the hole. Problem was, once they

had the meat in their fist, they couldn't get their hands back out."
Susan's sponge slowed. Jolene tipped the soda and took a long drink.
"All they had to do was drop the meat. But they wouldn't let go and so
they'd just hang there, holding on, until the monkey hunters come and
beat 'em to death."

***

*She found out Tom was married the night he met her husband. It
was a betrayal of epic proportions, his somehow greater than hers.
She'd told him the truth. He withheld information. A novice in adultery,
she'd never thought to ask. Susan told herself she wouldn't have done it
if she had known, more willing to honor another woman's marriage
vows than her own. She didn't like to think about that.*

*It was a party at DNKY. Bill was supposed to go, the buyers, all
the Macy's muckety-mucks, lots of good champagne and cracked crab
at a hip Tribeca restaurant. Two days before, Bill came down with a
bug, eyes and nose running, his chest rattling like a baby's toy. He
offered her his tickets. She meant to go alone. She meant to call Tom
and tell him she was coming. She meant a lot of things that never
happened.*

*She bought new shoes, metallic bronze with ankle straps and spike
heels. She had her hair highlighted and her nails done. Instead of the
customary black, she chose an ice blue dress that hugged her curves
and floated away from her legs. A chunky necklace made from pieces of
glass worn down by the sea, bought on the trip to the Caymans.*

"Wow!"

*She turned, mascara wand in hand, shocked. "What are you doing
here?"*

*"I live here." Sean stood behind her in the mirror, sliding an arm
around her waist.*

"You're never home this early."

"Expecting someone else?"

"What are you doing here?"

"I had a client in midtown, we finished up faster than I thought, so I decided to come home instead of going back to the office." He set his laptop on the bureau. "So, what's with the getup?"

"I, I have a thing for work. Bill's sick, he asked me to go."

"Must be fancy." He kissed her neck. "Looking pretty hot."

She stepped away from him. "Can you fasten my necklace?"

"Where's the party?"

She watched him in the mirror, peering at the clasp. "Downtown."

"Got it. Is this okay?" He held out his arms.

She turned to face him. "Is what okay?"

"What I'm wearing. I'll go with you."

"Go with me? Why?" Stomach acid crawled up her throat.

"Because you're my wife and you've gone to a million things for my job. And because you look good enough to eat." He kissed her with an open mouth.

"Sean, my lipstick." She turned her head. "You don't have to go, I didn't expect you to be home."

"I know." He paused. "I'm trying to hear you, Suz."

She turned back to the mirror, leaned in close to block his view, tears welling. *Now he hears me.* Well it was too late. She blinked rapidly, pretending to add mascara. "You can't wear that, it's all rumpled and you smell like the subway."

"It will take me five minutes to change."

"I have to go."

"You're still doing your makeup. We won't be late, I promise."

The restaurant was in Tribeca, minimalist and chic, a long and narrow room in silver and charcoal. Large textured art work hung on the walls, black and white abstracts with a bold splash of red or purple. The floral arrangements were tall and lush, bursting from their vases, ornamental grasses and orchids and birds of paradise. The place was packed when they arrived.

Susan gave the tickets at the door and Sean took her arm. They both took a glass of champagne from a waiter that materialized in their path. Sean took a sip and looked around.

"Nice place."

"It's okay."

"Didn't we read about this in the Times?"

"I think so."

"We'll have to give it try some night."

"That would be good." Her eyes kept scanning the crowd. He had to be here. She wasn't sure if she wanted to avoid being seen or find a way to find him. It was less than a week since the missed afternoon at the Marriott. He'd stopped by work, told her he understood. As much as a man who loved a woman could, he added.

"Earth to Suz!"

"I'm sorry, what?"

"Isn't that that model, the one who's married to David Bowie?"

"Iman. I don't know."

"Right over there, in the corner. You don't think he's here with her, do you?" She still didn't see him. "Let's go see." Sean took her elbow, maneuvering through the crush.

"You know what, I want a martini. Please?"

He told her to wait where she was and fought his way to the bar. She smoothed her skirt and adjusted her shoulder straps. Played with her necklace and discretely sniffed her wrist to check her perfume. People moved around her, she smiled and nodded without speaking. Then she turned and suddenly he was there.

"Susan!" Surprise bordering on shock.

"Tom, hello." Her voice was carefully modulated, party polite. "How nice to see you." She leaned in to kiss each cheek. Let her lips linger.

"You look, well... That dress is amazing."

"Donna Karan, of course. You're looking good yourself. More than good," she murmured, stepping closer.

"You here with Bill?" He adjusted his tie and widened the space between them. She tried to meet his eyes.

"He's sick. Disappointed?"

His laugh was too hearty. "A beautiful woman or an old queen? Gee, let me think." Something was wrong.

"Are you mad? I meant to call you but..."

"There you are!" A woman pushed to his side, snaked her arm through his. "Honey, I want you to meet Claudia."

Honey. Susan blinked. The woman was petite and slender, thick red hair that tumbled across bare shoulders, skin as pale as milk. Her green eyes sparkled up at him. Like the diamond solitaire that sparkled above the wedding band on her left hand.

"I'm sorry, I didn't mean to interrupt." She glanced at him, waited, then said, "Hi, I'm Ashley."

"Susan." Somehow she extended her hand. Tom shifted his feet.

Ashley's hand stayed on his arm. "Nice to meet you. Do you work with Tom?"

"At Macy's. I work at Macy's."

"Well, I love your dress, it's gorgeous."

"Here you go," Sean announced, arriving with martini in hand. A migraine started behind her right eye, pounding like a fist. "Sean Kearney, Susan's better half." The men shook hands.

His wife smiled. "Ashley," she said, extending her hand. "I've been his better half for years." She smiled at both husbands. "A dirty job, but someone has to do it."

Susan couldn't swallow. Tom wouldn't look at her. He was looking at his wife.

"That's why she makes the big money," he said, his arm around her waist. Ashley shook her head and playfully punched his shoulder.

"Yea, right. It was nice meeting you both. Would you mind terribly if I dragged my husband away? There's someone waiting to meet him."

"Of course not." Susan's voice was forced. "Please, take him." The last with just enough edge to make Sean glance her way. Tom didn't look, hadn't looked. She wanted to scream, make him to look. "Have fun," Susan called after them. "Enjoy yourself!" She took a gulp of her martini.

"So which one was it?"

"What do you mean?"

"You don't like one of them, which one was it?"

She polished off the rest of the drink. *"He's a jerk. Just some jerk from work."* She forced a laugh. *"Gotta love an open bar. Let's have another drink."*

"I still have the first one."

She leaned into him, pressing her breasts into his shirt front, arms around his neck, empty glass dangling over his shoulder. *"Well drink up, sailor, because tonight's your lucky night."* She took his ear lobe between her lips, bit gently. *"And I mean lucky."*

She made a fool of herself. As if to prove she hadn't been making a fool of herself for the last six months. She drank too much and ate too little and danced with wild and sensual abandon, wrapping and rubbing her arms and breasts and legs around Sean. Eyes bright with booze and challenge. She would show him. Him and his beautiful wife. His wife. The bastard!

She tried to feel Sean up in the cab on the way home. When he pulled her hands from his zipper, she got mad. Upstairs in the apartment, she accused him of not loving her and tried to slap his face. Just as quickly she started crying, telling him how much she loved him, how much she wanted him. All over him, flipping on a dime. He was hard against her belly, her thigh. He bent her over the back of the couch, fast and urgent, blue dress flipped up over her shoulders.

Afterwards she insisted on a cognac. They took it in the shower together and she threw up at the first swallow. He went naked and dripping to get her robe. She sat on the cold tile floor, retching, miserable, the water raining down, vomit swirling toward the drain.

***

She was sitting on the porch watching the kittens play in the yard. Callie watched from the rail. "Zoey," she called. "Zoey?" Susan scratched at her knee. It was early evening, the dusk settling on the yard like a cashmere throw, luscious and soft. The bugs were starting to sing, just warming up. She could hear the faint sound of cars in the distance, an engine slowly growing louder, coming closer.

A motorcycle turned into the driveway and Jack pulled off the helmet. He settled it on the back of the seat. "Just wanted to see how you were doing," he said.

"Not so good." Surprising how easy to was to tell the truth. "Nice bike."

"Can't drive around with a bug on my head all the time."

He had a nice smile. He was a nice man, a good boy, his mother said. "I don't think I ever apologized. About the bug."

"It's okay. I probably would have thought the same thing." He settled himself on the steps, reached out to pet the cat. "Anything on Zoey?" Susan shook her head. "Somebody will find her."

She didn't answer. They sat for a minute or two, then she said, "It's hard to imagine you being married to her." He grimaced, settling on the steps. "You're nice, I mean, I know I've been a jerk but you've been really nice. Under the circumstances."

He looped his arms around one knee. "The first time I saw her, I was just blown away. She's beautiful, but it was more than that. She's like a force of nature, when she came in a room, people had to stop and look." He twisted over his shoulder. "You don't have a beer, do you?"

When she came back, she brought two, a picture frame tucked under her arm. "This is Sean."

"Noticed you were wearing your ring." He glanced down at the photo. "Looks like a nice guy."

"He was, kind of like how Becky was for you. Sean always got things done, he always knew what he wanted, where he was going, how to get there. I liked that, that he was always so sure," she said wistfully, taking the picture from his hands. "I was never sure about anything. Even before I went nuts," she added.

"You're not nuts."

"No one's that nice."

He raised his beer, she did the same. Both took a drink. "Sometimes when I see you, it feels like a mirror. The way I'd look if I was turned inside out and everybody could see how I feel." He looked over at her. "Must be hard."

She sighed. "I'm not good with people, never was. That was Sean's job. Everybody liked him. Like you."

"Not everybody."

"You know it was her, right? This wasn't your fault," Susan said.

"I could say the same to you."

"Touché."

"But you know, that's what eats my lunch, I do know. I see her now, how she acts, and I know I wouldn't even ask her out if I'd was meeting her for the first time."

"But you're still sleeping with her." He turned in surprise. "She made a point of letting me know."

"Like a dog peeing on a bush," he muttered. She winced at the word. "Sorry. Zoey's gonna come home, Susan. She has to," he added.

He dropped his hand over hers, gave it a squeeze. Her fingers twitched beneath his touch but for a few seconds she let it sit. Then she said, "I think sometimes people do things for reasons that they can't explain. It always seems so different from the inside, not the way it looks from the outside. I don't think she meant to hurt you. She just got herself tied up in knots, worrying too much, looking for things she already had."

"She didn't want what she had."

"I don't think that's true. Maybe somewhere inside she was so afraid of losing you, so sure you'd wake up one day and look at her, and wonder what you were doing there. Wasting your life with her. It would be unbearable, the waiting, all the time, watching. Maybe she had make it stop."

"You don't know her," he said, shaking his head. "And you of all people don't need to defend her.

"No," she replied, scratching her elbow. "I suppose can't."

212

Chapter 27: September 2, 2006

Islam literally meant surrender to the will of God.

The Prophet Mohammed had been visited by the Angel Gabriel, carrying revelations from the one true God. The same true God of Abraham and Moses and Jesus, just with a different spin on who was who. These revelations were captured in the Qur'an. A second book, the Hadith, had been written by Mohammed's followers to capture his life and his teachings. Like the New Testament had been written about Jesus. There were specific texts prohibiting murder, punishment by fire, the slaughter of women and children. A third book, the Shaddith, was a code of law derived from the two.

Terrorism was a crime against Islam.

Thou shalt not murder, it was religion's one common thread. Always unraveling. Crusades and holocausts, clinic bombings and suicide bombers, occupations and fatwa's. Men acting in the name of God. No matter how well intentioned, mankind just couldn't play in the big leagues. And so they choked, temple after church after mosque. Killing in the name of love, brutalizing in the name of mercy, man ostracizing and executing and judging in the name of their God. Giving credence to the absence of any.

***

Cordelia heard the doorbell, settled herself on the pillows. She'd known Susan would come. Once you knew how to play it, the cancer card was a winner every time.

"Hi." She stayed in the doorway. "Your husband let me in," she added, holding a white box tied with string.

"Thank you for coming. Is that...?"

"Brownies. Jolene brought them and I thought...."

"Dottie makes brownies just to hear people compare them to her cake. Thank you. Ben will appreciate them." Cordelia gestured to a slipcovered chair. "Please come in, sit down." The girl didn't look good. Her hair was greasy, a big stain on the front of her shirt. Lips chapped at the corners, nails to the quick. What looked like a rash creeping out from under her shirt. "Are you getting settled in? Were you able to use any of the drapes?"

"Drapes?"

"When Jolene brought you by the first time, I had some drapes and she thought you might be able to use them."

Susan scratched at the base of her neck. "She didn't tell me."

"Nice girl, Jolene, always has been," Cordelia replied. "Is it allergies?"

"What?"

"That rash. Did you need something, some Benadryl?"

Susan's hand dropped to her lap. "No, no, it's fine. Ummm, is there something…"

"Have you found your dog? Jack said she got lost."

"Not yet," Susan said softly. "I have to get some flyers done today." Cordelia could see the wheels turning, why was she here, how soon she could leave. She felt badly for that, but had to ease her way into it.

"Jack's very fond of you. I'm glad for that. You've met his former wife?" Susan nodded. Wary. "There's something I need to tell you and I want you to know that I feel badly about having to say it."

"Mrs. Wyle, there's nothing going on between me and…"

"Oh no, honey, it's not about Jack." She laughed, coughed, frail fingers on her throat.

"Are you all right?"

"Just need a sip of water, that's all." She gestured toward the pitcher. Susan poured and handed her the cup. "That's better. Thank you. Feel like a two year old, got my own sippy cup." She settled back on the pillows, took a deep breath.

"Jackson and I have always been close. He loves his daddy too, of course, but there was always something special between us. I suppose it comes from me being home when he was little. I think that's so important, don't you?"

Susan nodded.

214

"He's my only child, you know. Would have liked to have a bunch, but God didn't see fit for that to happen. Jack's been a blessing, my pride and joy." She took another sip from the cup. "I'm beating around the bush, aren't I, but I feel so foolish. I don't want you to be angry with him because of me."

"I'm not sure I understand."

"Course you don't. And I'm taking my dear sweet time telling you. He told me about you. About your husband and how he died. I think you'd had a spat, he was mad and... so he came and talked to me about it."

"He told you."

"He wasn't trying to gossip, I promise you that. He just felt badly about how things had gone. It was a confidence, you see, between mother and son." She paused. Susan didn't say anything. "Came back and told me he'd spoken with you, said he gave you his word. That he wouldn't tell anyone." She glanced up, then back down to the bed.

"But it was too late," Susan said slowly.

"I am ashamed of myself, that's the truth. And I am truly sorry."

"You don't have to..."

"It was gossip, pure and simple. I never should have...it was so...to know someone who was...not that I knew you, but still, right here in Wendell." She played with the edge of the blanket, the cup nearly dumped.

"Let me take that for you."

"There's no excuse for it. Queenie Britton, she came to visit with some ladies from our church and I...her husband's sister is married to a Howe, Becky's uncle I believe, though it could be her cousin, I can't quite remember." She sighed. "It doesn't matter"

"It's all right."

"I know it's not, I heard what happened. Jack was so upset." Her fingers continued to fidget with the covers.

"You didn't tell him," Susan said. "That you told."

"No." She ducked her head, purple flowered scarf incongruous on shiny pink skin. "I let him go on about it, agreed with every word.

Becky was never what I would have wanted for him, but that's neither here nor there. I lied to my son because I didn't want him to think less of me."

"You didn't really lie."

"That's kind of you, but not telling can be just as bad as an outright fib. Maybe worse." She lifted her eyes. "But I think you probably know that."

Susan stood up and walked to the window. The rash was climbing up her shoulder, a new blotch just behind her ear lobe. "Some things you just can't tell."

"Still, it can be too big a burden for one person to carry."

"That's the thing, how it looks, it doesn't bother me like it bothers everybody else. This is how I am now. No one understands that, but I can't be...normal again."

"Maybe you were never normal." Susan turned. "A song bird in a hen house is bound to think itself strange. Maybe you were always extraordinary, Susan. That's why God could hand you what he did. He knew you would survive."

"I'm tired of surviving."

"Me too," Cordelia said.

***

"I been thinking that if we shorten the run from the bait and set the switch four inches closer, that might do it," Skeeter said. "Then we could scale the whole durn thing down, do different sizes based on what they wanna catch. Whaddya think?"

Billy was pondering when his Nextel came to life. "Billy, where are you?" He and Skeeter looked at each other. Skeeter tiptoed to a crate next to the case of beer. "Billy, pick up. Over."

"Go ahead."

"Where are you?"

"You ain't calling me from the lock-up, are ya?"

"I told you a million times, I slapped her one time, that's it. So don't change the subject." Skeeter popped the top on a beer. Billy winced at the sound, Skeeter slurping the foam that oozed out the top. "I heard that."

"I'm busy, woman, what do you want?"

"Busy drinking beer. Skeeter, I know you can hear me. Billy's got things to do."

"Last time I looked, you weren't his momma," Skeeter called. A drunken giggle. Billy frowned, waved a hand to shut him up.

"Jolene, what do you want?"

"I gotta go out and put up some flyers, for the dog. Might not be home in time to make dinner."

"And just what am I supposed to do?"

"Hear tell, I'm not your momma." Billy muttered under his breath. "Don't cuss me," she warned. "Go by the drive-through and get yourself some barbecue. We'll talk about the rest of it when I get home. Over and out."

Billy sighed. Both men sat for a second, enjoying the silence.

"Don't know how you do it," Skeeter finally said.

"Ain't so bad."

Skeeter lifted one butt cheek and passed gas. "Once you learn to pull your own pud, don't hardly notice them being gone."

***

"It's the best way to find the dog, simple as that," Becky said, sipping her sweet tea.

"Don't try to weasel your way around me, little girl."

"Dottie, it's TV. Works a lot better than a bunch of stupid flyers," she added. "Look, I'm not pretending that it's not a win-win. I get the interview, but she gets the dog."

"Person didn't know better, they'd be wondering if you took the dog yourself," Dottie muttered.

"Too bad I didn't think of it," Becky drawled. "Oh come on, I'm joking. This is not victims and villains. I want something, she needs help, makes sense for everybody. I'm gonna put something on anyway." Betty Jane snorted, disgust plain on her face. "I'm a reporter, that's what I do."

"Lots of things you do, Becky Lee, that don't make them right."

"Here's my numbers." She slapped a card down on the counter. "Tell her to give me a call." She slung her purse over her shoulder and sauntered out the door. The bell jangled as she left.

"I'm not one for cussing but that girl is a b-i-t-c-h! No other word for it. Don't know what her momma and daddy were thinking when they were growing her up." She glanced at Betty Jane. The old lady nodded. Dottie picked up the card, tapped it against her palm. Debating. She walked to the phone and dialed.

"Jolene," she said. "It's Dottie."

***

"Will you marry me, Suz?"

They had just finished dinner. He'd suddenly suggested that they go to the Rainbow Room. "Rockefeller Plaza," Sean told the cab driver. "At 49th."

The restaurant was an icon, up on the 65th floor, floor to ceiling windows with a southern view of the city. They found seats at the bar and ordered after dinner drinks. Sean excused himself. Susan thought he was in the bathroom. She sipped her Remy Martin and gazed at the view. The twin towers glowed against the night sky, she raised her drink to them. "Here's to your new job," she said. .

"Pretty cool," he replied, clinking her glass.

"It's so beautiful."

"Like you." She loved him so much, leaning in for his kiss. "Look they have a table in there. I thought we could dance."

"Dance? Really?"

"Let's go," he said, tossing a twenty on the bar.

The maître seated them with a flourish. Another twenty passed hand to hand. The dance floor revolved, spinning gently as he spun her around the floor. He was a good dancer, Susan a bit stiff, afraid of not being able to follow. She rested her head on his shoulder, listened to him hum.

"I've never danced to an orchestra before, you know that? I never have."

Her toe caught his shoe, she stumbled. He held her. "Only have eyes for you," he sang.

After two dances, he whirled her back to the table. A bottle sat in a bucket, two slender flutes at each chair. "Champagne!" She was delighted. A waiter materialized, lifted the bottle from the bucket. "Good champagne," she added.

This was the New York of her dreams. The beautiful room, the well-dressed couples, dreamy music, dancers gliding across a backdrop of the city skyline. "It's like a movie," she murmured, her eyes on the dancing.

"Suz."

"Look, look at that woman in the pink dress, she is amazing."

"Suz," he repeated. She turned her head. His eyes on hers, he pulled a small box from the inside pocket of his suit. She was dumbfounded. Was he....he couldn't be. Her mouth dropped open.

"I've loved you from the minute I saw you. Remember those butt ugly paintings? But you were so beautiful. I thought for sure you'd blow me off if I tried to talk to you."

"Sean." Hand trembling on her throat.

"My life is so much better with you in it." Her eyes filled with tears. "So I talked to your father..."

"My dad, when did you..."

"And he gave me his blessing. Now it's up to you. Will you marry me, Suz?"

The ring in the box was just under a carat. A large stone with two smaller stones set to each side. It was stunning. She loved it. She cried and cried, staring at her hand. She couldn't wait to show Maggie. They danced until the band stopped playing.

She stopped wearing the diamonds two years before the end. She'd started picking at the ring like she picked at the marriage. She wished that it was white gold, that the diamonds on the side had a different setting. They catch on my sweaters, she told him. The stupid prongs, the way the jeweler set it was so dumb. He didn't answer. It didn't even cross her mind that she was hurting him.

Men don't get hurt. They're men.

She'd left the engagement ring in their apartment. Not even in a box, just thrown in the drawer of the nightstand next to her bed. She would have left the wedding band too, but she couldn't. Couldn't leave it on, couldn't leave it behind. She didn't want to think about why. So she bought a chain at Walgreens and compromised. That was what marriage was all about. Everyone said so.

***

She didn't answer the phone fast enough. Can't even answer the goddamn phone! Dumb bitch! He'd thrown it at her. Caught her on the cheek, raising a lump, blackening an eye. He took her by the throat, his nose inches from her face. How stupid she was, how ugly. He throttled her, stopping only to slap or kick. A woman didn't learn as quick as a dog does. It took what it took to teach 'em. He finally bored of it, let go, tossed her to the floor. She lay there, gasping, while the little girl chewed the hem of her blanket, watching from the bedroom door.

***

Jolene wasn't sure what to do. She spent most of the afternoon putting up flyers, staring into the puppy's eyes as the staple gun chugged. Ker-plunk, ker-plunk, ker-plunk. She'd papered a wall with them, down the street from Lyman's, an old wood fence put up to keep kids from running between buildings and getting into mischief.

Someone should have seen Zoey by now, someone should have called. It scared her to think what it would do to Susan if no one did. "Not exactly a hot bed of mental health as it is," she muttered.

She had to tell her. It wasn't her call. And it sucked.

She stopped at the Food Lion on the way, got two steaks, some greens, the last-of-season tomatoes. "Becky Howe does not deserve to be on this earth," she muttered, throwing the bags in the truck. "God,

220

I'm not trying to say you don't know what you're doing, but...you might wanna give that another look. In Jesus name, amen."

Susan was at the computer, four or five websites open. She clicked from one to the next, down the line, back to the first. She hadn't showered, her hair was lank, knots and snarls. An ugly rash working its way around the insides of her arms. She hated to have to tell her.

"I brought some food."

"I'm not hungry."

"Well I am, so we're gonna eat." Jolene took the food to the kitchen. The window by the back door was still covered in cardboard. She looked at it for a minute, then went out to the truck, grabbing a bag from the back. As she headed into the house, her phone rang.

"There's money in the jar on the counter, just drive over to..." Jolene stopped, listening as she came in the door. "No, I am not gonna..." She stopped again. "Yes, I was in the Food Lion, I told you that I...Fine, go there then. But don't come crying to me if you're soppin' up gravy with rat poison biscuits." She snapped the phone shut. "Lord, he tries my patience."

Susan didn't answer, click, click, click. Nothing moving but the mouse. Hot pink blotches climbing up her neck like roses on a trellis. "You got any Benadryl for that? It's spreading."

"It's fine." Eyes on the screen.

"Oh yeah, lovely. I brung something for ya. Suz! Stop! Just for a second, okay," she added. "It's curtains. A whole bag of 'em. Look." She dumped the pile out on the floor. "Mrs. Wyle had 'em, for the rummage sale at the church, but she got sick, and they never got there, so I ...."

"She told me."

"When?"

"I went over there. She wanted to see me."

"Why?"

"She just did."

"Well, well, well, meeting the boy's momma. Booo-ha."

"No boo, no ha." She stood, looked over at the pile. "I don't like them."

"You haven't even seen them." Jolene held up a pair. "I think these would look good on that window by the door, let the light in."

Susan sat back down at the computer. "I don't want any curtains."

"These are nice," Jolene continued, feeling the fabric. "Come from Sarah Delacorte's momma house, got Alzheimer's real bad, had to put her in a home. It liked to kill Sarah."

"Great, dead people stuff." Before Jolene could respond, she added, "And I'm not feeling sorry for myself."

"Hold that thought, I'll run to the truck for my violin." Jolene held the drapes against the window. "Knew they'd fit."

"You're not putting those up." Jolene ignored her. Dropping the curtain on the floor, she pulled a stub of a pencil from behind her ear, marking the corner of the window frame. "I said I don't want them," Susan said. "I don't like them. They're ugly."

"Yeah, well, you would think so, used to cardboard and all." She marked the over side, held the fabric up. Susan grabbed at them, both holding on. Tug of war. "Stop it," Jolene grunted. "They're just curtains."

"I don't want them. This isn't home."

"Where's Zoey supposed to come back to then!" She felt bad the second she said it. Susan's face went white, rash like paint splatter. She dropped the drape and turned away. "I didn't…Suz, I'm sorry."

"I pretend that I'm gonna find her and she's gonna be all right but…" She shook her head. "Someone would have seen her by now."

"We're gonna find her. We are." Susan didn't answer. Jolene sighed. "All right, look, I wasn't sure if I should tell you, but Dottie called me and well, Becky told her that she'd put Zoey on the TV."

"What?" Susan slowly turned around.

"But only if you come on too, talk about…you know." Jolene looked miserable. "This sucks, it really sucks."

***

He couldn't believe he was doing it. But she had called and he had answered and now here he was. The party was at a restaurant, out near the airport. Capital City Chophouse, lots of polished wood and subdued lighting. The menu was elegant, without pretension, steaks and seafood, perfectly cooked. Prices about the same as week's worth of groceries. But tonight was on the house, or at least on WRAL. He got himself a drink and looked around for her.

She was glowing, the center of a group, mostly men. All captivated. She wore a leaf green dress, the neck high, shoulders cut away on the diagonal, the rest hugging all the way down to just above her knees. Surprisingly demure. As he watched, she laughed at something someone said, turned to touch an arm. A beautiful shoulder. No back on the dress at all. He swallowed some Jim Beam. Then she saw him.

He'd been waiting so long for that look. Her eyes smiling into his, lips parting, the sight of him making her draw a breath. He felt the pull, leaning like a plant to the light. She disengaged herself and came toward him, eyes never leaving his. He was suspended in time, watching her come. Smooth, hips and legs, the silk flowing, nothing to catch on underneath. Beyond beautiful. Unreal.

"Jack." Becky took his arm, leaned into him, kissed him. Not on the cheek, on the mouth, perfume dancing up his nostrils, filling his head. "I was afraid you wouldn't come."

"You're not afraid of anything." Taking a swallow, ice swirling in the glass.

"You might be surprised," she said, waving a hand. The bartender was right there. "I'll have a Bellini please, and can you give my husband another drink." She smiled, at Jack, giggled. "Look," she said, turning his head toward the mirror behind the bar. Her lipstick on his mouth. She ran her finger across his bottom lip, perfect oval nail, the softest shade of pink, sparkling flecks in the depths. "There," she said, looking into his eyes. "I got it."

"Nice party," he said, forcing his eyes away. "Isn't that the guy who does the weather?"

"Would you like to meet him?"

She never wanted him to meet anyone. People were his or hers. Either or, it had never been both. "What's going on, Beck?"

"What do you mean?"

"What's with the sudden interest? A drink for my husband," he added, emphasizing the word. She bit her lip, glanced around.

"Let's go over there," she pointed. "I don't want to talk here." She led him to a pair of barrel chairs, tucked into an alcove. A wall of windows faced the parking lot, but beyond, the airplanes soared, wing and tail lights trailing in the night. "Isn't it gorgeous? So much better after dark. We come here for lunch a lot, it's not the same..." Her voice trailed off.

He waited as long as he could. "So what's this about?" Set his drink on the table, votive candles turning the bourbon to fire.

She leaned from the chair, crossing the space between them, and pulled his head to hers. Her lips came down, parted and warm, tongue gentle, then probing, pushing, their mouths desperate to combine, teeth to teeth. Leaning into him, her breasts suspended in midair, his fingers itched for the green silk. She twisted her body to hide the touch, nipple falling into his hand. "Jesus," he whispered.

"That's why," she said, breaking the spell. Taking herself away, back to her chair. How did two feet become a chasm? He exhaled, heart tripping, trying to slow its beat.

"I've missed you, Jack. And before you say anything, let me say this. I'm sorry. I screwed up, okay? I see that now. I was wrong but I want to make it right." She crossed her long legs. "Because when it's right with you and me, it's not like anyone else."

He had to keep his head. "I've got nothing to compare it to."

"I can't change what happened but I want to start again. If you'll let me."

Were those tears in her eyes? He fumbled for his drink. This was what he dreamed of hearing. What was wrong? Something was wrong. "So what prompted this epiphany?"

He caught the flash of irritation in her eyes. Gone as fast as it came. "I hadn't seen you for a while, I mean, I'd been thinking about you, but then when I saw you again." She hesitated. He let the silence stand. "And that day, in Pilot, when you went with her, over me, you know, it made me…"

"Susan is a friend, that's all."

"I didn't like it," she said quietly. "I was surprised by how much I didn't like, actually." Candle light flickering, dancing in her eyes. "It made me realize what I'd given up."

"You didn't give me up, you threw me away."

"It was the stupidest thing I've ever done." She faced him, wide open, defenses down, head bowed. His heart contracted and he reached out to touch her face. She turned her cheek into his hand, sighed, covering his fingers with her own.

"I've always wanted you, Beck, you know that."

"Then have me." She smiled into his eyes. Her cell phone rang, startling him, but her gaze didn't waver. At the third ring, she broke away, pulled the phone from a small lavender bag.

"Rebecca Howe," she said, keeping a hand on his knee. Whoever it was surprised her. She raised one finger, begging for a minute. "Glad to hear it," she replied, inching away. He sat there, a little dazed. It was surreal, getting exactly what he wanted.

Chapter 28: September 3, 2006

"It's a deal with devil," Jolene groaned. "You got any of those fancy creamers, the vanilla ones?"

Dottie nudged a bowl toward her. "She loves that little dog."

"I know but...Becky's a snake." One creamer, two creamers.

"That ain't in question, but why all the hiding in the first place? Doesn't make sense."

"I know. She's messed up. But you can't go from zero to a hundred and fifty, all in one shot." She took a sip of the coffee. "Wooo, that's hot." She picked up another creamer, poured it in.

"Maybe I should put those on the menu," Dottie said tartly, folding her arms. "What you think, Betty Jane? Why bother with coffee at all when you can drink free creamer."

"Sorry," Jolene replied, "I'm just worried. It's like finding Zoey is a way to make up for not finding Sean. That's the husband," she added. "I mean, I understand, but it scares the pants off me. What if the dog doesn't come home?"

Dottie folded her lips, hands quiet on the counter. Betty Jane stared the window.

"Exactly," Jolene said. "And she'll have put herself through all this crap for nothing. Then I'm gonna hafta kill Becky Lee Howe, and that's about the only good news."

***

They shot it in front of the wall Jolene had covered with flyers. To air at noon, six and eleven, part of a two part-deal, another interview to follow.

It started with Ground Zero, of course. The planes, the towers, the smoke. They'd found stock footage of Susan, young and pale, walking President Clinton along the wall, Sean's face on the flyer. The clip faded into the flyers of Zoey on the fence, then panned out to Becky, mike in hand.

"Susan Kearney was only 28 years old when her husband was killed in the attacks on the World Trade Center. His body was never found. Like all the victims of 9/11, she has struggled to regain some sense of normalcy, find a way to carry on. For Mrs. Kearney, normal came with four legs and tail, but now tragedy has struck again and she needs our help." The camera cut to Susan. Too thin, dark circles under the eyes, hives not quite hidden by the makeup, she fidgeted, fingers picking at her shorts.

"I'm Susan and this is my dog, Zoey." She pointed to a flyer. The camera obligingly zoomed in on the puppy's face. "She's lost and I'm really worried. She's just a baby," her voice quavered. "I love her so much and I want her back. Please if you see her, she's very friendly, please call me," she said, reciting the number. "There's a reward and if you've been keeping her, I'm happy to reimburse you for food or toys or..." She blinked hard. "She likes toys." The camera closed in for the kill. "We never found my husband," she said, choking on the scripted line. Part of the deal. "Please help me find my dog," she whispered.

"The greatest tragedy in American history," Becky intoned. "Five years ago we all felt helpless. Five years ago all we wanted to help. This is your chance. Do for Susan Kearney what couldn't be done that fateful day. Bring her loved one home. This is Rebecca Howe in Wendell, on the hunt for little Zoey."

They went back to the anchor, who promised more in-depth coverage with Susan Kearney, wife of a fallen hero. He segued into a traffic jam on I-40 and Susan turned off the TV. The phone rang.

"Hello?"

"Miz. Kearney, this is Louise Merry, we met at the Pilot Firehouse. Jolene Mayes introduced us?"

"Oh yes. I...umm..."

"Miz Kearney, I wanted you to know how sorry I am about your little dog. I lead a Girl Scout Troup, number 449 here in Wendell, and we'd like to volunteer to look for little Zoey," she said. "You're at the Garrett place as I recall, so I will swing by to get some flyers and we'll get the girls started going door to door."

"That is so kind of you, thank you."

"Bless you, Miz Kearney, you're in our prayers."

Susan hung up. The phone rang in her hand.

"Is this the gal who lost the dog?" A raspy voice, thick with southern drawl.

"Yes, did you find her?"

"Ain't started looking just yet." As if she was dumb. She felt dumb. "I got me a couple of dogs. Labs. Buster and Beau. We go hunting mostly." Another pause. "I'm retired now you know."

"No I didn't."

"You're not from around these parts."

"No."

"Well, I reckon that we're gonna know places a dog might get that a gal from up north wouldn't. Beau's got a right good nose. Yeller puppy, right?"

"Yes, with big ears and brown eyes. She had a collar, a blue collar and she comes to her name. Zoey."

"Zoey," he repeated. "Wanted to let you know we'll be going out lookin'. "

"Thank you so much, Mr...?"

"No thanks needed, right thing to do. Marines, you know, Vietnam. Two tours. Sorry for your husband, ma'am." He hung up without saying his name.

She walked to the front door and stood at the screen. The sky was moody, gathering clouds and the dank smell of coming rain. The kindness of people had always seemed such an intrusion. Reaching in when she least expected, trying to touch her heart. So eager to show her how much they cared, to share her grief as if their own. They couldn't have it. It was hers.

Thunder rumbled, lightening flashed in the clouds. Susan wondered where Zoey was, if she was scared. Inside, outside, on the run, sound asleep at someone else's feet. Dead on the side of the road. The thought stabbed her. It hurt so much, it didn't seem possible it could hurt this much.

She tried so hard to be nothing, feel nothing, do nothing, want nothing. Her life played out as if she stood in front of a movie screen, a projector running behind, bathing her in moving pictures of planes and buildings and smoke. No forward, no back, always the same. Building one, plane, smoke, fire, papers, bodies. Screaming. Building two, plane, smoke, fire, papers, bodies. Boom! The second tower falls. Boom! The first one goes down. Sean is inside. Sean is in that building. As many times as she saw it, she could never quite wrap her brain around it.

The phone rang. "Hello?"

"You the one who lost the dog?"

"Yes, did you find her?"

"You paying cash money?"

"Five hundred dollars. Did you find her?"

"You're a Jew girl, ain't ya, from New York?"

"What?"

"Oughta gas the lot of ya, Jew bitch. And the fucking dog too."

She hung up the phone. Terrorists. They were everywhere.

***

"Is Sean all right?" Maggie shrieked.

Susan was in Starbucks near Herald Square, waiting less than patiently behind a woman digging through her purse for exact change. The girl at the register, the one with the hot pink hair and a ring in her nose, was calling out an order. "Lo-fat mo, whip, decaf cap, skim, frost it."

"Sean's at work. What's a matter?

"Susan! My god, you haven't...Susan, there's been... you have to find a television."

"You're scaring me. What happened?"

"Just find a TV!"

Susan looked around. People were running in the street, pointing. Traffic stopped, doors opened, people staring a cell phone to every ear. "What's going on?" There was a TV near the door, sitting on a shelf on the wall over the tables, a crowd grouped around it. The volume was on mute, everyone talking. A crawler running along the bottom of the screen. Breaking news.

"Oh my god, I don't believe it."

"Holy shit, man, that pilot musta had a major buzz on."

"Turn it up, someone turn it up."

The woman on CNN was saying that a plane had hit the World Trade Center, that the building was on fire. The World Trade Center. A plane had crashed into the World Trade Center.

"Susan, are you still there!"

"Did she say a plane?" Susan asked the man in front of her.

"Yeah, sounds like it flew right into the side of the building."

"Which tower?" No one answered. "Which tower!"

"Dunno," the man muttered, eyes on the screen.

"Be quiet," said a woman near the front.

"Maggie, which tower?"

"The north," Maggie sobbed.

"Oh my god!" Susan ran out the door. She looked downtown. Sixth Avenue was full of people and cars. Looking downtown, the towers no longer twins. One was on fire.

She couldn't see any plane. Only black smoke. Plumes of black smoke, the blackest smoke, so much smoke, tumbling out into the sky like a thunder storm on fast forward. "I can see it," she whispered. Black smoke everywhere, up high. How high?

"Susan, he's gonna be okay, Sean's okay."

"The building's on fire." Trying to process. She started to jog, moving south. "I can see it, oh my god, the building's on fire!" She was crying now. There was so much smoke. Running, dodging in and out of the people stopped in their tracks, pointing and staring. Sean. Sean! "Maggie, I've gotta...Maggie?"

The phone crackled static. She broke the connection, still running. Hit two, speed dial to Sean's cell. Busy signal. Shouldn't be busy, call waiting, voice mail. No busy! She hit the phone against her palm, dialed again. Busy. Busy. Busy. Busy. Busy. Busy.

The second plane hit the second tower.

She was just above 18th Street, running, dialing. Busy. Busy. Busy. Busy. A collective gasp so loud it forced her to a stop. Someone screamed, then someone else. More smoke, new smoke, black smoke, blooming like fungus in a petri dish. She panted, staring, mouth open. Two planes. Both towers. Two planes. She couldn't breathe. No accident, not an accident. It was on purpose! How could that be!

Busy. Busy. Busy. Busy. Busy. She tried Patrick. Busy. Busy. Busy. Maggie. Busy. Busy. Busy. The stupid phone, the fucking phone! Busy. Busy. Busy. Busy.

"Sean, answer the goddamn phone!" She leaned against a telephone pole, wracked by sobs so strong she couldn't run. "Sean, please! Answer the phone!"

"Are you okay?" A stranger stopped.

"My husband," she gasped.

"Is he...oh no, I'm so sorry." The first of so many to come.

"My phone...can I use your phone?"

"I can't get a signal. I think everything's jammed."

"Sean, God, oh God, Sean!" Susan screamed, both hands to her head, spun in a circle. Couldn't breathe, couldn't look, had to look, hated to look, couldn't tear her eyes away. People ran past her, heading downtown or running for cover. Fear in the streets. She had to call him. He had to answer. Home. There was a phone at home. A land line. Get to the phone, get to the phone, get to the phone. She turned uptown and ran back from where she'd come.

She was running up the stairs to their apartment when the South Tower collapsed. Still dialing. Busy. Busy. Busy. Busy. She didn't know what she didn't know, through the kitchen, past the blue papers on the counter, had to get to the phone. She dialed, struggling to remember his work number, mind overcome. She turned on the TV, live footage, camera crews in place now. She paced, phone to her ear, stopped. Only one. There was only one. She froze, phone to her ear. Busy, busy. Watching. The second plane hitting the second tower. The people jumping. The fireman dying. The building falling. Busy. Busy. Busy. Sean! Fist in her mouth, watching. Busy. Busy.

The North Tower fell as she watched, phone falling, building falling. Everything falling. No busy. No more. No nothing.

***

"Hey mom," Jack said, trying to keep his smile straight. She was disappearing. The woman on the bed was a bird, twig arms and legs, flesh gone from her face, just bones covered in skin, nose poking forward like a beak. Bright eyes. "How are you feeling?"

"Better today," she lied. "So good to see, honey."

"I'm sorry I haven't..." he started.

She waved a hand. "Please, one of us has to have a life," she said. He winced. "Jackson" she scolded, "everything's going to be all right."

"I know," he lied.

"Sit, tell me," she said, patting the edge of the bed. "What's been going on?"

They talked for almost an hour. He made her laugh more than once. It was so easy between them, if they ignored the elephant in the room.

"So what did the doctor say?"

"Oh honey, please I am so tired of talking to doctors and then having to talk about what they said. Did I tell you I met your Susan?"

"She's not my Susan, mom."

"You know what I mean. Pretty girl. Seems sweet, sad as she is."

"She's had a bad time. Her dog got lost too, I told you that, right?"

She nodded. "I saw it on the TV."

"What?"

"It was on the news."

"What! Goddammit!" Up off the bed.

"Jackson, please!"

"She did it, she knew I didn't..." He shook his head, a harsh laugh. "I'm so frigging stupid. Goddamn it!"

"There will be no cussing in this house, Jackson," she scolded. "Now what is a matter with you?"

It all poured out, the visits, the phone calls. The need. So much more than she already knew. Her heart ached for him. "She's sitting there, telling me that...what is wrong with me," he demanded, eyes dark. "I keep chasing after her."

"Honey, it's her job to get stories. Maybe she was trying to help," Cordelia soothed. "It's not as if..."

"She did it on purpose," he interrupted. "She knew I didn't want her to, she doesn't care about anybody. Susan's been through living hell, I mean if you could see that house..." he paused, shook his head. "She thinks I like her so she's got to..." Cordelia sighed, hand to her chest. He stopped in mid-sentence. "Mom, I'm sorry, I didn't mean to get..."

"I'm the one who told her," she interrupted. "Becky. Not her exactly, but that doesn't matter. You asked me not to tell but I did. I wasn't...oh there's no excuse. I told her that too. Susan, I mean, not Becky," she added.

"Oh man," he groaned, plopping down in the corner chair.

"I'm so sorry, honey."

He waved it off. "That's the least of it." He ran his hands through his hair.

"Are you in love with her? Becky?" She saw him hesitate. "No more lies now, I'm not here to judge."

"I don't know. I know I shouldn't be, if I am. It's all screwed up. I want her back so bad I can hardly stand it and then I see who she is and..." He shook his head.

"If you love someone, you have to accept all of them. What's pretty and what's not."

"What if you can't?"

"Then it isn't love."

He didn't answer. He got up, then sat back down. "The treatments aren't working," he said. It wasn't a question. He took her hand. "No more lies," he added.

"No." She squeezed his fingers. "But don't tell your daddy, he can't bear to hear."

***

Jolene managed the girl scouts, all fourteen of them and Mrs. Merry. Susan stayed in the bathroom, staring in the mirror. They were disappointed, she was sure. They wanted a look at her. Live and in the flesh. Seven more days.

Susan peered in the mirror. She couldn't see it, but she could feel it. The grit, the ash, the tiny bits of concrete or bone, hard to tell which. She leaned into the glass, rubbing her cheek. It was there. Blowing up her skin, rash spreading now, to her chest, her scalp. She could feel it, creeping in under her clothes, between her teeth, on the soles of her feet. Every year. She couldn't get it off.

"Suz, they're gone." Jolene tapped on the door. "Suz?"

"I have to take a shower."

"You already took a shower."

"I'm taking another one.

"I thought you wanted to go look for the dog.

"I have to take a shower."

"Don't make me come in there and get you," Jolene sighed.

***

They peppered telephone poles with flyers and stopped at two mobile home parks, Jolene dealing with the folks who were home, Susan sticking them in the doors of those that weren't. Susan called Zoey's name out the window, her eyes darting between the road ahead and the mirrors. Each time the truck went around a bend, she would be convinced that Zoey was back there. That she had heard her name, trotted to the side of the road, looking for Susan, hopeful, looking, one little ear cocked. Abandoned again.

"Jolene, go back. She's there, I know it."

"Did you see her?"

"No but I know it. Go back! Please." She wasn't there. Jolene turned around every time she asked.

"Come on, girl. Here girl, come on, let's have a biscuit." Zoey. Zoey. Zoey.

***

They recited the names at the memorial. The heroes, not the villains. So many. "Sean Patrick Kearney," she whispered. There was a Keasler after Sean, two Keatings, a Keene. She wanted to remember them but there were too many. She picked up the double frame, talked to Waleed. "We haven't found her." He didn't answer, he never did. "How did you get so lost," she whispered.

Her skin crawled. She couldn't stand it. She scratched her neck, her chin, her under arm. It was driving her mad. In the bathroom was a razor blade. She could scrape off a layer, get to the skin.

The phone rang in the other room. She stayed put, scraped the blade over her neck, the hives like little moguls on a ski slop slope. Nothing on the blade. She pressed harder, blood swelling at the starting point, just under her jaw. She scraped again. Blood rolling down her cheek. Slippery. The machine picked up.

"If this is the woman who was on TV looking for her dog, I think I mighta found it. We live over on Arendell in Zebulon. Little fella, kinda yellow, been feeding it for a day or so, then I saw you on TV and well, I guess you're not home, so I..."

Oh my god, wait! "Hello! Hello?"

She ran to the car, stopped and ran back for Cowboy Rhino. Zoey would want Cowboy Rhino. "They found her, the woman said they've been feeding her," Susan told him. He stared straight ahead, safety pin glinting on his leg. "She's coming home."

The house was small, a brick box with lots of plastic toys scattered through the yard. Susan could hear a baby screaming as she knocked on the door, children yelling. A woman yelling too. It took forever. Susan knocked again.

"Yes?" The woman opened the door a crack, sobbing baby on her hip. Four small children surged forward around her legs.

"I'm here about the dog?"

"Oh, I'm sorry, I didn't recognize you," she said. "You bleeding?"

Susan touched her cheek, blood still oozing. "It's...allergies. I shouldn't scratch. Can I...do you...where is Zoey?"

235

"Uh-huh." Suspicious. "Jake, go get the puppy."

"Ma, I wanna keep him," the boy whined.

"I don't care what you want, that dog belongs to this lady here and you go get him right now."

"No!" The child's chin quivered.

"Don't make me whup you, boy, go get the dog!" She snapped, smiled at Susan. "He's been wanting a dog but his daddy says he can't have one until he's old enough to take care of it. Got enough mouths to feed as it is." She shifted the baby. "So there's a reward, is that right?"

"Yes, oh yes, here." Susan pulled the envelope from her purse. "And I am so grateful to you for taking care of her. I'd like to reimburse you for the food."

"Shoot, nothing but table scraps and the like." The woman fingered the envelope, light in her eyes. They waited awkwardly. "Jacob!" She bawled.

The boy turned the corner and started down the hall, in silhouette, a lump in his arms. He bent his head to whisper, the lump began to squirm. He stepped up next to his mother, dog in his arms.

It wasn't Zoey.

***

How could she have been so stupid? He was just trying to get laid. That was all. He was married. Tom said that he loved her. No doubt his wife heard the same. He must think she was stupid, another dumb blonde, just a piece of ass. Who was he having lunch with now? How many women met him for drinks at their little bar. His little bar. He was a slimy creep, preying on innocent women. Absolving herself. A victim, not a volunteer.

It was four days after the DKNY party. She was walking past Bill's office and heard his voice. She stopped. He sounded just the same, laughing and sparring with Bill. No change. Nothing different at all. Anger flushed her cheeks and before she could think, she swung through the door.

"Well hello," she said, eyes like lasers. "Tom, what a surprise."

236

"Hey, Susan, how are you?" He smiled like always, didn't even squirm.

"I am fine. Really fine." She bit the words off one at a time. Bill glanced at her.

"There's donuts in the break room," he said.

"I love donuts. Absolutely love them. How do you feel about them, Tom?"

"I brought 'em, if that helps." He and Bill exchanged glances, warning code for 'that time of the month.' "Well, I should probably get going," Tom said.

"Let me walk you out," she offered.

"That's okay." He shook Bill's hand. "I'll have the order here by Thursday."

"Is that a promise," Susan asked brightly. Tom walked out the door, Susan on his heels, feeling Bill's eyes on her back.

"Look, Susan" he said, "I don't think this is the best place to have this discussion."

"This is where it all started."

"I'm sorry you're upset, but..."

"You're not sorry. Oh that's right, I forgot, you lie a lot." Her voice rising. He took her arm, turned her down the hall and into the break room.

"Look, it was fun, we had a good time. Why can't we just leave it at that." He shot his cuff, gave her the smile. "Donut?" He held up the box, trying to keep it light.

"You think I would cheat on my husband for fun?"

He narrowed his eyes. "You were just as into it as I was."

"You lied to me!"

"Okay, I did, but it's not like you weren't doing the same thing to what's his name. Sean."

"How dare..." Susan sputtered. "I told you I was married!"

"Right before you stuck your tongue down my throat," he snapped. "Don't blame me for giving you exactly what you were looking for. 'I'm married,'" he mocked. "You sure as hell didn't act like it." She started

237

to cry. *"Jesus,"* he groaned, glancing toward the hallway. *"Susan, look, we had some fun. It's no big deal! God, we didn't even..."* He stopped, reconsidered. *"And I do care about you. I wouldn't have bothered otherwise."*

"Bothered." There was a roaring in her head. It wasn't supposed to go like this. *"You wouldn't have bothered to try and screw me?"*

"This is getting us nowhere. I have to go."

"So what does Ashley think?" Susan crossed the line.

"You don't want to go there." His eyes went cold.

"Hey, we were just having some fun. Nothing wrong with that." She squared her shoulders, crossed her arms to hide her trembling hands. He had to feel something. She would be damned if he would leave here without feeling something.

"And the hubby, how's he gonna take it?"

"I've already told him," she lied.

"Bullshit." He stepped up, took her arm. His nose inches from her face. *"This is done, right here, right now. Like it never happened!"* He dropped her arm and walked out the door.

"You son of a bitch," she yelled, following him into the hall. *"I'm gonna call your wife,"* she screamed. *"I am!"* He didn't slow down. She threw her coffee after him. It landed short and splattered in the hall, two co-workers jumping back. Everyone staring.

"Susan!" Bill had her by the arm, dragging her back into the break room. He pushed her toward a chair and slammed the door. *"What are you doing!"* She burst into tears. He groaned. *"This is why you don't shit where you eat!"*

"I'm sorry," she snuffled. *"I didn't mean to..."*

"Get your stuff and go home." Susan sobbed harder. Bill sighed, patted her shoulder. *"Look, we'll talk about it tomorrow. Go on now, Susan. Go home."*

She couldn't go home. She was humiliated and hurt and suddenly wanted Sean desperately. He would make this better. He loved her. She ran for a downtown train, rode it to the Trade Center stop She would quit her job. Get another job. A real job and a real life. She would be a

238

real wife, love and honor her husband. He was good, a good man. It was her, she was screwed up. She'd go to a counselor, start running, become a Buddhist. Something. She could change. She could.

Susan rode the elevator up the 84th floor, got off before she remembered his office had moved. She got back on and found her way to the back of the 101st. A corner office, all windows, his secretary guarding the gate. The woman looked up and smiled.

"Mrs. Kearney, hello."

"Is Sean here?"

"I'm sorry, he's not. Was he expecting you?"

"I'm his wife, I don't need an appointment," she snapped. The secretary flushed. "Just tell him I was here." Stalking to the elevator. A woman scorned. Twice.

Chapter 29: September 4, 2006

It was just after one a.m. Jack sat up, half awake. The doorbell rang again. He got up, headed for the front door. He glanced out the window by door, didn't turn on the light, not with Miz Childress across the street, fully expecting to see Becky on the stoop.

It was Susan. She waited on the steps, shivering as if it were cold. He unlocked the door. "Susan?" Bare chest and feet, boxer shorts and rumbled hair.

"I woke you up."

"It's okay. Come on in." She followed him into the living room. "Give me a second," he said. He came back in jeans and a T-shirt. She was still standing where he left her. He flipped on the light. Her left cheek and neck were smeared with dried blood. "Were you in an accident?"

"I don't know how it happened."

"Are you hurt?" He repeated. She laughed. "Okay, just answer the question because you're starting to freak me out," he said, leading her to the kitchen.

"I was going to Wal-Mart but it's too early so …"

"Not helping," he interrupted. He got a paper towel, wet it and took her chin. He dabbed at the blood, a long clean cut just under her cheekbone. The skin on her neck was scraped. Some kind of rash beneath. "You're a mess," he said. She didn't disagree. "I got some Neosporin, I think." He opened a cupboard. "Do you want a BC powder?"

"What's that?"

"Never mind, here, come sit on the stool." She did as she was told. He squeezed some ointment on his finger, dabbed at her face.

"I was on TV today."

"I heard." He hadn't seen it. Had called Becky twice but she hadn't called back. A text message arrived around nine. So sorry, super busy, miss U.

240

"I got calls afterwards, somebody thought they found her, but they didn't." Beneath the blood, another slice along the side of her neck. He smeared the Neosporin on it. She winced, looking up at him. "Your wife said the two of you were back together. Are you?"

It caught him by surprise. "You came over here in the middle of the night to ask about Becky?" He sighed. "Not trying to be rude but that's the least of your problems. Why did you do this? And don't pretend you didn't."

"I had to get it off."

"Get what off?" He put the cap on the tube, wiped greasy fingers on his jeans.

"It itches."

He gave up. "So what are you doing here?"

"I wanted to know if you forgave her."

"What?"

"I need to know."

It was irritating. All of it, both of them, women in general. "What difference does it make to you? Not like you're interested." He stepped near the stool. "Or are you?" He was too close, in her space, suddenly, surprisingly very interested himself. She twitched but didn't move. No place to go. He reached out and touched her cheek. "Why did you hurt yourself?"

"It doesn't matter," she whispered.

"It does matter."

He kissed her. Didn't plan it, didn't think about it, just did it. So simple, not a big deal really, just as easy as lowering his lips to hers. Her whole body trembled. He pulled her to him, like a rag doll she fit to his chest. The kiss growing, expanding, her lips parting under his, stirring a passion he'd thought was reserved only for Becky. Their mouths rising and falling, soft and hard, teeth gently pulling at her bottom lip. The taste of salt opened his eyes. She was crying. He went to let her go, but she clung, burrowed into his chest, arms wrapping him tight.

AP picked up the story and put in on the wire. Maggie called at quarter of eight. Zoey had made the Today show. The phone was already ringing, the media entranced with the freebie - a lost puppy and a nine-eleven widow, didn't get better than that.

"I gotta go, Maggie."

"I'm so sorry about Zoey, Susan. You're gonna find her."

"I know."

The phone started ringing. More reporters. They were coming.

***

The kitchen door flew open, screen door bouncing off the wall as Jolene burst in the house. "Shoot, Suz, you're on the TV, I mean the real TV, Katie Couric, for real, Katie Couric! There I was flipping eggs, nursing Billy through last night's bout with a forty and there was Zoey on the TV! I couldn't believe...What happened to your face?"

"Nothing."

"And I'm the queen of France."

"There is no queen of France."

"My point exactly," Jolene replied.

***

They gave tours there now, promising paying customers the chance to stand on the actual floor of the actual World Trade Center. An unobstructed inside view was offered in the case of inclement weather. No money back for rain. Visit the single most historic site in American history. A moving tribute, the marketing materials said. Just fifteen dollars, plus tax and gratuity. See the spot where Sean died and buy yourself a souvenir.

There really wasn't much to see. It was a construction site, slowly obliterating the old with the new. Right afterwards, St. Paul's Chapel had become the dropping spot for flowers and notes and pain. The staff put up a wooden wall to display the pictures, the flags, the baseball hats, the love letters in all different languages, all the mementos left behind by people grappling with their loss. Even those who lost nothing

242

needed to come and bring something. It was compelling. Sean's sister Mary took his old baseball glove. He'd left it at her house, teaching her son how to throw curve balls. It was packed up in some basement somewhere now because at some point, St. Paul's had taken the wall down. Life goes on.

The mangled remains of the fountain that had stood in the middle of the Trade Center complex ended up in Battery Park. That was the first year, the first ceremony, she'd watched as they lit the eternal flame. It would burn there until they rebuilt, then it would move to a permanent site. Another stop on the walking tour. It would look good on a t-shirt. Nothing was sacred.

***

"I'm sorry I've been out of touch," Becky said. "How are you, baby?"

"Had a busy day, huh?"

"What's wrong?"

"I'm sick of being played!"

"What are you talking about, I meant to call you but work was a madhouse and…"

"Surprised you had time to look for a dog." Silence. He waited. "Hello?"

"You aren't gonna tell me how to do my job, Jack."

"It's a witch hunt, not a job."

"This is about her, isn't it?"

"Damn right it's about her, Becky, the girl is barely holding on, did you have to…"

"Help her find her stupid dog?"

"You only did the dog to get to her."

"I didn't realize you had this much of thing for her."

"I don't have a thing for her." Remembering Susan in his arms. "And don't try and turn this around on me."

"Because you never do anything, poor little Jack."

"You do enough for both of us."

"Oh please, man up!" She snapped, disconnecting the call.

***

Jolene had the bathroom tore up, trying to find the leak in the pipe from the upstairs toilet. The phone rang continually, the machine picking up unless Susan lifted the receiver to drop it back down. All the producers, Larry King, Diane Sawyer, Charlie Gibson, Connie Chung, all of them. Good morning, America.

The curtains looked strange on the windows. The ones in the living room puddled on the floor. They were burnt orange, a color Susan never would have picked. Like fire against the glass, glowing in the sun. She liked them. The house liked them too. Zoey would have loved them, giant tug of war.

"So I heard you gave Debbie Miles five hundred dollars," Jolene called from the bathroom.

"Who? Oh, she thought she found the dog."

"You coulda taken the money back."

"What difference would that make?"

"A lot to Debbie."

"Then it worked out, didn't it?"

A thunk, a yelp. "Crap," Jolene yelled. "I'm stuck! Hey, c'mere."

Her arm was up inside the drywall, to the shoulder. The front of her shirt was wet and smelled suspiciously of sewer. It took the two of them to work her free, Jolene's crescent wrench lost behind the wall.

"You stink," Susan said, wrinkling her nose.

"Pipe's from the toilet." She wiped her forehead with her sleeve, smearing dirt and god knows what else. "Geez Louise! You mind if I take a shower?"

Susan got her a towel, a T-shirt and shorts, threw her clothes in the washer, holding them by her fingertips. She was out on the deck, watching Callie watch the kittens when Jolene poked her wet head out the door. "You got anything to eat?"

They made tomato sandwiches with mayonnaise and bacon bits, grabbed a couple of sodas and took lunch to the deck. The afternoon was lovely, just a hint of breeze, the air fresh and light. The rose bush still bloomed and purple, pink and white phlox clustered next to the deck, delivering a spicy scent.

"How much money you got, Suz?"

"I don't know, a lot."

"You don't seem too happy about it."

"Most of it's from Sean getting killed."

"You don't have a million dollars or anything, not as much as that?"

"Yeah, probably." She turned toward Jolene. "Do you need some?"

"No, course not." Her cheeks pink. "How did it go yesterday with the witch?"

"I've done it a million times, coulda been worse." Jolene sputtered. "I did it for Zoey."

"Shouldn't have had to, that's all I'm saying."

"You don't like her because she cheated on him."

"Among other things, but that's a good enough place to start. If you're gonna get married, you should get married, you wanna sleep around, okay, not my choice still that's up to you. But the two don't go together – it's one or the other. "

"I thought God was supposed to forgive people."

"Yeah well, that's why He's Him and I'm me." They sat looking out at the yard, caught up in the antics of the kittens.

"Jackson kissed me."

"What!" Jolene was up out of her chair. "Shoot, you give it up, girl, all the details! "

"I went over there to find out and…" she stopped, shook her head. "It shouldn't have happened."

"Find out what? And could we skip to the good part, please?"

"Becky said they were back together and if they were, he must have forgiven her."

"Did you kiss him back?"

"I cheated on him."

Jolene stopped dancing around. "What?"

"I cheated on him. Not Jack," she added.

"Sean," Jolene answered slowly. She sank back down in the chair. "Well, that explains a few things now, don't it."

***

"You ever see him again? Tom?"

"No, not after the fight at work. He never called, you know, not even after Sean…I don't know why I thought he would, everybody else did but…"

"He didn't. Did you try and call him?"

Susan hesitated, nodded. "I did, one night. His wife answered and I hung up, two times. The third time, it was him, he didn't know it was me, and he was mad, you know, about the hang ups. I felt so stupid. I don't know what I expected, because I knew…" Her toe traced patterns on the deck, sandwich barely touched.

"He sounds like a real piece a work. Reminds me of John Chestner, hot as a pistol that boy. Knew it too. Had all the girls jumping through hoops, at least until he dumped them and then still, half of them after that." She dangled a sneaker, laces driving the kittens crazy. "Always felt sorry for his…" She stopped short.

"Wife," Susan finished. "Go ahead. You can say it."

"Not easy being married to that kind of man." Or woman was left unsaid.

"I didn't sleep with him." She knew she sounded defensive.

"You sound like President Clinton."

"I'm not trying to make excuses, but Sean worked so much. He was never home, never had time for me. I still don't really understand why I…"

"Selfishness. Pure and simple, not that hard to figure." Jolene was matter-of-fact. Susan flushed. "No point in sugar coating it, honey, that'll only rot your teeth."

"It wasn't like I planned it, it just happened," she replied. Jolene laughed. "It did."

246

"Come on, you knew what you were doing, I betcha thought about it all the time. It's just us girls here now, Suz. You got him good, didn't you?"

"No, I wasn't trying to…it wasn't about him."

"You were married," she hooted. "He spent more time providing for you than he did admiring you. And you didn't like it."

"You don't understand." Jolene shrugged. "It's not like here, thumping bibles in Bumfuck, North Carolina," she snapped. "It just happened. I made a mistake."

Jolene's irritation rose, the self-pity getting on her nerves. "You made a choice. You knew what you were doing and you didn't care who got hurt."

"I shouldn't have told you."

"Then you got dumped," she continued. "And he upped and died."

"I wasn't dumped," she answered hotly. "Drop it, okay?"

"Look around," Jolene insisted. "Connect the dots, Suz, one way or another we're all held accountable for the choices we make."

"Like putting a seven year old on the back of a tractor?"

Jolene paled. She stood slowly, leaned over, one hand on each arm of Susan's chair. "I finally get to see the real you," she whispered. "Okay, fine. I let my little girl climb up those big wheels most every day with nothing more than a 'Hold on to Grampa and be a good girl.' I helped her up, you hear me, those very same wheels that rolled over her little body and crushed her ribs into her lungs, left her drowning in her own blood. You hear me, I helped her up." She pushed herself away from the chair with so much force that Susan's tipped back. "Top that!"

***

After the bombing in '93 they built a system to boost the capacity of handheld radios inside the towers. A repeater channel it was called. Before they had it, there was only one channel, hundreds of firefighters trying to talk, to listen, to share information. To hear an order to evacuate the building.

There were two buttons required to activate the repeater channel. The first one got pushed. No one remembered to push the second.

Everyone makes mistakes.

Chapter 30: September 5, 2006

He brought work home like always. He was cranky, distracted, not inclined to talk. She should have seen the warning signs but she was caught up.

"I'm going to quit my job." Sean didn't look up, laptop open, papers spread across the kitchen table. *"I think I wanna go to school."*

"Be sure that's what you really want."

"What do you mean by that?"

"I mean that you should make a commitment before we spend the money."

"It's always about the stupid money."

"Don't start, you don't want to start with me tonight," he snapped.

"Be nice if you could..."

"Just some jerk from work, right?" That shut her up. *"That's what you said, right? At that party. What's his name, Tom?"*

Susan flushed, red creeping up her throat. *"I have no idea what you're talking about. I'm going to take a bath."*

"No you're not." He followed her through the kitchen, cornered her by the couch. *"Let's talk. You always want us to talk, let's talk about Tom."*

"What is a matter with you?" Her heart was racing. She tried to step back, bumped into the couch. *"He's a guy at work, a salesman, I told you."*

"What didn't you tell me?" He didn't wait for a reply. *"About the bar, right? Did you just forget to mention you were meeting him in a bar?"*

Susan's throat closed, her mouth dry, mind darting frantically. *"I don't know..."*

"Don't," he shouted. Furious. *"Someone saw you, they saw you!"*

"Sean, it was just a drink," she stammered.

"Why would you need to lie about a drink!" He slammed his fist on end table, rocking the lamp. She steadied it before it fell. *"How do think it made me feel, when he told me. And it wasn't just a drink, he*

didn't even want to tell me, but his wife, his goddamn wife told him he should!"

"Who was it?"

"Yeah, that's important. Are you fucking him?"

"No!" She reached for him. He jerked away. "I should have told you, you're right, I shouldn't have...." She licked her lips. "It was just one time."

"How stupid do you think I am." Dismissing her.

"Sean, don't, I'm sorry, I love you. It was just a drink. I never slept with him, I would never do that," she pleaded. He didn't answer, his back to her. "He flirted with me, that's all. It was...he paid attention to me." He had to understand. He never listened to her! "Maybe you should try it some time!"

He turned, stared. "So this is about me?" Incredulous, almost shrill. "You're out whoring around and it's my fault." He turned without another word, grabbing a jacket off the back of a chair.

"No, wait, please!" She scurried after him. "I didn't mean that. Don't go, please." He shrugged her hand from his arm, still moving. "Sean, it was just one time. I shouldn't have done it. Please," she begged, grabbing at his shirt. "I'm quitting my job. I'll never see him again." She tried to turn him around, he jerked away. "Nothing happened. It was just a drink, that's all. I shouldn't have gone."

He groaned, covered his face with both hands. She stepped close to him. "I love you" she whispered. He stiffened but didn't move away. She leaned her cheek against his back, stroked his arm, tiny kisses on his shoulder. "I'm sorry. I was wrong. I'm so sorry." Over and over. After forever, his hands fell to his sides. "I love you."

He turned. "Do you?"

"Sean, please, it was stupid and I'm sorry. It was just one drink, nothing more."

"One time?"

"I promise."

***

He called again, the man who said he'd seen the dog. She answered the phone this time. He'd tried to catch the puppy but it ran from him. He thought it was sleeping in his barn. He put out some table scraps in a bowl but he couldn't be sure that the coons weren't eating them.

"But they're gone, that's for sure. I'll keep trying, ma'am."

"Thank you."

"Little yeller dog, no collar, right?"

"She had a collar, just no tag."

"Musta lost it then. I'll catch her, don't you worry."

She wouldn't. It wasn't Zoey. Zoey was gone.

A little after ten, Little Charlie showed up to mow the lawn. Old Charlie came to chat, coffee and cake in tow. Dottie had sent along a bag of cinnamon biscuits. "She said to keep 'em in the refrigerator, stay better for when you find her." She put her hands behind her back. He set it on the table. "Curtains look nice," Charlie added, looking around. "How you feeling?"

"Not so good."

"Uh-huh." He took a sip of coffee. "Was sorry to hear about your husband."

"Thank you." She waited, fidgeting. He didn't say anything. She rolled her neck, tried to loosen her shoulders.

He glanced at her. "Something wrong?"

"No. No, it's just...most people they, usually they..."

"What?"

"Nothing."

He didn't push. "Sure you won't have any cake?"

"No thank you."

"Dottie Washington has a way with baked goods." He took another sip. "And coffee too. Can't get..."

"What were you doing?" It burst from her. "When it happened?"

"When...oh, you mean?" He set the cake aside and patted her hand. "Wife and I were talking about that just last night. All those times on the TV, how hard it must've been for you to see it. We all watched it, couldn't not, but I never thought of what it must've been like for y'all. The folks who had to live through it. Wife and I felt badly, I can tell you that." Susan blinked twice. Speechless.

"Have some cake," he coaxed. "Not much that can't be helped by butter cream icing, at least that's what the wife tells me. I swear sometimes she'll pick a fight just so I'll go and get cake to smooth things over."

"Sounds pretty smart," Susan said, trying to smile.

"Married me, didn't she?" He winked.

***

They finished the kitchen floor together, stripping away the last remnants of dark varnish and spattered paint. The floor was calmer, the room changed. Sun streamed through the windows, golden and serene.

"Now you just take that rag and dunk it in the stain there and smear it on." He demonstrated. "You can't do it wrong, it's not like paint. Rub it on and rub it off. That's all there is to it."

"Is this right?"

"That's perfect. You start from here, I'll go over there and meet you at the door."

She'd chosen the cherry. Deep, dark and rich with an undertone of red. It warmed the room. The curtains on the kitchen windows had little flowers, some of them with red centers. A real house. She tried to ignore it, so used to being on the outside looking in, but it called to her. It was a real house. Her house.

"You made a good pick with this one," Charlie said sitting back on his knees. "Look how nice that is."

"It is pretty, isn't it?"

"You wait until we get the shellac on it. Shine like a ruby when the sun hits it, I promise you that."

"What's your wife's name?"

"She goes by Annie, though her given name is Louise. After her grandma. Ann's her middle name." He leaned down, rubbed a spot.

252

"Got one last board here, you best catch up or I'll paint you right into the corner."

"Not fair, you've done this before." Susan dipped her rag and rubbed. He stood, stretching his back and legs.

"Lord I'm feeling my age today. This your husband?" Sean's picture was on the counter. She nodded. "Fine looking man. Not that I'd expected less, pretty as you are. No," he warned, "plain as the nose on my face. And," he paused, eyes twinkling, "I hear tell Jackson might be of the same mind."

"That's the last thing I need." She bent over the floor.

"Could be, you're the only one who knows. Course, there is the other school of thought," he said. "You missed a spot, right there, by your heel."

"What's that?" She dabbed where he pointed. "The other school."

"Well, just an opinion, mind you, but some might think that a person who's been through what you have, well, they deserve a chance at some happiness."

"You mean I shouldn't feel guilty for being alive."

"Don't mean anything but I might point out that you're not the one who died."

***

Patrick had left a message on the machine. She cringed at the sound of his voice, the message sandwiched among the reporters and dog finders and Maggie and her mom.

"Susie, sweetie, I saw you on the news. Hated to hear about your dog. I'm sure you've found her by now but I worry about you, honey, still got dark circles under your eyes. Why don't you come up and visit? It would do me good to see you. We all miss you." A pause. "There's a memorial for the anniversary. I reserved you a seat, just in case you want to come. Be good to have you."

Show up for Sean, message received. She might as well tell him now.

"Hello, Paddy?"

"Susie, sweetheart, so good to hear your voice. Mary, it's Susan."

"Hi Susan," Mary called from the background.

"How are you, darlin', did you find your dog?"

"Not yet, but we're still looking. Everyone says we'll find her."

"You listen to them, honey."

He chattered for a while, telling her about the grandchildren, a neighborhood feast, the new priest at church who just about put everyone to sleep. Finally she got to it.

"Paddy, I can't come for the ceremony."

"Ahh Suzie, are you sure?"

She paused, not sure she could do it. Their common bond had always been off limits, by her decree. She took a deep breath. "Remember that day Sean took us to breakfast after mass and did the nun imitation? What was her name? You remember?"

Of course he did. He remembered it all, held it special and dear. Not like china in a cabinet, for ceremonies or special occasions. Not boxed up and packed away and moved from place to place. Everyday memories, he cherished them. He kept Sean alive.

"...so many times," he laughed. "His mother was always getting called to the school. That boy, if he wasn't plugging up the toilets, he was kissing girls in the coat room. More novenas said for him than all the souls in purgatory." Abrupt stop. The novenas had paid off way too soon.

"I miss him too."

"He's with his mother now." His voice cracked. He was old, she realized. An old man, aged further by the loss of his only son. She heard a raspy breath, a fit of coughing.

"Susan?" It was Mary.

"Is he okay?"

"Hold on a minute. I want to go outside," she whispered. "He's been sick."

"Is he all right?"

"It's his heart. But I'm glad you called. He thinks about you a lot, and I didn't have any way to reach you."

254

"I'm sorry."

"I know you're moving around, but it would be nice if you could call him once in a while," she added, frosty. "He shouldn't have to lose both of you." Susan didn't answer. "He had me send you a box, after he saw you on the news. Just open the package when it comes and call him. It's important to him, Susan."

"Mary, I don't..."

"Get over yourself for once. He's an old man."

"I'll try."

"Don't try, do it," she snapped. Clearly not a fan. "And if you can't do it for him, then you can damn well do it for Sean. Because you owe him, Susan, and you and I both know why." The phone slammed down.

The secret wasn't a secret after all.

***

Jack sat in the kitchen in the dark. Becky was asleep, long legs tangled in the sheets, auburn hair tossed across the pillows. They'd argued heatedly at first, then slowly worked it out. Everything was fine now. So why was he in the kitchen, instead of in the bed, playing at human spoons, tucked up against her, fingers splayed across her belly. He couldn't sleep, that was all. It wasn't anything more than that. He opened the refrigerator, looked around, closed it. Opened it again, stood there, looking.

He kept thinking about what his mother said, that if you couldn't accept all of someone, it probably wasn't love. He did love her, he just didn't always like her, or at least like the things she did. That wasn't something to end a marriage over. He closed the refrigerator. It wasn't ending. It was starting. Their new beginning.

Susan had sat on that stool, right there. He went and sat on the other one. That scraped up face, the dirty hair. The fingers always moving, picking, twisting. Not so pretty. Her frailty took his breath. Even remembering, he felt the urge to call her. Hear her voice. It was instinctive, that's all, part of being a man, coded into the DNA. Defend and protect. That was why he was out here thinking about her.

He wasn't thinking about her. He just couldn't sleep.

He wondered about calling her. Just to check in, make sure she was okay. She'd be up. But what would he say? She'd left without a word the night before. Suddenly, gently, separating herself from his arms. She'd touched his cheek, let her fingertips run over his lips. Electric. He couldn't explain it. Then she slipped away and he heard the door close behind her. Strangely final. It left him restless. Discontent.

He didn't have a thing for her. He just liked that Becky was jealous, for once the shoe was on the other foot. That's all this was, keeping Becky on her toes. That's why he wasn't going to call her, it wasn't right to use her. Just for that. That's why he was thinking about her, he should apologize. He was married, or at least he would be. Becky was back.

He should call her, tell her he was sorry. That he shouldn't have kissed her and that he hoped she'd be okay. He remembered kissing her. Like falling, the sadness inside her endlessly deep. He felt such a compulsion to grab her, to catch her, keep her safe, his whole body charged. It was pity, compassion. Nothing more.

Maybe he should just call her now, get it over with. He didn't need that kiss hanging between them. It could be awkward. Sooner or later they'd bump into each other. If she stayed. She might not stay. That hadn't occurred to him until right now. He got up, went back to the refrigerator, fingers on the handle, thinking. She had no ties here, there was no reason to stay. Except the dog and sooner or later, if the dog wasn't found...

He paced a circle around the kitchen. If she left, he'd never get to tell her, to explain. She'd be gone, no trace, nothing but pictures of a puppy on a fence. He should call her.

"Baby?" Becky's voice floated down the hall, throaty with sleep. "Where are you?"

***

"Zoey, come on. Zoey." She called every time she went outside.

The night was so dark. The stars were so bright, just a sliver of a moon.

Of course Sean would have told someone. Of course it would be Mary. They had always been close, Mary and Sean. They were the two oldest, her like her mother, him like his dad. They watched out for each other as kids, as adults. They talked once a week at least. Susan couldn't believe that she hadn't thought of it before.

She sat on the grass, staring at the sky. Heaven was up there, or so Patrick thought. Jolene too. Mrs. Wyle. They all took such comfort from it.

Bin Laden believed, Atta too, all of them, even Waleed. Was Allah enough when the plane started to dive, she wondered, looking up to the stars. "Did you worry, even for a second, that you might not go to heaven, that there might not even be a heaven?"

Sean believed in heaven. Hell too.

"Waleed," she whispered. "Where did you go?" Was he with the angels, all the promised virgins? Or burning in hellfire for all eternity? Maybe he was just nothing. Gone, vanished, done.

Sean would hate that.

Chapter 31: September 6, 2006

They were supposed to shoot the planes down, they just couldn't find them. It wasn't clear who was supposed to know or who was in charge. There were so many agencies, so many chiefs in charge. They rarely played in the same sandbox. It was a hell of a time to learn.

Almost forty minutes after American Flight 11 had hit the North Tower, the FAA was telling NORAD that it was heading for Washington. There was a plane, but not that one. No one was concerned about American Flight 77. The plane had fallen off the radar in Indianapolis, but the controllers there hadn't been informed about the other planes. They assumed it was a mechanical error, a radar problem, nothing outside the norm. So no All Points Bulletin was issued. The plane flew unhindered for more than a half an hour before Dulles air traffic controllers found it on their radar. A National Guard cargo plane that had just taken off was diverted to investigate and got there in time to watch Flight 77 dive into the Pentagon.

Now the government stepped up their game. United Flight 93 was the wild card, missing in action. Even as it crashed and burned in Shanksville, the President, fresh from an elementary school in Florida, had authorized shooting it down. They thought the plane was sixty miles out of DC, FAA officials mistakenly reporting on a simulation instead the actual radar data. The Vice President issued the order. Any plane, all planes that won't divert on command. Shoot them down.

But despite all that had happened, there was second guessing all along the chain of command. The military, where following orders is drilled into every raw recruit, did not comply. The fighter jets flying overhead were never told to shoot. Identify tag and tail, that's all. If the passengers hadn't taken the plane and forced it to the ground, no one would have stopped it. The Vice President was pissed.

***

"You mad?" Jolene asked, standing at the screen door.
"Kind of."

"Me too." They both waited. Neither apologized. "You gonna let me in?"

She went straight to the bathroom, not a word about the floor. Susan checked the computer, no news on the dog. Jolene went in and out of the house, looking for the shut-off on the water, getting tools, not saying a word. It went on until almost ten, the only voices from reporters leaving their messages on the machine. Finally she came and stood in the doorway. "I gotta go to Lyman's, get some stuff. Be good if you could call over there, give 'em a credit card or something. I wasn't planning to hafta ..." she stopped, rolled her neck. "I don't got the money to put upfront." Cheeks slightly pink.

"No big deal," Susan murmured, eyes on the monitor.

The lack of concern was a match to gasoline.

"Course not, no big deal, no big goddamn deal! Nothing is, if it ain't about you!" Jolene stomped to the front door. "You know what, you don't have a clue, sitting here, all caught up in yourself, you got no clue," she shouted.

"Stop yelling, I'm not ..."

"There you go, that's just what I mean." The cooler she was, the hotter Jolene got. "'What's got you so upset, Jolene?' That's what a normal person would say, but not you, you're not gonna and you don't wanna, and that's the end of that! When did you become queen of the world, huh?" She opened the door, slammed it shut, stormed back to the table.

"Here's a news flash for ya, shug. Not everybody's got the money you got, some of us are working our damnedest just to keep a roof over our heads. We don't have the luxury of sitting around all day playing on the internet, money to throw around so we can have what we want the second we think of wanting it," Jolene yelled, so mad her eyes were tearing.

"Some of us can't even pay to keep what we got, much less get what we need, or what our boy needs, because he's in college and he doesn't understand that his momma and daddy are...are doing their best, the best...best they..." Her voice cracked. She burst out crying,

259

hard, wracking sobs that shook her body. She bent over, trying to catch her breath, arms around her middle.

Susan hovered beside her, uncertain. She tried to remember back when she had a different life. Jolene continued to weep, trying to stop, long hiccupping breaths to no avail. She'd held it all in for so long, so hard to get it back in the box once it was out.

"Jolene," Susan murmured. "Don't cry." Jolene didn't stop, couldn't stop, even when Susan finally, gingerly wrapped her arms around her. Letting her cry it out. Nobody was mad anymore.

***

More cars had been broken into over in Stallings Crossing subdivision near Bunn Lake. Second time in a month. It was the topic over coffee. Big Jim, Bubba, Billy, Dick and Skeeter, opinions flying. Ben walked in as the debate was heating up.

"Don't mean it's kids," Big Jim argued. "I'm telling you there's a whole bunch of spics living over off route 97 that got…"

"Nate Parsons' boys are running wild all the time," Bubba insisted. "Already been caught once trying to get into cars at the Wal-Mart."

"Ben," Dick called. "Jack ever find out who messed with his car?"

"That was different," Big Jim answered. "I saw one of those mex girls the other day, got more kids than I can count. How you think they're feeding 'em?"

"Government money, we're paying for it, that's how. Paying through the nose to keep them foreigners in our country, that's what." Skeeter threw in his two cents.

"Don't even speak English." Bubba spat.

"I still say it was kids," Dick replied. The bank had signs in English and Spanish. "Ben, you hear about Stallings Crossings?" Ben poured sugar into his coffee.

"A person's car ain't safe in their own driveway, don't know what this country's coming to," Skeeter griped.

"That's what I mean, all those damn Mexicans, filling up the schools, living off food stamps."

"Billy, you got some working for ya, ain't that right? Should be hiring Americans."

"Find me some that work for cheap and I will."

"See, right there. That's what's wrong with this country."

The door opened and three men came in from a landscaping truck. Hispanic. Everyone shut up. Ben stepped aside as they filled their coffee cups, browsed the aisles for chips and sweet rolls so preserved they could sit on a shelf for years.

"So how's Cordelia doing, Ben?" Dick wasn't one to let a silence sit. "She feeling okay?"

"Keep your eyes pealed," Big Jim muttered to Skeeter. Loud enough to be heard. The men knew enough to ignore it. Escoja sus batallas.

"Don't take no debit cards," Skeeter called out. "Cash money, that's all."

"No," Ben said.

Bubba turned. "No what?"

"She's not feeling okay." Stirring the coffee like there was no tomorrow, the plastic stirrer stick trembling in his hand.

***

"Feel like a total fool," Jolene grumbled, wiping her nose, still sucking up tears that tried to run free.

"Yeah, well, remember who you're talking to."

She choked on a laugh. "Don't make me laugh when I'm trying to be miserable."

"Why didn't you tell me that you needed money?"

"It's not the kind of thing that folks..."

"But people talk to their friends," Susan interrupted. "We're friends. You could have told me, I can fix it."

"You're not gonna fix it."

"Why not?"

"You're not gonna fix it," Jolene repeated.

"You're just like Sean," she said, shaking her head. "Like money is important."

"Trust me, you ain't got any, it's real important."

"Of all the things…I've been broke, I know how it…" Susan bit her lip, frustrated at finding the words. "Look, money is the least of it, between us. What we share, I mean, I've told you things I haven't told anyone. You talk to me like nobody else does."

"I shouldn't be so judgmental, I'm…."

"No, you talk to me like I'm real. You say what you think. Instead worrying that I'm gonna break apart every single second."

"Suz…" Jolene started.

"Don't be dumb, I can help you."

"I'm not taking money from you. And that's that," Jolene added.

"Really," Susan replied. "So who's crazy now?"

***

Jack stowed the last of it and slammed the trunk. He handed Miz Tyler the invoice, she offered him some sweet tea while she wrote the check. He drained the glass, thanked her again and got on his way. Last call of the day. Before he realized it, he was driving toward his mother's, so normal to point the car that way around supper time. Go to the house, uninvited, always welcome, something always smelling good. His stomach growled just thinking about it.

She'd be busy, order him to wash his hands, get out of her kitchen. He'd join his father, both glad to be banished, to have food made for them. She delighted in their pleasure. Her chicken-fried steak with pepper gravy, not the white gravy, but real chicken gravy, golden rich, it melted in the mouth. There would be homemade coleslaw, crunchy, tart with vinegar dressing. Mashed potatoes, zucchini squash, all hot and buttered. Maybe black-eyed peas. Or snap beans. All piled high on a plate, biscuits in a basket. She'd slap his hand as he reached, reminding him to bow his head. Give thanks to God. For what? She was wasting away, killing herself in the process. It was so like her to do it for them.

He ended up at Susan's. He told her he was there to pick up flyers, to check in about the dog. Her face was looking worse, the scratches gone to scabs.

"Here you go," she said, coming back with a Coke, a handful of flyers. "I've got some cake, if you want some. Mr. Lyman brought it."

"How did you hurt your face?" His phone buzzed in his pocket. He knew who it was. He didn't answer. "Look, about the other night…"

"You don't have to be nice."

"What if I want to? Is that a problem?"

"Why are you here?"

And then he was talking. He told her about his mom, how she was before and how things were now. Memories and stories, good and bad, all wonderful now. Desperate to hold on to them. How worried he was about his father, his mother's sacrifice. His fear. All so jumbled, hard to see the right thing, much less know how to do it.

"I don't know what to say. I'm sorry." A wry grimace. "I hate it when people tell me that."

"I probably haven't heard it as many times." Her hand was dangling off the arm of the chair, he wanted to take it, hold it. "Everything is a mess."

"I know."

Four more days, he thought. He wondered how she'd be after it came. How he would be. "I can't imagine my life without…but people say it gets better?"

"It's supposed to. I guess you have to want it to, maybe." She scratched at her neck. "I'm probably not the one to ask."

"Do you miss him?" He stopped, embarrassed at the obvious question. It was needy. To need to know if she was still… She gazed into the yard, profile defined in the dwindling daylight. Straight nose, long slender neck, the slightest lift to her chin. "He was a lucky guy."

"No. He wasn't."

"I didn't mean…"

"I know." She sighed. "I don't think I'm the one to ask about how to handle this," she repeated, trying to smile. "Crazy, remember?"

"Eccentric."

She laughed. "On steroids." Quiet for a second. "Every year it comes. I can't seem to stop it, even if I wanted to...it's like I just have to wait for it to happen."

So many things he wanted to say, none of them enough. "I want so bad to change the ending. For Mom, me, you."

It was so beautiful out here. It felt so right. He reached over and took her hand. She let him, swinging gently between the chairs. Fingers intertwined. His cell phone rang again but he'd turned the volume off.

***

She'd known he was going to kiss her. Just like Tom, just like in the bathroom of that bar, looking in the mirror knowing what she was about to do. Just like Jolene said. Jack had a wife too. But Susan kissed him anyway. More than once. Caught up in the moment, wanting to believe. Nothing changes if nothing changes.

After he left, she went to Wal-Mart to buy something for Maggie's kids. Because Maggie was right. Everyone was right.

She wasn't sure what to buy them. Matt was seven, Maggie said. Zach was four. What did you buy for that. Susan went to the front of the store, looking down the cashier lines. Only two open, Ellie not at either. She'd have to figure it out.

She bought Harry Potter movies and Harry Potter books. Spiderman sheets and Batman sweatshirts. She got markers that glowed in the dark and the paper that made them do it. She found light sabers and Darth Vader masks, a game about baseball, a water gun that shot bursts of over ten feet.

Susan had been hurt when Maggie said she had stopped being friends. But it was true. She sucked up all the love and concern, and gave nothing in return. Everyone so willing to help her, give as much as took. It took Susan to want it and she wouldn't. So comfortable under her rock, all the worried people peering in around the edges. Saving Susan.

She didn't want to be saved, like a spoiled child, an adolescent doing the opposite of what was told. She thought about herself all the time. They made excuses for it. She let go of their lives without so much as a glance back. Not even a flyer on a fence.

She had a sense of entitlement, maybe she always did. A secret fault, nurtured by the infamous nine eleven. *Poor Susan.* She deserved special treatment. Despite her constant attempts to evade, pity was available upon demand. That day, it was the ace up her sleeve. *It's so sad, she's can't seem to get passed it. How could she be expected to remember a little dog when people were being so mean to her? Poor Susan.*

Zoey was all about unconditional love, so rare in human beings, so instinctive in dogs. Anytime of day or night, all Susan had to do was whistle and love came running. Tail wagging, ears flopping. Rampant joy.

She blinked back tears. What was she doing? Thinking she could have friends, make a life. Kiss someone, as if maybe they could…what, start a life? It was a joke! She fumbled the cell phone from her pocket and checked the messages. She left the cart in the middle of the aisle, went to groceries and got a box of soaped-up steel wool. SOS.

Chapter 32: September 7, 2006

The drive to the station was uneventful, if riding with Jolene could ever be considered as such. The news director was brisk, no nonsense. Becky less so when she saw Jolene. Susan insisted. After a huddle with the producers, it was agreed to let her stay. "If you're quiet and can act like a human being," Becky demanded.

Jolene was unfazed. The only thing that shocked her was the blue screen for the weather reports, couldn't believe that the maps weren't really there. "How does he know where to point," she kept asking.

Susan sat passively as the makeup girl fussed over the rash, listened while she told her where she'd been when she heard. One of the cameramen came up to tell her he was from New Jersey. His mom worked in lower Manhattan. For five long hours, he hadn't been able to get through. His mom was all right, stuck in the Holland Tunnel after they closed it down. Susan said she was glad.

"Mrs. Kearney, I want to thank you for being with us today," Becky said. The two of them on set, matching chairs, the Raleigh skyline projected on a fake window behind them. "You were married to Sean Kearney for six years, is that right?"

"Almost seven."

"Susan," she stopped, smiled. Exuding warmth. "May I call you Susan?"

"No."

Her jaw tightened, she made a cutting motion in front of her throat. The red light over the camera went out. "I'd appreciate if you'd work with me here," she said tersely. Royally pissed.

The camera rolled again. Becky walked her through the day, where she was, how she found out, what her initial reactions were. Susan had told it so many times. "It wasn't much different for me than anyone else. I couldn't believe it. I thought it was an accident and then…"

"Where were you when you realized it wasn't?"

"I was on the street when the second plane hit. I was trying to call Sean, to make sure he was okay and..." She paused, squared her shoulders. "But I couldn't get through. The lines were jammed."

"We've heard so many stories of victims calling their loved ones. From the planes, the buildings. Did you talk to your husband before he died?"

"I just told you the lines were jammed."

Becky's interest was peaked by the edge in her tone. "So you never had a chance..."

"This is still hard to talk about it," Susan interrupted, stalling with a sip of water. She wasn't going to stop. "Loss is very complex. A friend of mine and I were talking about that last night. His mother is ill and he's trying to find ways to cope."

Jolene coughed, smothering a laugh. Becky glanced her way, back to Susan, eyes of ice. "It must be difficult, making new friends. All the baggage you're carrying," she said. "I didn't mean that to sound..."

"I know what you mean."

"So did the two of you have breakfast that morning? You and your husband," she added.

"No, not that day."

"But you did usually?' Still sure there was something hiding.

"He went into work really early, sometimes we did and sometimes we didn't." Bringing up Jack had been a mistake. "Are there any other meals you're interested in," she asked politely. One of the crew chuckled behind the cameras.

"So how did you wind up in Wendell? Not exactly a big city." Becky was looking, a wasp buzzing for a place to sting.

"I like the quiet. And the people are really nice."

"And yet tragedy is always so close on your heels. That poor little dog dying and..."

"Cut," Susan said, on her feet. "Cut!" She yanked the microphone off her blouse.

"My goodness, do you still think? I thought...I didn't mean...It's been gone so long. Oh Mrs. Kearney," Becky said. "That was thoughtless of me. I'm so sorry," Becky added, spite sparkling in her eyes.

"Let's finish up," the director ordered. "Get her mike back on."

Susan talked about Zoey, Becky asked about Sean. Finally, she said, "Thank you so much for coming today, Mrs. Kearney. I'm sure everyone is hoping that Zoey comes home." She crossed her legs, leaned forward. "Just one more question. If the lines hadn't been jammed, what would you have said if your husband had called?"

Susan met the camera lens without flinching. "That I loved him, Ms. Howe. What else would there have been to say?"

***

The package sat on the front porch, next to the door. Innocent enough, a medium sized box, a UPS post-it stuck to the side. Jolene carried it inside. The sun had ducked behind the clouds. A storm was building, Indian summer heat driving the clouds to new heights.

"What do you think it is?"

"Sean stuff."

Jolene plopped in the cardboard chair, noticed the empty charger. "Hey where's the phone?"

"In my pocket." Susan squatted down and read the address. Mrs. Susan Kearney, 241 Old Wilson Rd, Wendell NC 27591. She had a sudden urge to call Maggie and tell her where she lived.

***

The lamp caught her by surprise. That Patrick would part with such a precious piece of Sean's boyhood. Hans Solo, Luke Skywalker and Princess Leia with her cinnamon biscuit hair. Little hand-painted action figures glued on a revolving base. Chewbacca, R2D2, C3PO. Darth Vadar locked in a battle of light sabers with Obi Wan Kenobi.

The figures were grubby from tiny fingers. The shade was stiff and brittle, covered with ships and explosions and battle stars. It had sat by his bed until he was too grown up for toys. He remembered it though, had told her how cool it was, the posters he had, the ships and toys. A geek, she teased. And proud of it.

268

"Does it still work?" Jolene plugged it in. The star fights came alive, Princess Leia chased Hans, ray gun in her hand. "That is adorable."

"He loved Star Wars. He used to go on eBay all the time and buy stuff. There was so much of it, collecting dust, I...he took most of it to his office."

"There's a note in here." Jolene held up the envelope. She expected to see Patrick's sprawling hand. Sean's precise penmanship instead. Susan hugged herself and nodded. Jolene opened it up. "It's a letter to his dad," she said, scanning the page. "I'm not really sure why..." She flipped the page over. "Oh." She looked up.

"Read it."

Jolene cleared her throat. "'Remember that girl I told you about? The one from the art show? I'm taking her with me on spring break. Going to Florida for some fun in the sun.' He's got this next in brackets. 'I promise not to get arrested!!!'" She looked up, grinning. "'Suz is the best thing that's ever happened to me, Da. I'm going to marry her and I know you think that's crazy because I haven't known her very long, but she's the one. You'll see, you meet her and you'll see.'" Jolene folded the letter, eyes bright. "The rest is, he just tells him to have a good time on vacation. I can read it if you..."

"They sent him to Ireland, all the kids. For his sixtieth birthday." She stood up and walked to the fireplace. "I don't know if I can do this."

"Up to you."

"I broke his heart," Susan murmured. "He died with a broken heart."

***

"Slippery little rascal," Skeeter grunted.

"Not sure the flap closed right," Billy said. "Don't look the edge caught."

"Ya think? I thought it came down pretty hard."

"Box is empty."

"Yeah." Dispirited. "Not sure why it ain't catching. Gotta figure on it some."

"Wanna beer?"

"Durn thing!" He hit the empty trap with his fist. Billy was bending over the cooler, pulling out a long neck. "Yeah," he called, "pop me one."

***

Susan arranged the pictures he'd sent on the mantel, Tom and Waleed sent to the kitchen. One was of Patrick with Sean when he was little, no occasion that could be noted, just the two of them out in the yard, smiling into the sun. Sean wore a red checked cowboy shirt with fringe across the middle. She'd have teased him unmercifully if he was here.

The second was of the family, a Christmas picture, all the girls and their husbands and children, Susan and Sean crunched together in front of the tree. An ornament, an angel, hung eerily over his head.

The other three pictures were of the two of them. From their wedding. Gazing into each other's eyes, champagne flutes and arms entwined, her veil like a halo. A shot from their honeymoon, Sean and Susan sitting on the side of a boat, flippers on their feet, arms around each other's waist. She wasn't sure where the last one was taken. It might have been at Mary's house, but she didn't recognize the couch. They were lying together, Susan on her side, Sean on his back. Her palm resting on his chest, head tucked under his chin. Both of them watching something on TV. So much more real for being snapped unaware. She closed her eyes, remembering his breathe on her hair.

***

"Go on, take it." Jolene had printed one of the Zoey pictures, a big one, almost life size and cut the puppy from the paper. She held it out, camera in hand. Susan put her hands behind her back. "Take it," Jolene insisted. She did, reluctant to handle the little paper dog. Flat and lifeless. On the side of the road?

"Now hold it up, near your cheek, come on." Jolene raised the camera. Susan didn't move. "Will you just do this? Just hold it up. That's right, tip her tail down a little, like she's licking your face."

"I can't." Susan turned the picture against her chest.

"A person should have pictures of herself with the folks she loves. Not just pictures of them, but them together. I shoulda taken one before, but this will do for now." She coaxed Susan back, positioned the cutout. The flash popped. "One more, just in case."

"Did it come out good?" She didn't really want to see it, but she did.

The picture on the screen played with the eye. The paper puppy tucked under her arm, the angle of the head realistic. The tail and paws were off but if she cropped it right...

"You'll hafta get it off of here," Jolene said handing her the camera. Susan sat at the computer, connected the USB cable to the camera. The picture dumped to the screen.

"I don't have a frame." Staring at the two of them.

"Hold on," Jolene said. She was gone for a minute, to the kitchen. "We can use this." The gold frame, Tom and Waleed. Panic showed on her face. "They're in the drawer, Suz," Jolene soothed. "I didn't hurt 'em."

***

"Thank you for everything."

"I'd stay later but Billy will be whining for supper like a hound on a chain. I expect I'll hafta be cutting his meat before it's all over. There's something to look forward to," she added as they walked to the truck. "You did good today."

"I still have to call Patrick."

"Not today, for today you done good."

"Can you wait one minute? Just one minute," Susan promised, running back toward the house.

Jolene was in the truck, engine running. Susan waved away the exhaust and motioned her to shut it off. "Take your hat off. Okay, push your hair down, it's sticking up."

"What are you on about, girl?" Jolene licked her hand, wiped it across her hair.

"No, the other side, yeah, that's good."

Susan stood beside the truck, next to Jolene's window, bent her knees to be at the right height. "Lean forward a little," she ordered, extending her arm, holding the camera She pushed the button. "Don't move." Pushed it again.

Jolene looked away, turned back, eyes suspiciously bright. "Coulda warned me," she groused, "my hair's gonna look like crap."

"It's a two picture frame," Susan replied. "Suck it up."

***

They held classes in Afghanistan. How to fire guns from motorcycles, close contact combat, night operations. No expense was spared, the curriculum was rigorous and demanding. How much effort did it take to stab a flight attendant? They used computer games to practice. A special course was conducted in Karachi, Pakistan, only two weeks long, specific to the operation. There were all kinds of toys to play with, flight simulators, airline schedules and timetables. They watched movies with hijackings. No popcorn or milk duds, Uzi's resting in their laps.

The games they played helped them to identify gaps in airplane security. How the cabin was laid out, the protocols. Watch the doors when you board, they were instructed. Learn the routine. Who does what. See if the flight attendants bring the pilots lunch. As if anyone eats airplane food.

They were learned English in Karachi, were taught how to read a phone book. An entire operation entrusted to men who had to be taught how to use a phone book. Laughable, until you considered their success.

***

272

"I don't appreciate being embarrassed at my job," Becky snapped. "Helping her friend with his sick momma."

"My mother is sick. I didn't know about your interview." He got himself a soda. "What did you want me to do."

"You could try staying away from her."

"There's no reason to be jealous." He leaned against the counter, slid an arm around her waist. She turned out as smoothly as a square dancer.

"Jealous!" She snorted. "I don't need some Yankee girl throwing herself at my husband. With his consent," she added, under her breath.

"Okay. I won't go over there."

She opened the refrigerator. "Did I not ask you to buy diet Coke?!" She slammed the door. "I thought we agreed to let go of the past, Jack, or is this just a little payback?"

"You're reading too much into it."

"I hope so, because if I'm not..." She let it hang.

"What?" Annoyed. "I'm not much for threats, Beck."

"More like tea leaves, darlin', see into the future."

She flounced toward the living room, long lean legs bare, butt cheeks peeking out from under one of his shirts. His heart didn't race, his breath didn't quicken. It was strange. Feelings flipped as if they were a switch. Or maybe they had been turned off so long his eyes had just gotten used to the dark.

There was nothing about Susan that he couldn't overlook. And so much about Becky that he couldn't stomach. His mother was right, as she mostly always had been.

"What are you smiling about?" Becky stood in the doorway, arms folded.

"Nothing."

"Uh-huh," she replied, eyes narrowing

Chapter 33: September 8, 2006

The itching was getting worse. No more sleep. She walked the house, down and around, and up and around and down. Start again. The day was looming, like a late afternoon storm. She stuck Sean's picture in a drawer, as if to hide him from what was to come. Two steps away, she realized it was the same drawer as Tom's and Waleed's.. Horrified, she pulled it out, hung it on the calendar nail. She counted the days, took a pen, crossed them off again, X, X, X, X, X, X, X, X, careful not to rip the page.

She missed Waleed. She got his picture out of the drawer, duct taped it to one of the cabinets. It was crooked. She didn't fix it. She stood in front of the open drawer, staring down at Tom. All alone. She knew what belonged in there with him but couldn't make herself go get it.

In the living room, Sean's lamp sat on the mantle, a soft glow in the dark room. The little characters going round and round. Round and round.

"Atta, Suqami, Alomari, AlShehri, AlShehri," she murmured. "Alghamdi, Nami, Hanjour, Rashid." Round and round. She itched her neck. "Patrick, Mary, Helen, Gina, Ellen, Peggy, Katie, Sean. Sean, Patrick, Mary, Helen, Gina, Ellen, Peggy, Katie. Susan." It always ended with Susan.

***

Bin Laden had been the seventeenth child of fifty-seven children. Who could fathom that? Lost in the sea of siblings, he rose above them all in his own mind, a Messenger, or so he claimed. They were embarrassed by him, they said, his father's company brought almost to its knees. It was hard not to feel sorry for them, his family, their own names suddenly a burden they never asked to carry. Still she had to wonder, how could they not have known?

Takfiri, that was the word other Muslims used to describe Bin Laden's fundamentalist followers. It meant 'those who define other

Muslim's as unbelievers.' It was Bin Laden's constant refrain, if you weren't with him, you were against him. And it didn't matter who you were or what faith you followed.

First and foremost, he was a business man, with investment firms and construction companies. He skimmed funds so neatly he put Enron to shame. He was a man who longed to be king. But there are no kings in Islam. He tried his best to get rid of the ones in Saudi Arabia. He barely escaped and made another home in the Sudan, building alliances with other terrorists, a network of fanatics, feverish in their pursuit of Allah. They weren't opposed to his money. But something went wrong, he was nearly assassinated there too. He ran back to Afghanistan, where he would rise to glory. By 1996, he proclaimed himself ready to "cut off the head of the snake."

***

She went outside and gathered sticks from the yard. It took three trips to get the wood to the hearth. She built a teepee, smallest sticks on the inside, stronger, thicker around the rim. Then she went and got the picture of Tom. She looked at him for a long time. "This is done," she said, repeating his words. *Like it never happened.* She knelt down and carefully tucked him in between the sticks.

The match caught on the first try. Fascinated, she watched the fire nibble at his face, eat away his chin, red and black bites of his hair. He fought back, glossy finish hindering the flames. She threw on a stick, way too big, the teepee collapsing. The building falling. The fire struggling. She could still his face.

The room was full of boxes. BOOKS. She ripped it open, Tuscan Kitchen on top. The jacket was battered, a glob or two from some previous cooking endeavor hardened on the spine. She ripped it in half, half again, fed it to the flames.

She opened the book. Arista alla Fiorentina. A pork loin, dotted with herbs. She'd never made it. She ripped pages out, threw them on the fire. He was below the flames, the paper had to go underneath. She ripped another page. Tortellini al brodo. Peperoni arrotolati. Zuppa di

Pane. Crumbled. Stuffed. Tom finally burning in earnest. Like he never even happened.

She had more books. The Secrets of Baking, the Joy of Cooking. No one to cook for. The fire roared, rude, loud, the heat shoving its way into the room, flames licking the edge of the hearth. Hot enough to singe her eyebrows, the smell of burnt hair so distinctive.

The flames melted plastic pens and CD cases, gobbled up tax returns, sponges and dish rags. The bath towels fought harder, almost smothering the fire. She watched it choke, dense smoke, strangling on the terry cloth. She didn't intervene. The flames burned hotter and higher.

Two wicker baskets, an old checkbook, a handful of pennies in a baby food jar. The glass exploded. She turned her face just in time. Shards like shrapnel, the copper pennies turned the fire blue and green. She opened another box. A TV remote, magazines, Barron's and Kiplinger, pages marked with post-its. Articles that Sean had read or wanted to remember. Whoosh!

She wanted all of it gone.

She grabbed a box, ripped off the top folds threw them into the blaze. What the hell, she thought, tossing the rest of the box on the pile. The flames ran up the sides, foreplay, rippling waves caressing a cardboard beach. MISCELLANEOUS on the side, corners beginning to brown. Then it registered.

That was *the* box. The manila envelope still inside, its red string looped around the button at the top. She lunged forward in a panic, the fire circling her wrist, arm jerking back. The corners of the envelope were turning black. She grabbed a stick and clawed at the box until it tumbled out, past the hearth, on the floor, the fire now free of the flu. The envelope slid forward. She dragged it free with her feet, stamping out the red teeth that had just begun to chew. The box was still on fire, quivering heat. She sat on the floor, hugging the envelope to her chest, and kicked the box back into the flames.

Some things can't be denied.

***

Ben used to be a sound sleeper. When Jack was a baby, he rarely heard his son cry, or felt his wife get out of bed. It was different now. He was on alert, a sentry, eyes snapping open at every little noise. 2:42 AM said bright red numbers on the digital clock.

She was retching, leaning over the side of the bed, the bucket on the floor. Her body so thin, so battered, he could see every bump on her spine through the cotton of her night gown. No scarf now, the bare, bald head exposed.

His arms went under her, supporting her shoulders, holding her as she vomited. So little in her belly, not much more than bile. When she was done, he settled her back on the pillows, tucked in the blankets. She was spent, barely a squeeze for his fingers. Beyond tired. It was killing him. Watching it kill her.

He left the room, went to the bathroom to wet a cool cloth. His face was reflected in the mirror over the sink. He couldn't let her go. He wouldn't. He loved her too much. Blinking back tears, he stared at himself. Too much or not enough? He gripped the sides of the sink, shuddering with silent sobs. He raised his head and took a deep breath. He loved her. He did.

Back in the bedroom, he wiped her chapped lips with the washcloth. Her eyes opened, so innocent without their lashes. Eyebrows long gone. He smiled down at her, his heart breaking.

"It's done, baby" he whispered. "You don't have to do this anymore."

***

She was out of Meow Mix, off to Wal-Mart at four a.m. She found the cat food, tried to retrace her steps, get all the things for the boys that she'd left the night before. When she got to the checkout, Ellie wasn't there again. The girl behind the register was younger, with orangey-yellow hair, roots a dull brown. She wore a blue vest with smiley face buttons scattered across an ample chest. She didn't smile, didn't comment, just scanned. The bar code on the Meow Mix was messed up.

"Couldn't pick up one with a tag," the girl muttered. "Price check," she bellowed into the mike. A heavy sigh.

"Have you seen Ellie tonight?"

"Nope." She picked at the skin around her thumbnail.

"Do you know who I mean," Susan persisted. "Ellie, tall, older?"

"Why would I be saying no if I didn't know who you meant?"

"You need a price check?" An assistant manager appeared behind her shoulder.

"Yea, this lady picked up one that isn't marked." Disgusted.

"I'm sorry, ma'am, we'll get you a price right away." She shot the cashier a glance. The girl yawned, a letter tattooed on each finger to spell the word L-O-V-E.

"Excuse me, but is Ellie working tonight?"

"Ellie? Oh, no. She doesn't work here any more."

"What do you mean? What happened?"

"I'm not really at liberty to discuss that, ma'am. Kristine, you finish ringing her up while I get this taken care of."

Kristine rolled her eyes. Work was so annoying.

***

Her last name was Harrigan. Susan used the computer to look up the number. More Harrigan's than expected – no idea where she lived. She woke two people up and got machines on three others. Barely seven a.m. None of them were Ellie. She dialed again.

"Hello?" It was her. Susan was speechless. "Hello? Well, good morning to you too," she added tartly before she hung up the phone.

There was an address with the number. It took a while to find the road. Susan missed the house on the first pass. It was a trailer, set back off the street, behind another house, looking as if a tornado had flung it down in the far back yard. Cinder block steps and dirty beige flashing hiding the underneath, curling up on one corner.

There was a Ford sedan in the driveway, old enough to have the gear shift on the steering wheel. A few yards away, a red and yellow plastic slide sat next to a dirt pile. Some doll clothes and a battered

Playschool kitchenette on the sparse grass. A dog slept, tied to a tree, surrounded by a circle of smooth hard dirt. It didn't bark, it didn't move.

Susan hesitated at the foot of the steps, feeling like an idiot now that she was here. Then a little girl dressed in pink Wal-Mart pants and a flowered shirt, her hair caught up in pigtails, came out of the door.

"Nonnie, there's a lady," she piped.

Ellie stepped out, pulling the child to her legs, an instinctive mother move, her long bony fingers spreading across the girl's chest. One side of her face was misshapen, a black eye just starting to go green, purple knot on her cheek bone. There were bruises around her neck.

"Miss Susan!" She let go of her granddaughter, put a hand to her throat. "Lord, I thought you was child protective."

"Ellie, my god, what happened to you?"

Clearly she had forgotten. "It's nothing, took a tumble down the steps that's all." Her eyes darting.

"Poppie says Nonnie's dumb," the little girl added. "Dumb, dumb, Nonnie."

"You get in the car, tootsie pop, we'll be late for school." She gave the child a pat on the rump and handed her a brown paper bag. "Get along now."

"Who did this to you? Did your husband do this to you?"

"Miss Susan, what are you doing here?"

"I...I just, you weren't at work and they said that you weren't working there anymore and I..."

"A person's allowed to quit a job last I knew."

"Right, I know, but... I just...what about the WIC?"

"No offense, Miss Susan, that ain't your affair." She brushed past her. Susan caught her sleeve.

"Ellie, please. He beat you, this isn't..."

"I said this is not your affair." She pulled her sleeve free and got to the door of the Ford. There was no car seat. The child sat in the front, walking her fingers along the dashboard, singing to herself.

"We need to call the police. I'll help you, I prom…"

Ellie whipped around. "Police! Are you outta your mind," she hissed. "You think anybody's gonna leave this child here with me if they see this?" She pointed to her face. "No, that's right, they won't and you can think what you like but she's better off here than where she come from."

"Please let me help you."

For just a second, the hard eyes softened. Then the face that knew better slid back into place. "We ain't all high an' mighty rich ladies from New York, some of us just gotta make do with what we're given. Make do," she repeated. "I'll thank you to stay outta my personal business." Chin up, dignity showing. Susan stepped back, nodded slowly. "Now I gotta get her to school, so I'd appreciate if you'd move your car."

"Ellie," Susan called. The woman didn't turn. "Wal-Mart's not the same."

"Hope you find your dog," she replied, sliding behind the wheel.

***

She heard the door close. "Hi honey," she called. He didn't answer. She got up and walked into the kitchen. "Are you hungry? I was thinking I would make that Tuscan chicken thing, the one with the rosemary and peppers?"

He sat down at the kitchen table. A long manila envelope in front of him. No laptop. "Is something wrong?" He didn't answer. "Sean, you're scaring me." Now he looked up. Something in his face, something bad. Hand to her throat. "Oh my god, is it Paddy? Did something happen?"

"Just once." He picked up the envelope, slammed it on the table. "One time," he said.

"Sean, what are you…"

"I promise," he mocked. He unwound the red string from the button on the top of the flap. He pulled out a paper, pushed it across the

table. "Read it," he said. She didn't move. He slammed his palm on the table. "Out loud," he demanded.

Her knees were shaking. She took a step forward.

"Read it," he repeated, words hissing through clenched teeth.

She picked it up. Dear Tom, it said. All the air left her lungs. "Sean..."

"Read it," he roared.

She dropped the email. "Let me explain."

"Explain? Fine, explain this!" He didn't even have to glance at the paper. "'I want to feel your lips, your skin, to breathe your breath.'" He folded his arms across his chest, cocked his head. "So?"

"Sean..."

"I'm waiting."

"I can't talk to you when you're like this."

He laughed. "That's rich. Fucking classic!" He picked up the email. "Here's one, 'If you will only give me another chance, Tom.'" He mimicked her voice. "Or this one, this was good too. 'I can't even remember how dull my days used to be.'"

"Stop it!"

"Or my personal favorite, love, and lust, Susan."

She grabbed her purse from the counter and started for the door. "If you can't talk calmly, this conversation is over."

"You don't get it, do you? Everything's over!" She froze, hand on the knob. "Say good bye to the gravy train." She spun around, shock plain on her face. "What did you think I would do?"

He strode back to the table, picked up the envelope, pulled out thick folded papers. Blue on the outside. Legal papers. "Read it and sign it." Her heart beat so fast she thought it would explode.

"What did you...I'm not signing anything. This is crazy!"

"You're a liar, a liar and a tramp."

She started to cry. "I can't believe you ..."

"Don't you dare! Don't you fucking dare." He tossed the papers on the counter and walked out of the room. She ran after him.

"I told you I was sorry. I made a mistake."

281

"Just one time, right? Just one drink. Bullshit!" He picked up the mug she'd left on the coffee table and flung it against the wall. It shattered, coffee splattered across the wall like brown blood. "You make me sick."

"Sean, we have to talk. You can't just get a divorce without even talking about it."

"I should be so lucky. They're separation papers," he said. "You've got a week to get out." She gasped. He smiled. Gruesome. "Yeah, that's right. You want any money, that's how it's gonna go."

"Sean, please don't..."

"How's it feel," he interrupted, "getting screwed by someone you trust."

"Please, I know what I did was wrong."

"Before you fucked him or after?" He slammed the bedroom door. Susan sank on to the couch, lips as white as her face.

***

She headed for Dottie's. It wasn't right, she had to find Jolene, they had to do something.

Dottie was pouring coffees for the ladies from the Mortell Outlet. A flyer for Zoey was taped on the back of the cash register.

"That dog hasn't been found yet, it isn't going to be found," Donna was saying. "Never had a tag, you know. My grandson lost his dog, didn't have a tag, told him and told him but..."

"Hush your mouth, Donna Mayfield," Dottie snapped.

"Five hundred dollars for a dog," she muttered.

"Sound jealous to me. What you think, Betty Jane, sound that way to you?' The customary nod. "So what bothers you most, that you ain't got five hundred dollars or nobody who'd spend it if you went missing?

"Dottie Washington, I don't care for..."

The door opened, a little too hard, hitting the wall. Susan stepped just inside, one hand on the door frame. The first time she'd been back. "Is Jolene here?"

"If it isn't the hundred dollar dog girl," Donna muttered.

282

"Been and gone." A formidable glare in Donna's direction.

"Do you know where she went?"

"What do I look like, her momma? Yankees," Dottie muttered.

"Dear." The nice woman from Mortell tottered over, touched Susan's arm. "I wanted you to know how sorry I am, about your husband and all."

"What husband," Donna demanded.

"Don't you watch the TV?" Dottie switched back to Susan's side.

"I watch my shows. I like that Murder She Wrote."

"Hasn't been on in a hundred years!"

"We got cable," Donna informed her. "I didn't hear anything about a husband, but the dog didn't have…

"My husband died in the World Trade Center," Susan interrupted. "On September 11th, I'm sure you've heard of that." Donna flushed.

"Yes and we are so sorry, dear," the nice one said, trying to keep everything nice.

"Well, how's a person supposed to know," Donna huffed. "It's not like I could know about it."

"Be surprised what you learn if you stop talking long enough to listen," Dottie replied.

The two of them gathered up their purses, coffees, heading for the door. "How was I supposed to know," Donna was whining. "Nobody told me."

"Do you know where she's working today?

"And why would I know that?"

"If you see her, ask to call me please?" She was out the door, heading for the car.

"Hey! You there, hey!"

She turned. Dottie stood in the door. Susan had never seen her out from behind the counter. Her ankles were swollen beyond recognition, a solid line from calf to foot. Frayed blue slippers on wide flat feet.

"I never had a chance to say, well, you know, I wish I'd been paying more attention that day. Shoulda seen her. Caught her. Felt real bad."

"Zoey was crazy about you."

"Yea, well." Her lips twisted. "Somebody had to teach the little mutt some manners. Can't count on a Yankee for that."

***

Jolene's Nextel rang. She cursed at the phone, on her belly in the dirt under the porch. "What! Oh hey Suz." She listened for a minute. "Who? I don't know what…what did you say? Listen, I can't barely hear ya and…damn!" She slapped at a centipede crawling over her arm. "Big sucker, whoa. What? Look, hold on, let me get outta here and I'll call ya back."

"Babysitter, that's all I am, between her and Billy, like I got nothing better to do," she grumbled, backing herself out, dirt and god knows what else up under her shirt and pants. She got out, shook herself and called back. "I can't come right now," she said, "if this porch don't get painted today, Lucas is gonna mess me around when it comes to the money," Jolene said. "Can't blame him, between you and me, Billy's screwed up just about every nail and board in the floor," she added. "Hey, why don't you come here? I could use some help painting."

"I don't know how to paint."

"I don't like asking but you're the only person I know who ain't got a job already, cept Billy of course and he's why I gotta ask in the first place. Fishing! The man just up and goes fishing. Him and Skeeter, I'm saying! The two of 'em, a perfect set," she added.

"I don't know how to paint," Susan repeated.

"Not like its brain surgery."

It was a little past eleven, heat working up to its peak, when Susan pulled in the driveway behind Jolene's truck. She didn't see anyone. "Hello? Jolene?"

Her head popped up from a hole in the porch floor. "Thank god, the cavalry has arrived. Hot as heck under here." She climbed out, wiping sweat from her forehead, shirt wet on the arms and neck.

"I brought some soda."

"That's my girl." Jolene took the can, pulled off her hat and wiped it across her forehead before taking a drink. "The paint and brushes are right over there. Use the gray on the slats and the white on the posts." Before Susan could speak, she added, "Shake the can, give it a stir with one them sticks. Use that small brush there on spindles. We'll put that darker gray on the floor, if I can ever fix the mess that man made."

"How did Billy get in the construction business?"

"Who says he is? Lord, look at this, he's using quarter round!"

Susan shook the paint can and opened up the gray. "Do you know Ellie Harrigan?"

"Harrigan, you mean Big Jim Harrigan? Got a doublewide just this side of Zebulon?"

"I don't know, is his wife's name Ellie?"

"Not sure about his wife, but he's gotta a wild daughter, a real nightmare."

"That's the one."

"Girl's outta control, shoot, she was cooking up drugs in the trailer she was renting from the Tyler's, you might have heard me mention them. No? Well, anyway, she damn near blew the thing sky high. Think she's in jail now, but I'm not sure." She stopped to push a floorboard into place. Bam, bam, went the nail gun. "Why you asking?"

"His wife works at Wal-Mart."

"And…?"

"Well, she wasn't there and so I…" She hesitated. "I went to find her, at her house and he's hitting her, Jolene. Her face is all messed up, I mean, really bad, and she's got the little girl, from her daughter and…I think her husband beats her up.

"Big Jim's no pussycat, that's for sure. Never did care much for him."

"You know him?"

"They all hang out over at the store. Skeeter's place, where Billy always disappearing to? In Pilot, at the flashing light right after the trailer park," she added. "Every morning, the bunch of 'em collect there like dust bunnies under a bed. 'Bout as useless too."

"She wouldn't call the police."

"Wouldn't do no good." Jolene pressed the nail gun. Bam, bam!

"How can you say that!" Susan slathered paint on a spindle, wiped a drip with her finger. "He should be arrested."

"What's the sheriff gonna do? Nothing. She's gonna say she fell and he's gonna get pissed and then she's really gonna be in for it. You said she's got the daughter's girl?"

"Yeah, she was worried that..."

"Thought you was CPS," Jolene said, easing another board into place. Bam. Bam. Bam. "You got drips going all down the side."

"I told you I didn't know how to paint."

"The rags are over there on the back of the truck. Vamanos, muchacha."

"Funny." Susan set the brush down and grabbed a couple of rags. The cell phone in her pocket dug into her belly, the hives reaching down past her navel. She pulled it out, scratching her stomach and checked the messages again.

"I'm starving," Jolene said. "It's after one already."

"Two more spindles and then I'm done with the gray."

"Looks pretty good." Jolene went to the truck, rummaged in a cooler. "I got a chicken sandwich and a ham sandwich. Some macaroni salad too, from the Food Lion." She dug around, looking for a plastic fork. "Thought you didn't use the cell phone."

"I don't."

"You just did. I saw you."

"No I didn't."

"Yes you did. And I can keep this up all day, just so you know." She held out two paper plates. "Chicken or ham?"

"I'll have the chicken." Susan finished the last bit of the spindle and set down her brush. "Somebody has to do something."

"About what?" Through a mouthful of macaroni salad.

"Ellie!"

"Need to mind your own business, Suz. It's between them."

"I'm not afraid of him."

"Should be, ain't one of those things where they call him Big Jim cuz he's little." Jolene took a hit off a coke. "So who were you calling?"

"I wasn't calling, drop it, okay?"

"Can't a person ask a question? You're the one acting all mysterious-like."

"I'm here, I'm painting, could you cut me some slack?"

"Fine, fine with me, you wanna lie about the phone, that's fine. Us being friends and all, but hey fine, that's fine."

"You're getting huffy."

"I am not."

"Definitely are."

"Shut up, I'm not."

"Shut up, you are and..." Susan continued before Jolene could speak. "Just so you know, I can keep this up all day." She raised her soda. "Boo-ha."

"Suz," Jolene replied, breaking into a grin, "good one."

***

He'd left the phone in the car, missed three calls that afternoon. Becky was on point, like a hunting dog that had found a scent. He had to tell her, he would tell her, but not until after the day. Everyone around Susan thought in terms of the day.

He got in the car, knew where he was going. He opened the phone and dialed.

"Hey, it's me."

"Well, back from the dead."

"Sorry, I've been working."

"Really?"

"Yeah, been out over by Archer's Lodge, can't get a signal out there to save your life."

"Really."

"What's up?" Ignore, deny, delay.

287

There was a pause while she decided whether or not to let it go. "I thought we could have dinner, in Raleigh."

"I can't." Before she could speak, "I gotta go see my mom," he lied. "She's not doing so good."

"I know, I'm sorry. So you're going over there." The tiniest of waits. "I can go with you." Well aware of his parent's opinion.

"I don't know…" Jack replied. No explanation needed.

"Fine," she snapped. "Have a nice night." The phone cut out. He looked at it. "You too," he said, starting the engine. Whistling while he drove.

***

"Hey, tell me about Dottie. Who is Betty Jane anyway?"

Jolene laughed. "She's Dottie's husband's momma."

"She's married?" Somehow shocking.

"Not anymore. He's been gone now, like to fifteen years. No, not dead, just gone. Left one morning and never come back. Had his problems that man, always liked a drink or two but then he started messing with other things. Got real bad real fast." Jolene broke off a hunk of brownie, popped it in her mouth. "Right after Alvin left, that's his name, Alvin, Betty Jane turned sick. Hurt her terrible, him doing like he did. Stole her wedding rings, her grandma's gold locket and the TV in her living room. Sold 'em right out from under her and she wouldn't do nothing about it."

"Was he living with Dottie then?"

"When he was home. She was fed up, figured he'd be better off locked up. She and Betty Jane fought like two cats in bag."

"So they didn't like each other?"

"Lord no, like me and Billy's momma," Jolene said. "It was bad, what Alvin did, had everybody in a twitter. And the mess Dottie had to climb out of. Lost her house, everything, moved into a single-wide over at the park."

"Did she have the Coffee Cart then?"

"She didn't have nothing. But she trusted in the Lord and kept putting one foot in front of the other. Took up Betty Jane and brought her along."

"Why?"

"She's family," Jolene replied, surprised. "It's what people do."

***

Ben carried her outside. The sun was behind the trees, dappled deck, daylight and shadow dancing on the boards. The air was fresh, not yet cool but cool was coming. Her last autumn. They sat side by side in the deck chairs, waiting for the sun go down.

He'd tucked her in with a blanket and though she protested that she wasn't cold, how could a person be cold on such a warm day, she kept it snugged around her. He moved his chair closer, so he could touch her. All so special now.

Cordelia had called the doctors. Wanted to do it herself. They had thrown out most of the medications together. She still took something for the pain, but not so much that it made her tired. Life is worth being awake for, she said. He hated that she hurt, but was glad for the time with her.

She hated that his last looks, his last memories of her were of a sick woman with a bald head. Ben tried to understand but he didn't. It wasn't what he saw. He saw the woman he had loved for so many years. Some days, he saw her young, others he saw her old, but he saw her. As if hair would change that, he told her. It made her cry. They both cried on and off, every once in a while tears on one face or another. Sometimes both. It wasn't discussed. Goodbyes are supposed to be sad.

The sun was bright hot gold behind the line of pine trees behind the house. The trees had been there when they moved in. Older now than them combined. He'd put in a few fruit trees, with Cordelia's supervision, those were big now. There was a plot of dirt in the back where she used to have a garden. Peppers and tomatoes, squash, rhubarb. Pumpkins when Jack was a boy so he could run to the back yard and pick one for Halloween. Ben would carve, pretending to let the boy hold the knife. Cordelia would paint the same picture on Jack's face that his father carved on the pumpkin. My jack-o-lantern, she'd say. Ben remembered watching her blink back tears, her heart broken the first year he was too old, too cool, to let her to do it.

He wasn't the one dying and yet all the time now, his life passed before his eyes. Not just big moments, but little times. How she paired his socks. A trip they took to Asheville. The smell of freshly mopped hardwood floors, every Saturday morning. Greens and black-eyed peas on New Years Day. For luck and money.

He ached, all of him ached. He couldn't be left behind. As if she knew, she probably knew, they knew each other so well, she took one hand out of the blanket and reached for his. Her fingers were so cold. "There's Jack," she said.

"I know."

More silence. The sun an inch lower, the color a bit richer. The faintest tint of pink in the clouds. "Ben." He kept his eyes on the sun. "Ben," she insisted. He made himself look. Hurt so raw, always kept hidden. Strong for her. "We'll be together again, you know that." He nodded, throat too choked to speak. "We have an eternity ahead of us. Jesus made that possible." His heart hurt, wishing for the peace she had, it eluded him at every turn.

"Please don't be sad," she whispered, pulling at his hand.

"I can't help it," he whispered back.

"I know," she said. "But I gotta have time to get my hair figured out anyway. Don't think I'm gonna be sitting around heaven with a bald head, do you?"

He laughed to please her. To have the pleasure of laughing with her.

"That's better," she said, settling back in her chair. "And when you see me, make sure you notice, say something nice."

"I always notice," he protested.

"Three weeks later when somebody says something about it first."

"That's not true," he insisted. "I notice."

She rolled her eyes. Just like always. He loved always. It just wasn't long enough.

***

"Susan?" Jack had been so glad to see her car in the driveway. Now he stood at the screen door, looking at her. She made no move to let him in.

"I don't think you should be here."

"I need to talk to you."

"I don't think you should be here," she repeated.

He opened the door. The house smelled of smoke. She was so small, nothing but eyes, the rash clearly getting worse. Bold and blatant, on her arms, her neck. He knew it would be on her breasts, her belly. Ached to stroke the angry skin.. "Susan," he murmured.

"No," she said.

He ignored her. Standing so close, not a finger on her. "What do you need?" She didn't answer. "What," he whispered. She shook her head. "Did I forgive her, that's what you wanted to know. Why?"

"I can't tell you." She trembled.

"Yes, you can. Why?" She stepped away, rolling her neck, her back to him. He waited. She didn't speak. "He would have forgiven you. Whatever you did."

"You don't know."

"I want to."

"No you don't," she said, eyes and nose running. "You don't know me, you don't understand..." She stopped, half-laughed, shaking her head.

"I do understand," he said, realization dawning. "Don't I?"

Her body jerked, not making a sound, just jerked, as if fielding a blow. He tried to take her shoulders, turn her to him. She stepped away. "Susan, he loved you."

"He shouldn't have," she gasped. Each breath a hiccup. "He was so good and I was horrible, I was...was horr...horrible and he, he, he..."

291

He reached for her, against her will, pulling her close. She thrashed but he didn't let go. He wasn't going to let her go. "He would have worked it out," he said.. "He didn't have time, but he would have." He shifted his grip to her arms, held her out in front of him. "He died before he could tell you."

"No, no, no," she wailed, wrenching away. "I wouldn't listen, I didn't listen." She sank to the floor, he followed suit. It took forever until she leaned into his shoulder. His arm went around her, the sobs growing softer after a spell.

"You're hurt," he murmured, gently turning up her palm, red circling her wrist. She shook her head. "It's okay, it's going to be okay." She huddled on her knees, big choking breathes.

"I wasn't perfect, you know," he said. "People forget that. Because she made mistakes." Susan shuddered. "But I wasn't listening to what she needed, I took things for granted. I always wanted to be married. I guess I figured I was and that was that. Like nothing else was required. I wasn't perfect," he repeated. "And neither was he."

"Sean was good, I was…"

"He wasn't perfect," Jack interrupted. "You screwed up, okay, I get that. But he loved you. He would have forgiven you."

"Why do you think that," she whispered.

He paused, groping for the right words. "Because I can forgive her, and I don't even love her." Susan lifted her eyes. "For Sean, from Sean, I forgive you too. Because when you love someone, that's what you do."

Chapter 34: September 9, 2006

It was three in the morning. Jack was upstairs. In the bed. Susan paced the dining room, circling the sad cardboard table, the Rubbermaid chairs. The hives were completely out of control. Separate to start, distended rosy tendrils snaking the divide until two became one. Chin and cheeks. She scratched without thinking, fingers constantly on the move from throat to arms to under the breast.

She shouldn't have done it. Shouldn't have let him. Shouldn't have listened, her heart shouldn't have lifted. She shouldn't have loved the way he touched her, or even being touched at all. His hands sliding over her ribs, down the thigh, so gentle, her breasts cradled, cherished, hives and all. The cool of his skin going to sweat, sticking to her own, bodies entwined. His lips, soft and then stronger, from her mouth to her neck to her ear. Sweet whispers in her ear. Such sweet things. She'd forgotten herself, for the first time in years. Lost in him, hope glimmering on the horizon. Light at the end of the tunnel, surely not another train. Her hips had arched under him, rising up to meet him, wanting him. Some folks might point out that you're not the one who died.

She went in the living room and got the manila envelope off the floor. The room smelled smoky, huge pile of ashes in hearth. The planks were burnt where the box had landed, a black spot the size of a softball. Pitch black. Sean played softball but he didn't pitch. He played shortstop. She had to stop but she couldn't shut it off.

She took the envelope to the kitchen, covered it with aluminum foil, carefully double wrapping the corners, she put it in the freezer. It would be safe there. Now that Tom was gone. She picked up the box of SOS.

The shower was cold to start. She didn't notice, didn't care. "Atta, Suqami, Alomari, AlShehri, AlShehri." She scrubbed, matching the rhythm to the singsong. A blob of pink lather dropped to the floor, the steel wool harsh against her face. She knew the names. Say the names.

"Atta, Suqami, Alomari, AlShehri, AlShehri, Hanjour, Alhazmi, Mihdhar, Moqed and Alhazmi." She raised her chin, scrubbed down the neck. "Two Alhazmi's, two AlShehri's, no wait, another AlShehri on United, three AlShehri's and a Shehhi, two Alghamdis." Scrubbing, scrubbing, scrubbing. "There was another Alghamdi, the one in the field." The steel wool bit into her face. "The young one was Nami, the pilot was Jarrah, then Haznawi, then the other Alghamdi." She closed her eyes and scrubbed as hard as she could.

Pink lather slid down the shower stall, threaded here and there with red. She scrubbed harder. Her cheeks, her chin, the bridge of her nose. She could feel the grit fight the pad. Taking the skin with it.

You can't just change things. No matter how much you wish they were different.

This was the day, not tomorrow, today. This was the day she killed him. Tomorrow was the day he killed her back. Nothing could change that. Too many wrongs to right. She would have to make do. Sometimes a person just has to make do.

Except when she shouldn't.

***

"Jolene Mayes," she answered to the Nextel's chirp.

"It's Jack, have you seen Susan?"

"Hey. Getting an early start, huh?'

"Have you seen Susan?"

"Not yet. Something wrong?"

"She's not here, I woke up and she's gone."

"You woke up? At Susan's!"

"Not now, okay, she's gone. The car's gone. The bathroom looks like, I don't what it looks like."

"What's wrong with the bathroom?"

"The shower's…it's all pink. And not in a good way."

"Pink, what the in the name of…"

"Jolene," he interrupted. "Do you know where she is? Do have her cell phone?"

"Oh lord, don't start on the cell phone, take my word for that."

"Where would she go?"

"Only two places I know, Wal-Mart and Dottie's. I'm here now, so I'd start at there. Wal-Mart," she added.

"Thanks. Call me if you hear from her, okay?

"Sure, right back at you." Before he could hang up. "And hey, Jack."

"What?" He was already heading for the car.

"Good one, bud. It's about time." He hung up without answering. Jolene grinned. "Booo-ha!"

***

She appeared in the doorway like a ghost. The sun was behind her, in silhouette more like a girl than a woman. So small. Just standing there. No one paid attention, conversation in full swing. Ben and Randy and Dutch and Bubba and Big Jim. There was no one behind the counter. She didn't step inside.

"Do you know that he beats his wife?" Susan said, loud enough to cut through the chatter.

Every head turned. First to her, but then to him. A big man, near the corner, next to a coffee can on the floor. They knew. The big man spit a brown stream.

"Okay now, honey," Bubba started, "I don't know what's…"

"I'm not your honey," Susan snapped. "He beats her," she repeated. "He takes his fist and pounds his wife in the face, then he chokes her, right Jimmy?" She taunted.

"Who's this crazy-ass bitch!" He tried to laugh. The other men looked down, around, away. "Better go on home, honey, if your old man will have ya," he drawled.

"Big Jim with the little dick! Can't get it up without slapping her around?"

The room exploded. Big Jim roared, started for her, fist up, raised and ready. Ben and Bubba jumping in between, they fought to hold him. She never moved, his arms reaching over their shoulders, the place in uproar.

"You stupid bitch," Big Jim screamed.

"You're a piece of shit."

Another roar, another burst of fight. "Susan, stop it," Ben shouted.

"You should have stopped it," she yelled back. "Here's how it's gonna go, Jimmy, I've got more money than I know what to do with, so I'm gonna pay somebody to watch her, starting right now. And every time, any time, they tell me they see so much a scratch on her then I'm gonna pay somebody else to take a baseball bat and beat you to a fucking pulp. Got it?"

Skeeter came running from the back room. "What's going on out here?"

Susan's eyes never wavered, one last disdainful look at Big Jim. "Just getting my bitch in line," she drawled and walked out the door. Stunned silence left behind. Ben and Bubba slowly let go, Big Jim panting, face hot red.

"Jesus," Skeeter exclaimed, "what the hell's going on?"

***

"She did what?" Jack couldn't believe it. "Dad, is she okay? What…holy crap." He listened to his father, hung up the phone. Dialed Susan's number. No answer.

***

He was gone when she got back. She was glad. He left a note. She didn't read it.

Everything smelled of fire. She pulled her pony tail around and sniffed the frizzled ends. Her wrist was red all around like a bracelet. The phone rang. She ignored it, squatted at the burn mark on the floor, rubbed a finger through the char. Rough but not bumpy. Probably just the varnish, not the wood. That had to come off anyway.

The answering machine kicked on. She got up, thinking, walked to it, absently scratching her cheek. She yanked the plug out of the wall, the light on the machine going dark. What to do about the floor? She'd

296

burned the head of the mop, the sponges too. She had two bristle brushes but they were ruined from stripping. It would take more than cleaning anyway, she thought. The phone rang again. She pulled the cord out of the jack. Charlie would know what to do. It was after nine. The hardware store was open.

Her clothes were dirty. She stepped out of her shirt and shorts, leaving them on the floor. Sean's Bare Naked Ladies T-shirt was neatly folded on the table. It was huge, shoulders to her elbows. Perfect. The Sunday morning bagel hat. Good too. She found a pair of sunglasses on the bathroom floor, one earpiece chewed down to bare wire. Bare feet, bare ladies, bare wire. She rummaged in a Wal-Mart bag for shorts, the tag rubbing against her skin. She let herself have a good scratch, around her nose, under her chin, in her arm pit. Callie liked to be scratched under her chin. She poured a paper plate of Meow Mix, set it on the floor, propped the kitchen door open.

She stopped to pee, paused at the mirror. Red raw skin blushing her cheeks, a patch on the tip of her chin. It gave her some color, she thought.

She started out to the car, stopped. They might not let her in the store without shoes. No shirt, no shoes, no service. She found a red flip flop in the kitchen, a yellow one by the door. Keys and a credit card. Ready to go.

***

"She did what!" Jolene said. "Hold on, I gotta...just hold on a minute." She scrambled down the ladder. "Okay, tell me again." She listened. "Yeah, from Wal-Mart, I guess." Listening. "I know, but I didn't..." Listening. "She did?" Jolene chuckled. "Well, I know it's not funny, but..." Squawking from the phone. "Well, nobody else did nothing about it, Billy." More noise. "I got things to do, we'll talk at home." She cut off the phone, stood for a second.

"Damn, Suz!" She dialed Susan's number but the phone just rang and rang.

***

Charlie was helping a woman choose lawn fertilizer. Susan lurked in the surrounding aisles, ducking her head to avoid other customers. She pulled the hat brim lower on her face, hiked her shirt and itched her belly.

"Miss Susan? That you?"

"Hi Charlie." She turned. Ghastly smile.

He stopped and took her all in, the sunglasses, the hat, the rash, patches of raw skin, the blisters circling her wrist. A clear plastic strip was still glued on her shorts, Faded Glory, Size Small, Faded Glory, Size Small, Faded Glory, Size Small.

"Well, now." He waited. She rubbed her flip flop against her ankle. He was looking at her funny.

"It's poison ivy," she said.

"Poison ivy."

"Yea. I scratched it too hard." He didn't blink. "But anyway, look, I started a fire last night and it got a little...well, the floor got burnt. Not bad," she added hastily. "But I don't know how to fix it because...it's all black and I thought...you would know." She scratched her cheek, her nose, the part of her neck right below her ear.

"Let's have some tea," he said, taking her elbow. "It's sweet, don't have any unsweet but it's cold and wet." He steered her toward the back of the store and into a small office. It was wood paneled, an old metal desk with a computer monitor, file folders and family pictures. A browning dollar bill was thumb-tacked next to a sign that said Old Fishermen Never Die, They Just Get Reel Tired. Charlie opened up a small refrigerator behind his desk and got the tea.

"You get us a glass or two, over there on the shelf." Susan brought them to the desk. "Looks like more than the floor got burned."

She covered her wrist. "It's nothing."

He poured. "I'm a man inclined to mind my own business, Miss Susan, never much gained from sticking your nose in where it don't belong, that's what my daddy always said."

"I think it's just the varnish because..."

298

"But if that's poison ivy," he continued. "I will eat my sister Louella's fatback and greens. And I hate fatback, Miss Susan, always have."

"You're busy. I'll come back." She stood up.

"You haven't finished your tea." She hadn't touched it.

"Really, it's no trouble." She bent and scratched her knee. "I just wanted to get the floor fixed but I can come back. The floor will still be there, so will the hole I guess, though it's not really a hole, just a mark but it's pretty black and I feel bad about the floor because the one in the kitchen looks so pretty and..." She burst into tears.

"That's right, let it out." He came around the desk. "Let it all out."

Susan cried. Hiccupping, nose running, blatting like a baby. Blindly she reached for the chair back and sat down. He grabbed a box of Kleenex off the shelf

"Here you go, now take a deep breath." She choked on a sob, nose so clogged she could barely draw a breath. "Let's blow," he added, handing her a tissue. "That's right. Deep breath now, that's a girl."

"I'm...sor...sorry," she snuffled. Still whooping.

"You just sit quiet for a second." He rummaged in a drawer and brought out a mauve bottle, tipped its mouth to a tissue. "Steady now." He dabbed her cheek. "Calamine lotion," he explained, swabbing at her neck. "Should slow the itching some."

"I wish I would die."

"Dying ain't your problem. Hold still." He took her chin and held her face steady. More dabbing. Her chest heaved. "Steady now."

"I shouldn't be here," she said.

"Where should you be?"

"I can't be what people want." Tears rolling down her cheeks. "I can't."

"But you can do all this." He shook his head, dotted a spot just above her elbow. "Now you listen to me, young lady, and you listen good. People die. Good ones, bad ones, in between. One second they're here and the next they're gone. You got no special claim to fame, or misery neither, one second to the next."

"But ...what if you got trapped in that second and time won't go?"

"I'd say you're a mite old for fairy tales. Time doesn't stop. You gotta grow up, Miss Susan, that's what this is about. Face what scares ya." He picked up the tea, drank it down. "Now blow your nose and wipe your eyes and we'll get the fixings for that floor. Shellac for the kitchen too."

***

They carried the people who couldn't walk -the firemen, cops, the Port Authority police. They directed the civilians down the stairs, out through the lobby, keeping them safe from falling debris and jumping coworkers. There were somewhere between sixteen and eighteen thousand people in the building that day. Two thousand one hundred and fifty two would die. One could call it a small percentage, but no one ever did.

There was so much chaos, so much falling debris, people waiting at their desks, the authorities sending some of them back of the stairs. No one knew how many had listened. It wouldn't happen now. Not now, never now, lickety-split people would be pouring down the stairs. They wouldn't care what anyone said.

Hindsight can be so smug.

***

He stayed in the bedroom for what seemed like forever. She forced herself to wait. Take time to think. He didn't mean it. He couldn't mean it. She was wrong, she could see that now, even before she knew about Ashley it was wrong, but how to explain it.. The pedicure analogy wouldn't fly. It was amazing that she had ever believed it herself.

Why didn't she delete the email, she asked herself for the thousandth time. So stupid! One mistake, one stupid mistake and she was on her way to divorce court. He wouldn't divorce her. He couldn't. It was just a threat. She wasn't going to be bullied. He was partly to blame. She'd told him a million times. He worked too...no. That wasn't going to work. She had to beg for forgiveness. Be accountable. They could work the rest out later, after things settled down. Maybe they

300

could get counseling. Most couples did sooner or later. Most of them ended up divorcing anyway.

She didn't want it to be them. She didn't want it to be her.

She wouldn't look at the papers. Couldn't imagine what they said. Was adultery grounds for divorce? It was so unfair. She was married to a ghost for god sakes. He was never around, never. She couldn't remember the last time they went out to dinner, well maybe dinner because they ate last week at that new Japanese place but not movies. He never went to the movies. There was a reason to get divorced.

She stared at the papers on the counter. The folds bent up, the bottom flat, making a triangle of blue. What did he say about her? She wondered who the lawyer was, if it was his friend Gary. She and Sean and Gary and his wife Deena used to go out to dinner once and while. No more of that. She wasn't going to sit across the table making chit-chat with a man who was trying to get her divorced. What did Gary know? Did he tell Deena? Lawyers weren't supposed to do that, but wouldn't he go home and say, "Honey, you will not believe who's breaking up. Sean and Susan. She was cheating on him with some guy named Tom."

Who did he think he was! She'd file a complaint with the Bar Association. . It wasn't like he and Deena were a prize. Trying to get pregnant, always trying to get pregnant, if Susan had heard one more story about in vitro fertilization, she'd have thrown her salad across the table.

She snatched up the papers. He'd signed that afternoon. September 10, 2001, there was the date, buried in a bunch of legalese that made no sense to anyone. They should have to write in real English. If a person was being threatened with divorce the least she should be able to do was understand the stupid papers.

She didn't recognize the name of the firm. At least it wasn't Gary.

***

She plugged the phone back in and dialed. "Maggie?"

"I was just thinking about you," she said. "It's getting close, how are you doing?"

"I've got the rash, but I got some stuff. It's pink." Susan glanced down at her arms. Polka-dotted. "Ummm, look, I bought some things for the boys, but...I can't remember the address and I wanted to ship them ..."

"They'll be so excited." She didn't sound like she believed it.

"I didn't know what to buy. For kids. I didn't want kids, Maggie. It scared the shit out of me, the idea of kids. I don't know what's wrong with me."

"Not everybody wants to have children."

"Because I would have been a crappy mother."

"That's not what I meant."

"Look at Zoey. I lost her."

Maggie sighed. "Just a couple more days and we'll..." Her voice faded away.

"Hello?" No answer. "Maggie?"

"Susan....I can't do this anymore. Eric's been telling me and I didn't want to listen, but he's right. I can't."

"What do you mean?"

"It's never going to get better and I guess that's how you want it but I just can't..."

"I don't want it," Susan interrupted. "I don't like it, I just don't know how to..."

"See, here we go, it's always the same. Nothing can be done, poor Susan," she said, mocking herself. "If I had a nickel for every time I've said that..."

"You're my best friend," Susan pleaded.

"I used to be. I don't know what I am now. Eric says I enable you," she said. "All this time, I've been trying to make you let go and move on and here I am stuck in it right along with you. Maybe I'm not willing to let go."

"I'll try harder, I promise."

"No, you won't. You live for this. Every year, you can't get enough of it. It's not a day, it's your life. And I don't...I can't do this anymore," she repeated.

"You don't understand, I haven't told you..."

"You know what Eric said," she interrupted. "He said what would she do if he'd just gotten hit by a bus?"

"I've gotta go," she whispered.

***

Jack and Jolene waited on the porch. Jolene had gone inside. "The phone's on the floor," she reported, "and the machine's unplugged. And here's the pink," she added, holding up a mangled SOS pad.

"So she was just cleaning," he said. Jolene didn't answer. "Where is she?" For the tenth time.

"You're gonna wear a hole in that floor," Jolene told him. "She stopped by Lyman's earlier. Talked to Old Charlie in the back."

Jack nodded. He'd heard that too. "You don't think...that she'd hurt herself?"

"She won't kill herself, that'd be getting off too easy."

"Where is she?" The sound of a car, gravel under tires. They both looked up.

"Oh crap," Jolene said, shielding her eyes from the sun. Red head behind the wheel. Jack cursed under his breath, started down the steps. Becky slammed the car door, waiting for him to come.

"Hey Beck," Jolene called. "Surprise, surprise, surprise." Giving it her best Gomer Pyle.

"So. Fancy meeting you here." Becky folded her arms.

"Look, I know you're..."

"Pissed? You bet your ass I'm pissed. What are you doing here?"

"Something happened this morning and I just, I wanted to make sure she was okay."

"She's got the trailer trash for that," Becky snapped, jerking her head toward the porch. Jolene waggled her fingers. "This is not okay, Jack, we discussed this and I told you I wasn't okay with it."

"Could you lower your voice, I don't…"

"No," she interrupted. "I will not lower my voice. What are you doing here?"

"Becky, look…" He didn't know how to start. But she wasn't stupid, had never been stupid..

"You son of a bitch!" Staring at him.

"I didn't mean…"

"No, don't even! Unbelievable, unfucking believable." She shook her head. "I didn't know you had it in you, Jack."

"Becky, it doesn't work, we don't work."

"Oh but it works with the crazy girl. Well, fine, have at it." She swung into the car, fighting with the seatbelt. "I just got tired of seeing your pathetic face, following me around like a puppy. That's all it was. It was a joke, Jack, you're a joke."

"I never meant…"

"Oh fuck you, who gives a rat's ass what you meant!"

Her tires spun, a cloud of dust, backing down the driveway, furious speed. He stood there, wanting to feel bad, knowing that he should.

"I said it once, I'll say it again," Jolene called. "It's about time."

***

She drove around aimlessly. Long after dark. She would stop by the side of the road, near a patch of trees or by a farm, no idea where she was and call Zoey's name. Then she'd wait, watching, looking. She'd call again, wait some more. Finally she would be compelled to find another place, driving again, until she felt that she should stop. Call, wait, call again. For hours.

Everyone was gone. Zoey, Sean, Maggie. She had lost them all. She would lose the rest, Jolene, Jackson. Mr. Lyman, Dottie. Betty Jane. One more day. One chance to decide. One chance to grow up.

Chapter 35: September 10, 2006

Her hands were shaking, dotting herself with pink. Jolene had come in a few minutes before, walking in, assuming welcome. She didn't know what to say, had never shared this day with a living person since that day. "I don't feel good," she said.

"Don't look so hot either," Jolene replied, leaning against the door.

"Do you think this stuff will help?"

"No. Might wanna stay from the steel wool."

"Not today, okay? I just need to get…"

"Look, I got something to tell you and I don't think you're gonna like it."

"What?"

***

When the bedroom door opened, she jumped to her feet. "Sean," she said. He had a gym bag in his hand. She could see the garment bag on the bed. "Sean, please don't do this. Please talk to me."

"There's nothing to say."

"You have to give me a chance. We deserve a chance."

"You blew your chance."

"Please, just sit for a minute. I know you're hurt but…" She sank down on the couch, buried her face in her hands. After an eternity, the couch shifted under his weight.

"How could you do this?"

"I don't know," she whispered. "There's no excuse, I've been sitting here trying to come up with some way to explain, but there isn't any."

"I loved you so much." His hands trembled.

"It didn't have anything to do with you. No, wait, I know it hurt you but it was my fault. All of it."

"Why?" The all important question. The one she couldn't answer. He waited.

Susan cleared her throat. "I met him at work. He's a salesman. Nothing special. Not like you," she added, reaching for his hand.

"Don't!"

Hers dropped back in her lap, twisting with its mate. "It was just flirting. He made me feel, I don't know, pretty." A nervous glance. His face was stone. "I liked the attention, I just, I don't always feel...I liked being...wanted."

"Jesus!"

"I don't want to hurt you, I don't have to tell..."

"Wouldn't that be nice for you." He hated her.

"Not for...okay, okay." She hurried on. "We used to go to lunch, the three of us. Bill was always there and then one day, he wasn't and Tom and I...we went out by...and it didn't seem wrong because I told him I was married and he was..." Sean stared at the coffee stain on the wall. "I never slept with him, I didn't. I swear I didn't."

"Well, that's it, that makes it okay then." Biting off each word.

***

The trucks were lined up in the driveway, a couple on the street. A dark green Cadillac, almost as old as the house, sat at the end its tail sticking out in the road. Susan's mouth fell open as Dottie pushed her bulk out of the car.

"What is going on, Jolene?"

"I tried to tell them that you might not like it, so don't be mad at me."

"What are they doing here?"

There was Old Charlie and Young Charlie and Little Charlie. Dick Liddle from the BB&T. Willie Mayes. Mr. Wyle. Men she didn't recognize. Dottie supervised the unfolding of a long white table, two ladies helping, Mrs. Merry being one.

"Got a table cloth in the trunk," Dottie was saying. "Willie! That's right, I'm talking to you. We got stuff in the trunk that needs to be brought over, you boys think I'm gonna feed you for free and carry the food myself, you got another thing coming! Make yourselves useful for a change." She pointed, the men scuttled toward the Cadillac. She nodded to the other women, Betty Jane nowhere in sight. "Be careful with that," she yelled.

Susan stood helplessly on the porch. Jolene grinned. "It's a flagpole. Surprise!"

"Excuse me, Miss Susan, just wanna set these inside," Old Charlie said.

Susan caught his sleeve. "Charlie, I don't want a flagpole."

He gave Jolene a stern glance. She put her hands behind her back and shook her head. "She made me tell her."

"I don't even have a flag."

"Brought one for ya. Excuse me, these are getting a mite heavy." He pushed past her into the house, carrying a bucket in each hand.

"Was that paint?" Susan demanded.

"Jolene Mayes, you told me there was a barbecue," Dottie yelled, hands on her hips. "You best not be talking about this sad little excuse for a grill back here or..."

"Coming," Jolene called, scooting off the porch.

***

Jackson arrived on the motorcycle just as they were deciding where to dig. Dottie scolded him soundly about coming too close to her car. "Ain't a car, it's a bus," one of the men said offside, the others chuckling.

"I hear you, Duke Merry, don't think I don't. One less chicken for the grill, that's what I'm thinking."

"Aw, Miss Dottie we was just jokin'." Glancing around, suddenly standing alone.

"You don't see me laughing, do ya? And don't be trying to sweet talk me neither. You can practice your jokin' while everybody else is eating."

"Aw, Miss Dottie."

"How you doing?" Jackson walked over, touched Susan's shoulder.

"Not good."

It was hard to argue from the looks of her. "They just want to help."

"I know but...why don't people ask?"

"Maybe when you're in trouble, you don't always know what you need." He touched her arm. "Hafta to let somebody in." She turned away, hugging herself.

"Hey Miss Susan? Over here?" Willie Earl waved her over. "We figured that it would look best right here, don't have to dig up no bushes or nothing and ain't near any lines that we can figure. Could see it from the window up there." He gestured to the second story.

"How tall is this thing?"

"Fifteen feet. Nice pole too, got a pulley to bring the flag up and down. Charlie thought you'd want that, so is it okay to dig?"

"I guess."

"'kay y'all, listen up," he said, clapping his hands. "Duke, Jerry, Luke, you start digging. Jackson, if you can stop mooning like a cross-eyed calf, Randy can probably use some help mixing that cement."

***

There were no pictures. He'd found out too late for that. But there were statements from the bartender, one or two from strangers, regulars at the bar she guessed. A friend from work- former friend - explained the coffee in the hall. Another co-worker had seen them kissing in Bill's office. She didn't know anyone knew. Sean sat across from her like a prosecutor. Executioner. She shuffled through the papers. Her cell phone records. Tom's number highlighted in yellow. Three months back. So much yellow, too much to explain away. Then she saw the list of dates and times. The manicurist, the shoe store, the hair salon, the movies.

"You were having me followed?"

"Did you think I wouldn't check? You're a liar." Scorn in his shrug.

"You had me followed!" She stood up. "You went through my things."

"I checked your email. Oh and your buddy list. Your buddy Tom."

She had no right to be angry. She was suddenly so mad. "How long have you known," she demanded.

"Long enough."

***

Charlie was working on the burn hole in the floor. Young Charlie and Little Charlie were shellacking the kitchen. The smoke smell was overcome by varnish and stripper.

"Not much damage to the wood, should be able to get it up or at least most of it," Charlie said, leaning back on his heels. "You look a mite pink," he added.

Jolene popped her head around the doorway. "Is Suz in…hey, Suz, I need you for a second."

So many people. All together at one time. In her house. This is Sean's wife, Susan. "Atta, Suqami, Alomari," she murmured.

"Don't start, no time right now, come on over here. Charlie and Annie brought some paint from the store. The cream's for the kitchen, oil-based, stinks to high heaven, have to wait until they're done shellacking the floor. Which is looking good by the way, not bad work for boys," she called.

Susan's head ached. There were people everywhere. "So I'm thinking," Jolene said, squatting by the paint cans. "This gold would be pretty in here, not too yellow, you don't want to be eating somewhere that looks like a bathroom. Isn't that funny how certain colors make you think of certain rooms?"

"I have to sit down."

"Sit here by to the paint. He brung some nice green too, looks like army pants. Never woulda picked it myself but I think it's gonna look real nice in the living room."

"It's too much, Jolene." Her voice shook. "I can't do it."

"You just need something to eat."

"I can't."

"Suz, look around, you already are," Jolene said. "Okay, so we go with the gold. I just gotta hop out to the truck and get some spackle for the staple holes." She got up, put out a hand to help her up. "Come on, you can help carry stuff."

There were two more cars out on the road. Another couple of men to stand around the hole in the front yard. "What is it with men and holes," Jolene said. "Takes two to dig one and ten more to watch. There's painting to be done inside," she yelled. The men looked up, looked back down. "Don't matter which one you marry, they're all the same."

"Is Billy here?" Susan looked around.

"There's work involved, remember?" Jolene rolled her eyes. "He had to go meet up with Skeeter, two pea brains in a pod, I'm telling ya. They're cooking up some scheme, didn't want me to know nothing about it. Probably just as well."

"Who's paying for all this," Susan said suddenly.

"Don't think I heard anybody say. You can, if it makes you feel any better."

***

Atta and Alomari had driven up to Maine to catch a flight to Logan. No explanation of why, though employees at the Portland Airport remembered Atta was agitated when they told him he would have to check in again at Logan. Maybe that's why he went, thought he would just change gates, so many of them already boarding in Boston. Two flights out of Logan would explode that day. They took the red eye from Portland, arrived in time for the 7:45 a.m. flight to L.A on American. It would leave fourteen minutes late.

They hooked up with Waleed and company in the Terminal C. Atta called a friend. To say goodbye? To gloat about the impending doom? No one knows. Each of the five passed through the metal detectors. No problem. Nobody remembered them, not even afterwards when a memory would have bought more than fifteen minutes of fame.

Of the nineteen hijackers, nine set off warning bells in a system designed to identify potential threats to civilian aircraft. Their baggage wasn't allowed on the plane. Waleed was one of them, Alshehri and Suqami too. Three of the five on American Flight 11. Four if you counted Atta, randomly selected in Maine for additional screening. He passed with flying colors. She'd always wondered if he had been shitting his pants.

If only one of them had failed, if just one had been kept off the plane. United Flight 93, the one that was hijacked back, that plane only had four men. Four, not five. By then though, the passengers knew. They wouldn't have known on that first flight. But the passengers on United 93, they knew. They talked and they voted. Then they gave their lives for their country and they took that plane down.

***

"Here you go," Dottie said, passing her a coffee. "There's some sausage biscuits, over there, stick to your ribs."

The thought of sausage curdled her stomach. "Who's watching the store?"

"It's Sunday." Dottie rolled her eyes. "Don't work on the Lord's day. I swear, we got some schooling to do on you, missy." She peered at Susan's face. "Is that poison ivy? Don't you know enough to stay out of that? Leaves of three, let it be."

"Miss Susan, we haven't met. I'm Annie Lyman." She was a slight woman, sinewy, her hair cut in a bob, salt and pepper gray. Her glasses were bigger than what was in fashion, lenses lined in the middle. Pink lipstick, the color too young for her face. "Heard a lot about you."

"Your husband's the nicest man."

"Thank you. Married over forty years." She glanced around, lowering her voice. "Charlie told me about those hives. Only a man would think that a woman wants to run around with polka dots all over her face. I brought some Benadryl for you, honey. It's not pink," she added.

Annie got a bottled water and a napkin and led Susan behind one of the trucks. "There now, you clean off your face and I'll just put this on ya. Soaks right in, nobody will even know it's there, that would be better now, won't it? " She beamed.

***

"Wow! It's like a whole new room," Jackson said. "Hotter then blazes out there," he added, wiping his forehead.

"This ain't no hunting camp," Jolene informed him. "You're gonna hang out here, you're gonna pick up a brush."

"I just finished mixing two hundred pounds of cement, gimme a break."

"Ain't that just like a man, wah, wah, wah." Jolene slapped spackle on the wall. "I love the night life, I like to boogie," she sang, butt swaying to the beat.

"Holy crap," he muttered, sinking on the Rubbermaid box.

"You missed Muskrat Love," Susan informed him, paint in her hair.

"Thank god for that."

***

"I can't believe you had me followed. I don't believe it."

"You don't believe you got caught."

"I'm not the only liar in this house. You knew!"

"This isn't about me."

"Marriage takes two people, Sean."

"That's right, two. Not three."

"Fine! You want a separation, give me the papers."

"Poor Susan," he mocked. "Her husband's so mean."

"Don't you mean her ex-husband?" She walked into the bedroom, peeling her shirt over her head. She felt so dirty. She needed to take a shower. She pushed back the curtain and turned both faucets on. He followed her into the bathroom.

"I'm not going to feel guilty because you're out screwing around."

312

"Then don't. Saint friggin' Sean," she muttered, stepping in the shower.

***

Everyone ate while they waited for the cement to dry. The pole was in, wired and staked to stay in place. Dottie had outdone herself, the other ladies too, chicken and coleslaw, beans, green tomatoes soaked in Italian dressing. Biscuits with a squeeze bottle of honey.

Susan filled a plate and let it sit on her lap, listening to them. The jokes and stories, all the comings and goings of their lives shared by the nature of their proximity. She would never belong. But she found herself wondering if maybe she could fit.

"Not a gnat or a hair anywhere. Smooth as glass," Young Charlie was saying, about the kitchen floor.

"Course there ain't no hair, you ain't got any to drop," Willie Earl quipped. Randy Teator knocked off Young Charlie's cap and rubbed his bald head.

"Oh Charlie," he sighed in falsetto, "your skin's so baby soft."

"Get off." Charlie slapped him with the hat. "And stay off that floor too. Asshole."

"Charles Weldon Lyman," his mother said.

"Sorry. Sorry, ladies."

"You better be," Jolene replied, "Or I'll have Suz here kick your ass."

***

They never found a single square of carpet. Not a piece of fabric. Not a curtain, not a tie, not a sweater left on the back of someone's chair. All vaporized. Even the bodies were bare.

***

"Excuse me, Mr. Liddle? I was wondering if I could talk to you for a second?"

"Yes, ma'am. What can I do for you?"

"I wanted to talk to you about a mortgage."

"I'm happy to help, but I was under the impression…"

"Not mine." Susan glanced around. "Jolene's."

"I'm sorry, ma'am," Dick said, "I can't really discuss that with you."

"That's a shame, because I'm thinking I'd like to pay it off."

He gulped. "Pay it…"

"Yes. If that's okay with the bank?"

***

"There's nothing to discuss," he said as she passed by the couch. "Sign them."

She didn't answer, hair wet on her shoulders, heading to the kitchen. The papers were still on the counter. She ought to sign them, call his bluff. She couldn't touch them. She got a bottled water from the refrigerator, drank half in one swallow. Sean was there, standing in the doorway. He looked like such a little boy. So sad. No Christmas presents under the tree. Not picked for the baseball team. Betrayed by his very best friend.

"What do you think we should do," he said quietly.

"I thought you already decided that."

"I was mad."

"Oh and now suddenly you're not?" He didn't answer. "I'm not the only one, Sean."

"Did you ever love me?"

"Course I did. I still do." She waited. He didn't speak. "But you…?"

The words came so slow. "I don't know."

Like a stake through the heart, a bullet to the chest, a knife in the ribs, twisting. The pain was excruciating. It took everything she had to hold her face in place.

***

"I wanted to apologize," Susan said, catching him around the back, rolling up the hose.

"For what," Ben asked.

314

"What I said, at the store. It's not your fault he was hitting her." He didn't answer, kept winding the hose around his arm. "Okay, well, thanks." She turned to go.

"You weren't wrong." He tucked the end of the hose in the loops. "Folks round here talk." He hung the rolled hose on a big rusty nail. "Easy thing to do, just talk." He grinned. "Yankees just seem to hafta to do more."

She smiled back. "How is Mrs. Wyle?"

"She's doing much better."

"Really?!" Surprised by his answer. "That's so good, I'm so glad."

"Uh-huh."

Was there something in his face…in the tone? Something. "How are you doing?"

"I'm getting there."

***

The flag went up the pole a little after six. It looked so strange, the long silver pole, the six foot flag lying flat against it. No breeze to make it ripple and flow. Not like the flags on the TV. It hung there. All the men took off their hats. The joking and the talking stilled. She half expected them to break out in song, America the Beautiful or the Star Spangled Banner. Quick as it came, the silence was over and they were laughing and slapping each other, loading the trucks and taking down the tables.

Jackson and Jolene lingered behind, with a pile of chicken and beans, not much cake but enough for the night.

"Well, I guess I'll be going. Leave you two alone," Jolene winked.

"Good idea," he drawled.

"Jack!"

"See, you already sound like an old married couple." Susan drew a sharp breath. "Oh shoot, shoot," Jolene said. "Stuck my big fat foot in my big fat mouth. Suz, I'm sorry, I forgot, that's all. It's been such a good day."

"I'm really tired." Her voice quavered. "Do you guys mind if…"

"No, course not, I'm beat too." Jack stood, brushing cement dust from his jeans.

"I'm sorry, Suz."

"It's okay. I'm just tired." She leaned her head against the post. "I'll see you later. Thank you," she called.

She walked in the house. It smelled different. New. The dining room glowed gold, sun setting through the back windows. The kitchen floor looked dry. Twenty four hours, Young Charlie had said. The refrigerator was on the porch, the envelope still inside, with its email and pale blue papers. It was supposed to be on the counter. She made no move to get it.

The phone rang. "Hey, I just wanted to call and make sure you were all right. Feel like a damn fool."

"It's all right."

"Nice of you to say so, but geez Louise." Jolene hesitated. "Well, all right then. You try and get some sleep."

"I will," Susan lied.

"Okay then. G'night."

"Jolene? Will you come tomorrow?'

"Wouldn't be anywhere else."

***

He was already asleep by the time she called. Mary answered on the second ring, television low in the background.

"He goes to bed by ten, Susan." Chiding her.

"I'm sorry, but will you tell him I got the box, that I called?"

"Will you bother to answer if he calls back?"

Susan took a deep breathe. "I'm sorry, Mary. Really sorry, I didn't..."

"It's all about you all the time, isn't it," she interrupted. "The grieving widow!" She snorted.

"Mary..."

"Sean was devastated," she hissed. "How could you!"

316

"Tell Paddy I called okay? And I am sorry, Mary. I can't change what happened, but I was selfish and stupid. I never meant to hurt anyone, especially Paddy."

"Nothing is ever your fault, is it?"

"Everything's my fault and I can't ever make it right. I screwed up, I hurt him and lied to him and now he's gone and there will never be a chance to make it right. But I am sorry, unbelievably sorry." Mary didn't answer. "Tell Paddy I called, okay?"

"Susan, wait." Mary's voice called her back. "Wait." She sighed. "It hurt him because he loved you. Don't forget that, he never did."

Chapter 36: September 11, 2001

She stepped off the curb into the path of a cab. The driver swerved, horn blaring, shouting as he flew by, flipping her off. She jumped back, startled, heart racing, head already pounding. But now was nothing compared to what was coming. Every time she thought about it her throat shut down until she could hardly breathe. The light changed and the crowd carried her across Sixth Avenue.

She fumbled in her purse for a small bottle of Advil that she knew was in there somewhere. She couldn't fathom how she would work today. But she couldn't stay home. She finally found the pills, next to her cell phone, vibrating against her hand. Voice mail. She hadn't even heard it ring.

She stopped halfway up the block, dumped out couple of tablets and swallowed them dry. She flipped open the phone to check the missed call. She didn't need to, she already knew who it was, but she checked anyway. It was him. She rubbed her eyes. God, how was she gonna get through this day.

The vibration persisted, irritating, like a circling mosquito that she couldn't swat. She hadn't even had her coffee. She couldn't deal, okay, not right now. Starbucks was up ahead, slammed by the morning crowd. She pushed in the door, fighting to find the end of the line. The phone rang again. She ignored it. Another message. She hit dismiss to stop the buzzing, a battle of wills now. She wouldn't pick up, he couldn't make her.

She watched the girl with the hot pink hair and the nose ring, marking cups, singing out the orders. Like she did every day. Like everything was fine. The phone rang again. Screw you, she thought. You can wait.

***

It was just past dawn. The flagpole cast a long shadow up and over the house. Susan sat on the porch and played with the cell phone, flipping it open and shut. She paid Sprint to keep them. All three of

318

them. Open, close, open, close, open, close. She put the phone to her ear and dialed the voice mail.

"You have no new messages, three saved messages. First saved message, received September 11th at 8:27 am. "Susan. It's me. I'm at the office. We need to talk. Call me back.""

"To erase this message, press seven. To save this message, press three." She pressed three.

"Next saved message. Received, September 11th at 8:52 am. "Suz, something's happened. A plane, I guess a plane hit the building. It's…I don't know. There's smoke everywhere, I'm gonna get out of here now but I'm not sure the phone will work in the stairs. I wanted you to know I'm all right. I don't know what's going on, it's kind of crazy, the lights are out, so I don't know. I'll call you when I'm outside. I'm okay, if you see the smoke, don't worry. I'm okay. Call me." Press three.

"Next saved message. Received September 11th, 9:01 am.""

"Suz, I don't…we can't get down. The plane, it…the stairs are blocked and it's bad. Jesus, people are fucking jumping. I mean they're jumping. It's bad, it's really bad. I don't know what to do. We're gonna try to get to the roof but I don't know if I'm …Suz, all that stuff I said last night, about not knowing if I love you. That was just crap. It was…I love you so much. And I'm sorry. I should have been there, you know, like you wanted." His voice cracked. "I love you so much." Screaming in the background. "It's really bad up here. I don't know what's going to happen, but…I love you, okay? I need to know that you know." More yelling. Crackling. "Call me back, okay? Please? I just need to hear your voice. Okay? I love you, Suz, please call me. Please.""

She heard Jolene's truck before she saw it. Susan wiped the tears from her cheeks, walked over and before she could speak, handed her the phone.

"Press 1 for voicemail," she said.

"What is…?"

"Make sure you save them. There's more than one."

Chapter 37: September 12, 2006

The flag still flew at half-mast.

There was a knock on the front door. She was expecting Jackson. He knew a place that sold second-hand furniture, the kind you needed to fix up. She wanted to buy a table and a rocking chair. He wanted to go with her. He liked buying things that you need to fix up. She liked that.

A skinny man with white grizzle on his chin stood behind the screen. His face was creased, broken capillaries dotting gaunt cheeks with red. He wore a blue hat with ear flaps despite the heat. He shifted his feet, heavy half-laced boots.

"Miz Kearney," he asked. "Don't suppose you remember me?"

"No." She stepped out on the porch. "I'm sorry, were you here yesterday?"

"No, ma'am. Skeeter Jarvis, ma'am. You came to my store?"

"Oh. Right. How can I help you?" A lawsuit perhaps?

"I called about it earlier."

"I'm sorry?"

"The barn, you know? I built me this moose trap, and now turns out it don't work for moose so…"

"Excuse me, but…"

"Caught the dog," he said. She stared at him. "Earned every nickel of that re-ward, she's a slippery little rascal, I'll tell you that. Billy and me, waited there all day and half the night. But it's her all right." He turned and pointed to the truck. "She likes riding in the car just fine."

"Zoey!"

Made in the USA
Columbia, SC
05 March 2022

57227215R00193